Autonomous Agents

Edited by
Vedran Kordic

Autonomous Agents
Edited by Vedran Kordic

Republished by InTech
Janeza Trdine 9, 51000 Rijeka, Croatia

Technical Editor Goran Bajac

Cover Designer Dino Smrekar

Additional hard copies can be obtained from orders@intechopen.com

Autonomous Agents,
Edited by Vedran Kordic
p. cm.
ISBN 978-953-307-089-6

For EU product safety concerns:
IN TECH d.o.o., Prolaz Marije Krucifikse Kozulić 3, 51000 Rijeka, Croatia,
info@intechopen.com or visit our website at intechopen.com.

Meet the editor

Vedran Kordic is the founder and Board member of IntechOpen. After obtaining his Master's degree in Mechanical Engineering he continued his education at the Vienna University of Technology where he obtained his PhD degree in 2004. He worked as a researcher at the Automation and Control Institute, Faculty of Electrical Engineering, Vienna University of Technology until 2008. His studies in robotics lead him not only to a PhD degree but also inspired him to co-found and build the International Journal of Advanced Robotic Systems - world's first Open Access journal in the field of robotics. Vedran's background and experience remain crucial for the company's development as he is continuously engaged with overseeing the IT department.

Preface

Multi agent systems involve a team of agents working together socially to accomplish a task. An agent can be social in many ways. One is when an agent helps others in solving complex problems. The field of multi agent systems investigates the process underlying distributed problem solving and designs some protocols and mechanisms involved in this process. This book presents an overview about some of the research issues in the field of multi agents. In summary, this book presents a combination of different research issues which are pursued by researchers in the domain of multi agent systems. Multi agent systems are one of the best ways to understand and model human societies and behaviours. In fact, such systems are the systems of future.

Contents

1

State and Action Abstraction in the Development of Agent Controllers

Brent E. Eskridge
Southern Nazarene University and University of Oklahoma
USA

Dean F. Hougen
University of Oklahoma
USA

1. Introduction

The development of controllers for intelligent agents given a simple task is relatively straightforward and even basic techniques can be used to develop such controllers. However, as agents are given multiple tasks, using basic techniques for developing effective controllers quickly becomes impractical. Since each task may require distinct state information local to that task only, the resulting state space for the agent overall is simply too large to effectively cover. Furthermore, since each task places different demands on the agent, an effective controller must find the correct balance to achieve it's overall task. While each of these difficulties presents significant problems individually, their combination can make the development of agent controllers for these complex tasks impractical.

The potential avenues of investigation for this problem are vast and the literature on the subject covers the spectrum of algorithms and perspectives. This chapter's focus is on *composite* tasks that are the result of a combination of, in general, Concurrent, Interfering, and Non-Episodic (CINE) simple, or *primitive*, tasks. An example of a primitive task is COLLISIONAVOIDANCE. For our agents, COLLISIONAVOIDANCE is an abstract task that takes two inputs (relative direction to nearest obstacle and estimated time to contact with that obstacle assuming current speed) and provides two outputs (desired direction and desired speed). As such, it is simple enough that subdividing it further would not produce coherent subtasks, hence it is considered primitive. Note, however, that other formulations of COLLISIONAVOIDANCE that include lower-level information (such as the data from individual sensors or regarding all obstacles sensed) or actions (such as motor control values for individual components of the system) could be usefully subdivided into more primitive tasks such as TRACKOBSTACLE or PANCAMERA. If we combine COLLISIONAVOIDANCE with another simple task such as GOALSEEK, we arrive at a composite task. It is a composite task because the component tasks are coherent in and of themselves. Composite tasks composed of CINE primitive tasks have received comparatively little attention and are, for reasons discussed below, potentially one of the more difficult areas of focus. In contrast, many approaches focus on complex tasks that are composed of a series of sequential primitive tasks.

The challenge of correctly balancing CINE tasks, in addition to the complexity of the state and action spaces, must be addressed for the development of effective controllers for combinations of CINE tasks to be practical. Due to the variety of challenges, it is possible that a number of techniques must be combined to find an acceptable solution. As the complexity of the combined state and action space is a major challenge, it makes sense to consider state and/or action abstraction. For example, to coordinate the combination of COLLISIONAVOIDANCE and GOALSEEK it is important to know if a collision is imminent. If it is, the agent should probably try to avoid it.[1] If it isn't, the agent should head for the goal. If the answer is somewhere in between, the agent might give similar importance to both COLLISIONAVOIDANCE and GOALSEEK. Further, to determine if a collision is likely to occur soon, it isn't necessary to know whether the nearest obstacle is on the right or the left, only whether it is in front of the agent or off to either side. So state abstraction (in the form of ignoring right/left information) could reduce the amount of information used to decide the relative importance of COLLISIONAVOIDANCE and GOALSEEK. However, even if not all information is needed for all decisions, information cannot be simply discarded.[2] To continue the example, if the decision is that COLLISIONAVOIDANCE is at least somewhat important on this timestep, the agent will need to know which way to turn to avoid the obstacle.

The preceding example contained an explicit instance of state abstraction (using only the magnitude of the angle to the obstacle while ignoring its sign) but also an implicit instance of action abstraction. Note that the decision as to which way to turn was abstracted into determining how imminent a collision appears, then deciding how much importance to assign to each of the subtasks, then determining which way to turn. Such action abstraction is not necessary, however. In contrast, it would be possible to directly calculate turning angle as a function of obstacle and goal directions and distances.

Temporal abstraction, in the form of creating sequences of tasks, is also used in some systems to deal with composite tasks (Rohanimanesh & Mahadevan, 2002). However, such temporal abstraction will not work when the tasks are interfering as in our present research.

One approach that promotes the use of state and action abstraction while still allowing access to the unabstracted states and actions is the use of a hierarchical controller. A hierarchical controller leverages the hierarchical nature of the composite task by using smaller controllers responsible for each primitive task in the lowest level of the hierarchical controller and meta-controllers in the higher levels of the hierarchical controller to coordinate the lower-level controllers. Since low-level controllers are only responsible for a single primitive task, they do not need access to the full state space of the composite task, thus avoiding the combinatorial complexity of the composite task's state space. Furthermore, high-level meta-controllers are able to use state and action abstraction to simplify the state space since they merely coordinate the lower-level controllers that produce control actions instead of producing control actions themselves.

2. Adaptive Fuzzy Behavior Hierarchies

An example of a hierarchical approach to agent control, and the one used for the work described here, is an adaptive fuzzy behavior hierarchy (Tunstel, 2001). The hierarchy is orga-

[1] Only "probably" because if the goal is extremely close, the agent may prefer to reach the goal rather than avoid the obstacle.

[2] Some authors do deal with cases in which some variables are irrelevant and may be simply ignored by the controller with no loss of performance. We are assuming that all variables are relevant at least on some timesteps.

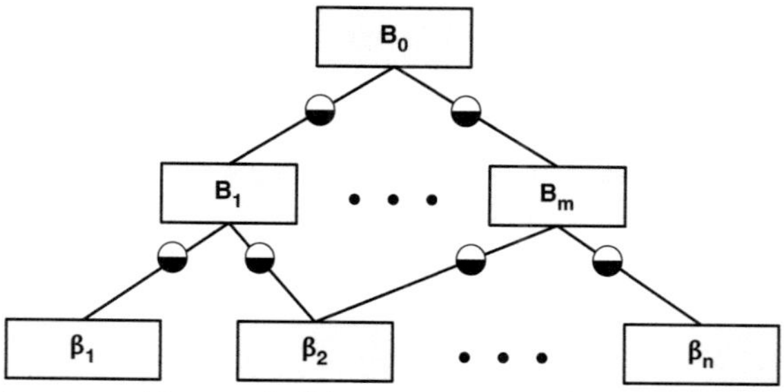

Fig. 1. Primitive behaviors (denoted β_i) are organized into a hierarchy and adaptively weighted by composite behaviors (denoted B_m) as described by Tunstel (2001) and redrawn here. The half-filled circles denote the weights and threshold values used to modulate behaviors.

nized using two types of behaviors. Behaviors responsible for accomplishing simple, primitive tasks are called *primitive behaviors* (see Figure 1). Primitive behaviors reside at the lowest level of the hierarchy and are responsible for producing low-level control actions for the agent. Since each primitive behavior is responsible for a single primitive task, inputs to the behavior consist of only state information relevant to the associated primitive task.

Following the formulation of Tunstel (2001), let X and U be, respectively, the sets of all possible input and output values, or universes of discourse, for a primitive behavior with a ruleset of size M. Individual rules within the ruleset have the following form:

$$\text{IF } x \text{ is } \tilde{A}_i \text{ THEN } u \text{ is } \tilde{B}_i \tag{1}$$

where x represents the linguistic variables describing primitive task state information, such as direction or distance, and u represents linguistic variables describing motor command actions, such as steering direction and speed, $\tilde{A}_i$ and $\tilde{B}_i$ represent the fuzzy linguistic values corresponding to the variables x and u. The antecedent proposition "x is $\tilde{A}_i$" can be replaced with a compound antecedent using a conjunction or disjunction of propositions. The consequent "u is $\tilde{B}_i$" could also be replaced with a compound consequent. An an example of a low-level rule in a primitive behavior responsible for steering towards a goal could be:

$$\text{IF } \mathit{goalDir} \text{ is } \texttt{LEFT} \text{ THEN } \mathit{steerDir} \text{ is } \texttt{LEFT} \tag{2}$$

The output fuzzy set of each primitive behavior can be combined in a similar manner to produce a single output. However, since primitive behaviors often have conflicting goals, their actions often also conflict. A method of assigning different activation levels to different primitive behaviors could address these conflicts and allow an agent to accomplish its overall composite task. In an adaptive fuzzy behavior hierarchy, this is accomplished by means of *behavior modulation* in which the activation levels of primitive behaviors are adjusted, or adapted, based on the current overall state of the agent. These activation levels are referred to as degrees of applicability (DOA) and are assigned to primitive behaviors by a high-level *composite behavior*. Composite behaviors are only responsible for modulating other behaviors, either primitive or composite, and do not produce low-level control commands. For example, a composite behavior that is responsible for modulating a COLLISIONAVOIDANCE primitive behavior and a GOALSEEK primitive behavior could determine that since a collision is not imminent, the GOALSEEK behavior is more applicable and should have a HIGH activation, while the COLLISIONAVOIDANCE behavior should have a LOW activation. Composite behaviors are also implemented using fuzzy rulesets, but, since they produce outputs specifying activation levels and use different output fuzzy linguistic variables and values, their consequents differ from those found in primitive behaviors. Fuzzy rules within a composite behavior have the basic form:

$$\text{IF } x \text{ is } \tilde{A}_i \text{ THEN } \alpha \text{ is } \tilde{D}_i \tag{3}$$

where $\tilde{A}_i$ is defined as in Equation 1, α is the scalar activation level of a given behavior, and $\tilde{D}_i$ represents the fuzzy linguistic values (e.g. LOW, MEDIUM, HIGH) corresponding to the activation levels which are used to modulate a behavior. If a behavior is not explicitly given an activation level, it is automatically given a default activation of 0 and does not contribute to the overall output of the controller. Furthermore, threshold values can be used to provide cutoff points for a modulated behavior's activation (Tunstel, 1999). Just as with primitive behaviors, the output of a composite behavior is a fuzzy set. However, when defuzzified, the crisp values provide the current activation levels of lower-level behaviors, and not motor control commands. Using fuzzy rulesets to produce activation levels results in smooth transitions between different sets of activation levels in response to the changing state of the agent.
The activation level α_p of a modulated behavior p is used to calculate the weighted contribution of the behavior to the overall controller's output. The output of each primitive behavior can now be combined using their respective activation levels to weight their overall contribution to the action generated by the controller. The output of the entire behavior hierarchy is calculated as follows:

$$\tilde{\beta}_H = \biguplus_{p \in P} \alpha_p \cdot \tilde{\beta}_p \tag{4}$$

where $\tilde{\beta}_H$ is the output of the entire behavior hierarchy, P is the set of all primitive behaviors, $\tilde{\beta}_p$ is the output of the behavior p, and $\biguplus$ is the arithmetic sum of the fuzzy sets over all the primitive behaviors. The fuzzy output values are then defuzzified using the discrete form of Center-of-Sums defuzzification (Driankov et al., 1996).
Since composite behaviors only modulate lower-level behaviors using state information, composite behaviors do not require lower-level behaviors to provide any information to aid in the modulation process. This is in contrast to other behavior coordination mechanisms which, for example, may require low-level behaviors to indicate the utility of a specific action (Pirjanian & Matarić, 2001). The only restriction that an adaptive fuzzy behavior hierarchy places on modulated behaviors is that primitive behaviors produce a fuzzy set as output since fuzzy inferencing is used to combine their outputs into a single action.
It is important to note that since a composite behavior does not produce low-level control actions, it may not need the full joint state space of the composite task to provide effective behavior modulation. For example, it is possible that the direction of the closest collision is irrelevant when determining the modulation for a COLLISIONAVOIDANCE primitive behavior. It may be that only the estimated time until the collision is important. As a result, it may be possible to reduce the state information used by the modulation process in a composite behavior that provides comparable performance. A reduced state set such as this would provide significant benefits not only in reducing the complexity of the composite behavior's ruleset, but also in the effort required to develop the ruleset itself.
Although there are a number of ways to reduce the agent's state space (de Oliveira et al., 2003; Guyon & Elisseeff, 2003; Guyon et al., 2006; Raymer et al., 2000; Yang & Honavar, 1998), in the work presented here we use the approach where state information is converted into a more abstract form. This approach can result in either (1) fewer state variables or (2) no change in

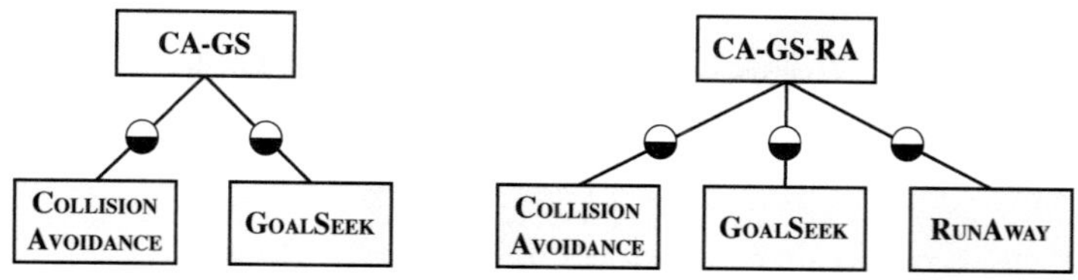

(a) CA-GS behavior hierarchy (b) CA-GS-RA behavior hierarchy

Fig. 2. The behavior hierarchies for the CA-GS and CA-GS-RA single-agent composite tasks are shown.

the number of state variables but simpler extracted variable sets. For example, a composite behavior may not need to know the exact relative direction to an object and only requires the magnitude of the direction for effective control. In this example, the original *direction* state variable is extracted to a more simple representation where both `SMALL_LEFT` and `SMALL_RIGHT` are abstracted to the same `SMALL` value. Since primitive tasks are, by definition, simple and straightforward, one can easily determine abstractions that may be beneficial

Although adaptive fuzzy behavior hierarchies have been shown to provide effective control, their implementation, as described by Tunstel, limits their application to two-level hierarchies. We have addressed this limitation by extending the architecture to properly function with hierarchies of arbitrary size (Eskridge & Hougen, 2009).

3. Problem Domains

For this work, a number of autonomous agent navigation problem domains were used. In each domain, an agent was given a complex task composed of N primitive tasks. In general, the primitive tasks used were active concurrently, interfered with one another, and were non-episodic (CINE). The only exception was the GOALSEEK task which terminated when an agent reached the goal location.

The composition of these N primitive tasks forms a composite task for which the agent should take an action at each timestep that maximizes the summed expected reward of each primitive task. An important aspect of this combination of primitive tasks is that an action that maximizes the reward for one primitive task could result in a penalty for another primitive task and, therefore, cause interference between the primitive tasks. While each primitive task had a (relatively) small state space, the state space for the composite task was the cross product of the state space for each primitive task: $S = S_1 \times S_2 \times \ldots \times S_N$. When this combined state space, referred to as the *joint state space*, was combined with the low-level action space, the resulting complexity made the traditional development of an effective controller impractical in some instances.

3.1 Single Agent Problem Domains

In the first single-agent composite task, an agent navigated towards a goal location while avoiding any obstacles in its path. This composite task, denoted CA-GS, was the combination of the COLLISIONAVOIDANCE and GOALSEEK primitive tasks. In the fuzzy behavior hierarchy for the CA-GS composite task, primitive behaviors were created at the lowest level for the COLLISIONAVOIDANCE and GOALSEEK primitive tasks (see Figure 2(a)). A composite

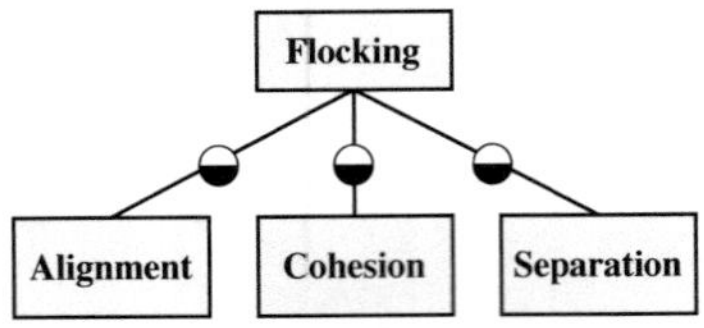

Fig. 3. The FLOCKING composite behavior composes the ALIGNMENT, COHESION, and SEPARATION primitive behaviors by using weights, denoted as half-filled circles.

behavior for the CA-GS composite task was then created at the level above the primitive behaviors and was responsible for weighting the primitive behaviors properly, given the current state of the agent with respect to the composite task as a whole.

In the second single-agent composite task, a third primitive task was added to the previous two. In this new primitive task, denoted RUNAWAY, the agent must avoid approaching too close to "hazardous" objects in the environment. The hazardous objects were not physical objects like obstacles with which the agent could collide, but instead represented areas that could be dangerous to the agent like areas of high-traffic or with difficult terrain. In COLLISIONAVOIDANCE, a penalty was only assessed if the agent actually collided with an obstacle. However, in RUNAWAY, an agent was penalized for simply being near hazards. The exact value of the penalty was dependent on the the distance to and strength of each hazard in the environment (a higher strength indicated a greater hazard). The new composite task was denoted CA-GS-RA. The fuzzy behavior hierarchy for the CA-GS-RA composite task was similar to that of the CA-GS hierarchy with the addition of the RUNAWAY primitive behavior (see Figure 2(b)).

3.2 Multi-Agent Problem Domains

In the first multi-agent composite task, a team of homogeneous agents must move together as a single unit, or *flock*, without explicit communication. This composite task, denoted FLOCKING, approximated the movement of flocks of birds or schools of fish (Reynolds, 1987; 1999) and was a combination of the ALIGNMENT, COHESION, and SEPARATION primitive tasks. In the ALIGNMENT primitive task, the agents were given the task of steering in the same direction and at the same speed as the rest of the team. In the COHESION primitive task, the agents were given the task of steering towards the other agents in the team in an effort to remain close to the team. Lastly, in the SEPARATION primitive task, the agents were given the task of steering away from other agents on the team which were "too close" in an effort to maintain a safe, minimum separation and prevent crowding. Agents relied only on the state information provided by sensors and did not communicate. Note that the goals of the ALIGNMENT and SEPARATION primitive tasks are diametrically opposed. Therefore, for FLOCKING to be successful, a policy that was able to effectively balance the two was necessary.

In the fuzzy behavior hierarchy for the FLOCKING composite task, primitive behaviors were created at the lowest level for the ALIGNMENT, COHESION, and SEPARATION primitive tasks (see Figure 3). A composite behavior for the FLOCKING composite task was then created at the level above the primitive behaviors and was responsible for weighting ALIGNMENT, COHESION, and SEPARATION properly, given the current state of the composite task.

In the next multi-agent composite task, we added the primitive task of COLLISIONAVOIDANCE to the FLOCKING composite task. In this task, each agent was tasked with avoiding collisions with other agents and with obstacles in the environment in addition to performing

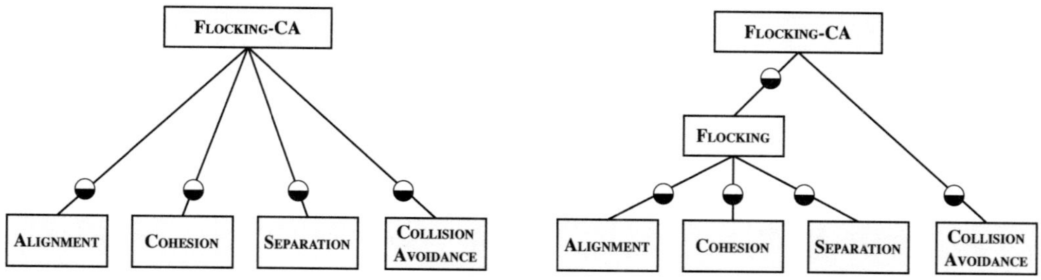

(a) 2-level hierarchy (b) 3-level hierarchy

Fig. 4. The two alternatives for implementing the FLOCKING-CA composite behavior are shown. In the first, the FLOCKING-CA composite behavior composes the ALIGNMENT, COHESION, SEPARATION, and COLLISIONAVOIDANCE primitive behaviors. In the second, FLOCKING-CA composes the FLOCKING composite behavior with the COLLISIONAVOIDANCE primitive behavior.

FLOCKING. The COLLISIONAVOIDANCE primitive task did not differentiate between collisions with other agents or obstacles. This new composite task, denoted FLOCKING-CA, presented the option of adding a new composite behavior, and, therefore, another level to the hierarchy (see Figure 4). Since the COLLISIONAVOIDANCE behavior was ignorant of the concept of a team and teammates, an argument can be made that it should be considered separately from the FLOCKING primitive behaviors. The use of an additional composite behavior at a higher level in the hierarchy not only simplified the action space of the FLOCKING-CA composite task, but it also had the potential to simplify the state space if the full joint state space of the composite task was not necessary for effective control. Furthermore, this hierarchical decomposition enabled existing policies for the FLOCKING task to be reused for the FLOCKING-CA task.

To further increase the complexity, the GOALSEEK primitive task was added to the previous composite task to create the FLOCKING-CA-GS composite task. While the COLLISIONAVOIDANCE primitive task could have actually assisted the task of FLOCKING by providing another means of avoiding collisions between members of the team in addition to the SEPARATION task, the addition of the GOALSEEK complicated the FLOCKING task. As with the FLOCKING-CA task, the clear separation between the FLOCKING composite task and the COLLISIONAVOIDANCE and GOALSEEK primitive tasks offered the potential for creating a separate composite behavior for coordinating the respective behaviors.

In the last multi-agent composite task, the RUNAWAY primitive task was added to the FLOCKING-CA-GS composite task to create the FLOCKING-CA-GS-RA composite task. As with the previous two composite tasks, a separate composite behavior which coordinated the FLOCKING composite task and the COLLISIONAVOIDANCE, GOALSEEK, and RUNAWAY primitive behaviors was possible. While the same potential benefits existed, the large number of primitive tasks which must be coordinated had the potential to exaggerate the results. As is described in Section 6, it was at this point that the complexity of the composite task's joint state space became too large for traditional methods of developing effective controllers to be practical and alternative methods were required. The use of this composite task represented the upper limit of complexity used in this work.

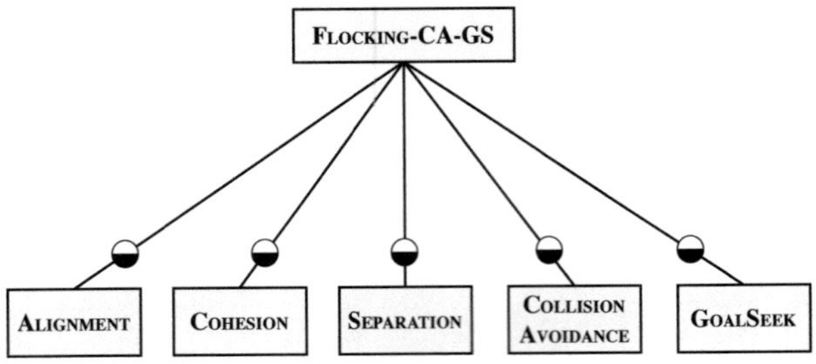

(a) 2-level hierarchy

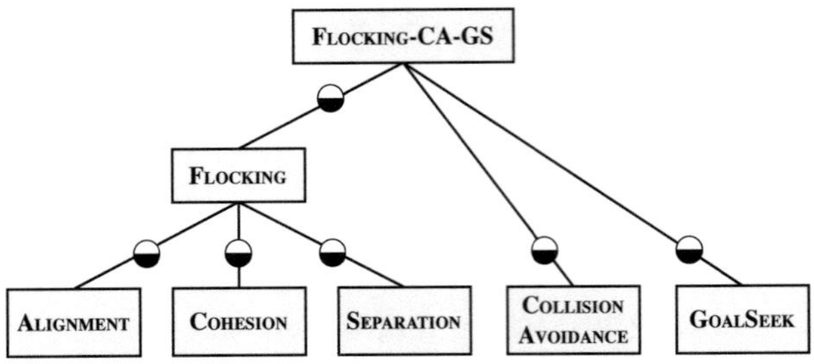

(b) 3-level hierarchy reusing one composite behavior

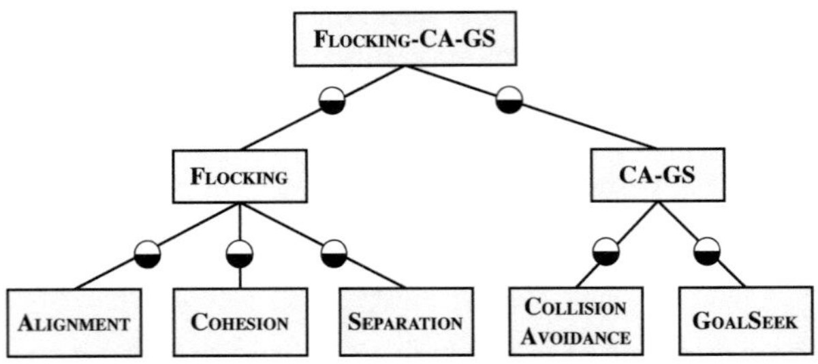

(c) 3-level hierarchy reusing two composite behaviors

Fig. 5. Three alternatives for implementing the FLOCKING-CA-GS composite behavior are shown. Each is similar to the corresponding hierarchy for the FLOCKING-CA composite task with the addition of the GOALSEEK primitive behavior

4. Development of Controllers

A standard approach to such complex tasks is to combine primitive tasks into a single composite task. A policy is then developed for the entire composite task, effectively developing a single policy responsible for addressing each primitive task and the coordination between them (see Figure 7(a)). The problem with this monolithic approach is that development of even the simplest composite task can be impractical due to the curse of dimensionality.

4.1 Modular Reinforcement Learning

Humphrys (1996) and Karlsson (1997) independently describe a reinforcement learning algorithm that is appropriate for the CINE types of problems under study here. In this algorithm, commonly referred to as *modular* reinforcement learning (Bhat et al., 2006; Sprague & Ballard,

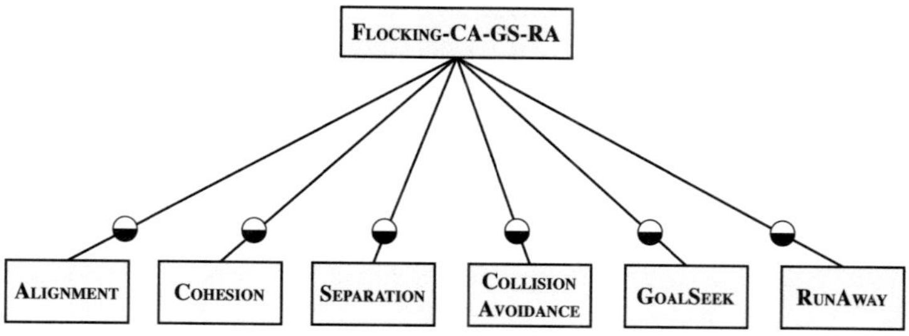

(a) 2-level hierarchy

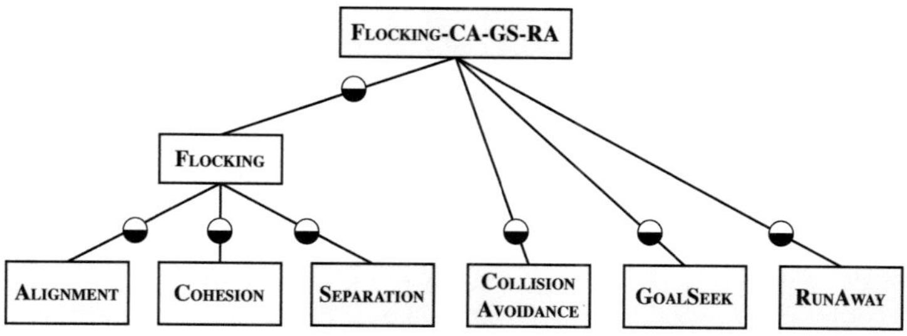

(b) 3-level hierarchy reusing one composite behavior

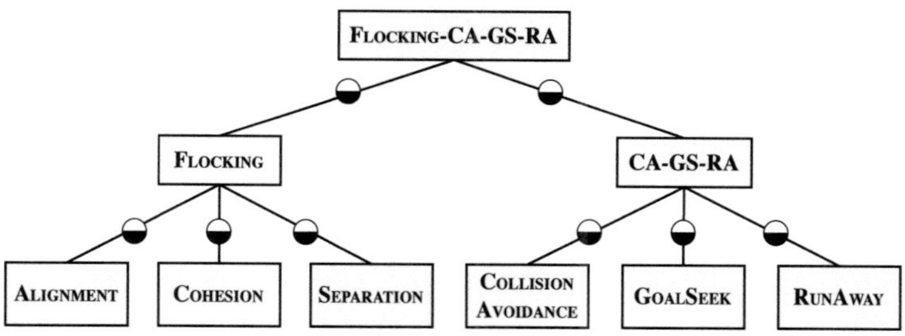

(c) 3-level hierarchy reusing two composite behaviors

Fig. 6. Three alternatives for implementing the FLOCKING-CA-GS-RA composite behavior are shown. Each is similar to the corresponding hierarchy for the FLOCKING-CA-GS composite task with the addition of the RUNAWAY primitive behavior

2003), a policy for each active primitive task is learned simultaneously using the state information and rewards local only to the task (see Figure 7(b)). At each time step, the policy for each subtask provides the action selection mechanism with a utility value for each possible action. This utility value is calculated using the value of taking a particular action from a given state, referred to as a *Q-value*, and is often simply the Q-value itself. These utilities are then used by the action selection mechanism to choose the action that the agent will take. The approach used in this work to choose the action, called the "greatest mass," simply chooses the action with the highest utility, or sum of Q-values, across all the primitive task policies (Karlsson, 1997).

Q-learning should not be used in learning the primitive task policies since it is off-policy and assumes the optimal policy will be followed (Watkins & Dayan, 1992). One cannot assume that the optimal policy will be followed for modular reinforcement learning since primitive

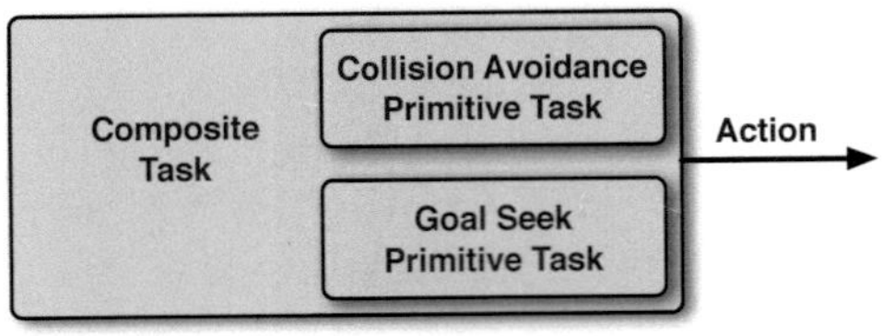

(a) Monolithic Reinforcement Learning

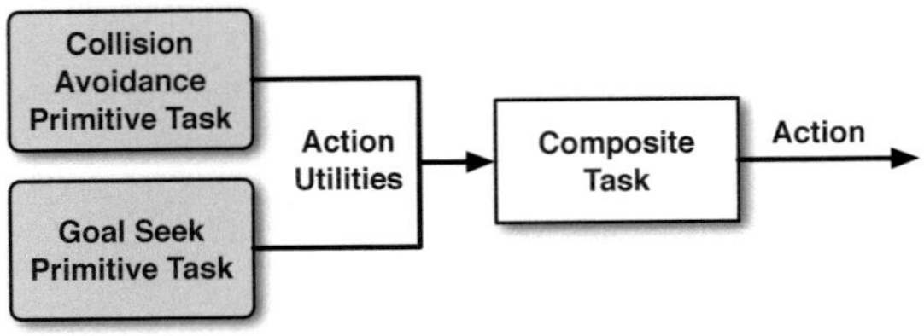

(b) Modular Reinforcement Learning

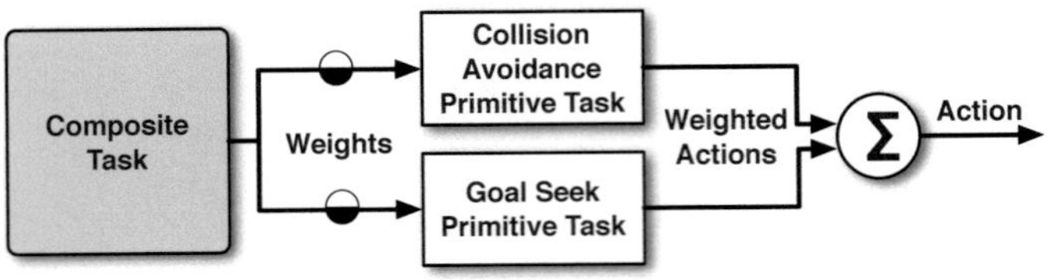

(c) Composite Reinforcement Learning

Fig. 7. A comparison of the different algorithms discussed in this work is shown using the COLLISIONAVOIDANCE-GOALSEEK composite task. The shaded tasks are where policy learning occurs in each algorithm. The half-filled circles denote the weights used to compose actions from primitive task policies for composite reinforcement learning.

task policies must share control of the agent (Russell & Zimdars, 2003; Sprague & Ballard, 2003). As a result, an on-policy learning method, such as the Sarsa algorithm, should be used (Rummery & Niranjan, 1994).

4.2 Composite Reinforcement Learning

As will be discussed in Section 6.4, experiments demonstrate that modular reinforcement learning does not perform well in the CINE tasks under study in this chapter. In light of this result, we introduce a modified reinforcement learning approach called *composite reinforcement learning* (see Figure 7(c)) which can be used to learn effective control policies for composite tasks built using CINE primitive tasks. Composite reinforcement learning leverages the architecture of the adaptive fuzzy behavior hierarchy to significantly improve the rate at which effective control policies are learned. Unlike modular reinforcement learning, composite reinforcement learning does not attempt to learn policies for the primitive tasks simultaneously. Instead, composite reinforcement learning learns an effective control policy for a given composite behavior only and reuses existing implementations of lower-level behaviors. These reused lower-level behaviors are viewed as black boxes and are modulated by the policy being learned. Therefore, instead of learning low-level motor control actions, composite reinforcement learning learns high-level modulation (i.e., weighting) actions on the lower-level behaviors. The reinforcement learning algorithm itself is largely unmodified except that the concept of an action has changed. The policy's actions are now weighting actions and after the policy's action has been taken, the lower-level behaviors are executed and the overall action of the agent is computed. The composite task policy being learned then determines the total reward and updates the relevant Q-value.

Note that the Q-values used by the learned policy are associated only with the modulation actions and not with the actions taken by the lower-level behaviors. While this means that the maximum performance of the learned policy is dependent on the performance of the lower-level behaviors in their associated tasks, in practice this appears to not present problems (see Section 6) and offers many benefits over other approaches, such as modular reinforcement learning.

One of the most significant benefits is the abstraction of the action space into high-level "meta-actions." As a result, the reinforcement learner is not required to learn the entire composite task from scratch. Rather, it only needs to learn how to best coordinate lower-level behaviors to accomplish the composite task. In a related benefit, existing behaviors can potentially be reused *without modification* by the learned policy and without specific requirements on their implementation method. Composite reinforcement learning does not require reused behaviors provide any information to aid in the learning or control process (e.g., Q or utility values). As a result, individual behaviors can be developed in isolation, simplifying the development process, using the method most appropriate for the task.

Furthermore, since the action space has been abstracted away from low-level motor control actions, it may be possible to aggressively abstract the agent's state for use in the composite behavior without the corresponding performance penalties commonly associated with perceptual aliasing (Whitehead, 1992). This is especially significant in light of our interest in directly comparing the effects of state and action abstraction on a controller's performance and learning rate. Note that this abstraction of the state only occurs in the composite behaviors; primitive behaviors still access the unabstracted state associated with the relevant primitive task to produce control actions.

While the idea of abstracting the action space into meta-actions is not novel and many hierarchical reinforcement learning approaches use it extensively (Dietterich, 2000; Konidaris & Barto, 2007; Rohanimanesh et al., 2004), our formulation of an action is novel. Since most approaches focus on episodic and non-interfering tasks, meta-actions in these approaches represent temporally extended sequences of actions. When a meta-action is executed, the meta-action assumes control of the agent either for the entire sequence of actions or until an event causes the high-level policy to re-examine the agent's state. In contrast, the meta-actions used by composite reinforcement learning are taken every timestep and represent the coordination of lower-level behaviors for that timestep only. In general, no one behavior is given complete control of the agent's actions.

5. Experiments

To evaluate the effects of state and action abstraction on the process of developing controllers for composite tasks, a series of experiments were performed in which controllers were automatically developed for each primitive and composite task using reinforcement learning and grammatical evolution (see Section 3). Experimental runs were evaluated using two different metrics. The first metric used was the best generalized performance of the agent controllers. This generalized performance was determined by executing agent controllers in environments that were different than the ones used in their development. The controller's performance was the mean undiscounted, total reward of the agent in all the environments. The second metric used was the computational effort used to develop the controllers and used the number of updates to the Q-values as the measure.

5.1 Evaluation Environments

For each composite task, forty environments were randomly generated. Agents were given random positions and orientations within a specified region of the environment. If a goal location was required, it was randomly placed within a specified distance interval from the agent(s). If obstacles were required, a random number of obstacles were generated and given random positions in an area surrounding the agent(s) and goal location. The same procedure was followed for hazardous objects, if required. These forty environments were organized into ten folds of four environments each for use in cross-validation (Cohen, 1995). Eight folds were used as a training set, one fold was used as a validation set, and a final fold was used as a testing set. Both validation and testing sets were used to evaluate the generalizability of the learned controller.

Each experiment consisted for forty individual runs initialized with a different random seed. Four experimental runs for each of the ten folds were performed. The same set of environments was shared between all experiments for a given primitive or composite task, while folds had different sets of training, validation, and testing environments. For example, all experiments using the two-dimensional CA-GS composite task shared the same set of environments, regardless of how the controller was developed or the architecture it used.

Agents were given a maximum of 1,500 time steps in each environment which constituted a single training episode. This was ample time for even the most risk-averse agent(s) to reach the goal location, if applicable, or to gain sufficient experience in the environment. While most of the primitive tasks used are non-episodic (the exception being the GOALSEEK primitive task), training was broken into episodes as a consequence of the nature of the evaluation environments and the primitive tasks themselves. Since the environments were unbounded, it was possible that in exploring the state space, agents could wander away from the finite number of obstacles or the other agents on the team and never have a realistic opportunity to return to the more "interesting" states of the environment. Furthermore, since much of this work is intended to operate on real robots, agent collisions warranted early termination of a training episode. Training episodes also ended early when an agent or the team of agents reached the goal location since the GOALSEEK task is inherently episodic.

5.2 State Space Abstraction

Since it is possible that composite behaviors in fuzzy behavior hierarchies do not require the full state space for effective coordination of lower-level behaviors, four different levels of abstraction of the agent's state space were used when learning composite behaviors. These were used to evaluate how abstractions affected both the rate at which effective composite behaviors were learned and their quality. Table 1 details the effects of each abstraction level on the state information for a composite behavior using the GOALSEEK primitive task.

Full This state space represents the original, joint state space of all the primitive tasks used in the composite task without any abstraction and acts as a baseline for comparison.

Large In this state space, state information describing directions, such as `SMALL_LEFT` or `SMALL_RIGHT`, are abstracted away into variables which denote the absolute value

Abstraction Level	State Information	States	Total States
Full	Goal arrival time	5	175
	Goal direction Θ	7	
	Goal direction Φ	5	
Large	Goal arrival time	5	125
	Goal direction $\|\Theta\|$	5	
	Goal direction $\|\Phi\|$	5	
Small	Goal seek priority	5	5

Table 1. The different state abstractions used in the development of a composite behavior using the GOALSEEK primitive task are shown.

of the angle, such as SMALL. State information not describing a direction remains unchanged.

Small In this state space, state information is abstracted into a single dynamic priority which is calculated using all the relevant state information local to each primitive task. This dynamic priority represented the task's determination of its applicability to the agent's current state. For example, using this state space, the CA-GS-RA composite behavior would only use dynamic priorities for the primitive behaviors COLLISIONAVOIDANCE, GOALSEEK, and RUNAWAY to determine how to weight its sub-behaviors. While this level of abstraction may appear to be too extreme, we have previously shown that rulesets using dynamic priorities can be developed which have similar performance to those using the **Full** state space (Eskridge & Hougen, 2006).

Minimal In this state space, the dynamic priorities from the **Small** state space were again used. However, instead of using the dynamic priorities for every primitive behavior, only the priorities of behaviors directly weighted by a composite behavior were used. For example, the FLOCKING-CA composite behavior would only use the dynamic priorities of the FLOCKING and COLLISIONAVOIDANCE sub-behaviors.

Note that these abstractions were only used by composite behaviors. Since primitive behaviors were responsible for producing low-level control actions, they still required the unabstracted state space relevant to their primitive task. Furthermore, since monolithic controllers were also responsible for producing low-level control actions, they required the unabstracted joint state space of the overall composite task.

5.3 Reward Functions

The reward functions for each primitive task as used in the development of composite tasks are shown in Table 2. Except for the terminal events of a collision or reaching the goal location, each reward was given per timestep. The reward values were developed with the maximum number of timesteps in mind and ensured that the total undiscounted reward did not create a bias towards controllers which "minimized the pain" by causing a collision as quickly as possible. While some portions of the reward function were not required (e.g., the goal distance penalty), they make the reward function more "dense" and act as progress estimators by allowing learning to make the most of each experience (Matarić, 1997; Smart & Kaelbling, 2002). While the addition of these unrequired components may have biased policies away

Primitive Task	Description	Value
COLLISIONAVOIDANCE	Collision event	-150
GOALSEEK	Goal reached event	150
	Goal distance penalty	$-0.03 \times Dist$
RUNAWAY	RunAway strength penalty	$-0.06 \times Str$
ALIGNMENT	Velocity heading difference penalty	$-0.02 \times \Delta Dir$
COHESION	Position error penalty	$-0.04 \times Dist$
SEPARATION	Separation strength penalty	$-0.02 \times Str$

Table 2. The reward functions used in developing controllers for composite tasks for each primitive task are shown. Note that while most rewards were given at each timestep, rewards for the terminal events of a collision and reaching the goal location are one-time rewards.

from the best solution, the benefit of allowing learning to make the most of each learning experience outweighed the potential problems in complex tasks such as the ones discussed in this chapter.

For the FLOCKING composite task, a survival reward of 0.09 was given for each timestep in which the agents were active, in addition to the rewards given by the primitive tasks themselves. This served to explicitly reward the agents for avoiding collisions with other agents and continuing to flock. In single agent environments, the agent merely needed to reach the goal for the reward to be given. In multi-agent environments, the reward for reaching the goal location was only awarded if the mean position of the team was within a specified distance to the goal. This served to explicitly reward agents that reached the goal with the other agents in the team and not agents that left their team to reach the goal faster.

Due to the complexity of the tasks and the randomness of the environments, an optimal performance value for each task would be prohibitive to calculate. As a result, the performance of learned controllers cannot be compared to the performance of an optimal controller. However, based on an understanding of the experimental configuration and experience with the tasks themselves, we can identify the approximate mean performance values one would expect from an effective controller.

5.4 Reinforcement Learning Configuration

The Sarsa reinforcement learning algorithm was used to learn policies for primitive and composite tasks. To speed learning, the replacing eligibility traces version of Sarsa, referred to as Sarsa(λ), was used (Sutton & Barto, 1998). The parameters used are shown in Table 3. Since the state-action space for many of the experiments performed precluded tabular storage of the state-action values, or Q-values, neural networks were used to approximate Q-values. The neural networks consisted of a single hidden layer in which the number of nodes was a function of the number of input nodes. Unlike previous work, we found that a relatively large number of hidden nodes (1.5 times the number of input nodes) were required for policies operating in our environments (Rummery & Niranjan, 1994). Previous work in the field has concluded that using a single network to approximate all the Q-values can result in unintentional modifications of the Q-values for actions other than the one chosen by the learning algorithm (Lin, 1993; Rummery & Niranjan, 1994). As a result, a separate network for each action was used in an effort to isolate the Q-values of each action.

Parameter	Value
Learning rate (α)	0.01
Discount factor (γ)	0.99
TD decay (λ)	0.25
Exploration (ϵ)	0.01
NN weight range	$[-0.25 : 0.25]$
NN momentum	0.01
NN hidden nodes	$1.5 \times N_{input}$

Table 3. Reinforcement learning parameters

The effects of a multi-agent environment further complicates learning as it makes the environment non-stationary (Claus & Boutilier, 1998). To simplify the process as much as possible, we chose to use the naïve approach in which all agents used and updated the same set of Q-values, or, more specifically, the same set of neural networks approximating Q-values. Experiments have shown that this form of cooperation does not impede learning and can even improve the learning rate (Crites & Barto, 1998; Tan, 1993).

While there are techniques for using fuzzy logic with reinforcement learning (Berenji, 1992; Er & Zhou, 2006; Glorennec & Jouffe, 1997; Jouffe, 1998), experience has shown that such modifications can increase the time needed to learn effective policies. Since fuzzy logic is not required to implement the behaviors (Tunstel, 2001), it was not used for behaviors developed using reinforcement learning. However, primitive behaviors that were developed manually and reused for development of composite behaviors did use fuzzy logic. While there are plans to use fuzzy logic with reinforcement learning (see Section 7), we were able to gather conclusive results without its use.

6. Results and Analysis

Figures showing the results of experimental runs reflect the mean performance of controllers on the validation set of environments. As stated in Section 5.1, environments were organized into ten folds for use with cross-validation. Each experiment consisted of four runs for each of the ten fold combinations for a total of 40 runs.

6.1 Developing Single-Agent, Composite Task Controllers

Figures 8 and 9 depict the results of learning for the CA-GS and CA-GS-RA composite tasks, respectively. For controllers developed using the **Full** and **Large** abstraction levels, composite reinforcement learning was able to achieve high performance within just a few updates for both tasks. However, the **Small** abstraction level was unable to converge to an effective policy in either task, although effective policies were learned. While monolithic reinforcement learning was able to learn an effective policy, results of a randomized two-way ANOVA test demonstrates that there was a statistically significantly difference between the rate at which effective controllers were learned between monolithic and composite reinforcement learning at the 95% confidence level. Modular reinforcement learning was unable to converge to an effective policy. It was able to achieve moderate success early and learned a number of effective policies, but was unable to converge to one.

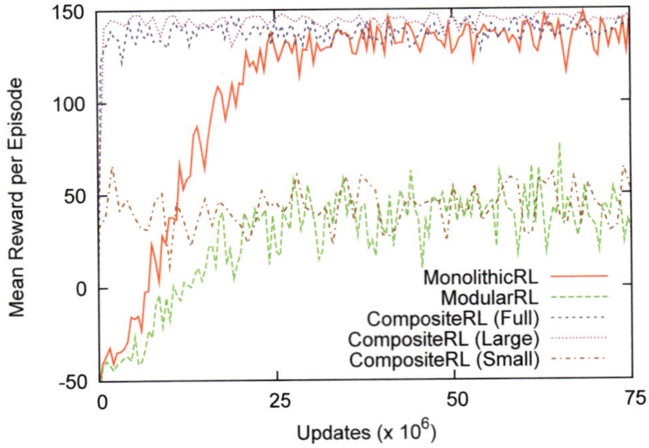

Fig. 8. Reinforcement learning results on the validation set environments for the CA-GS composite task are shown.

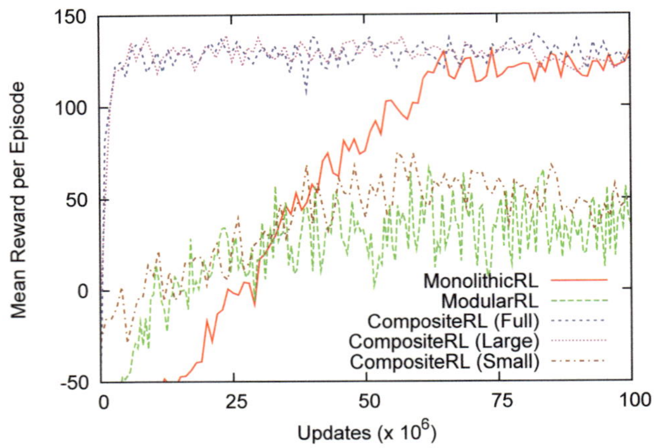

Fig. 9. Reinforcement learning results on the validation set environments for the CA-GS-RA composite task are shown.

6.2 Developing Multi-Agent, Composite Task Controllers

Figure 10 depicts the results of using reinforcement learning to learn a policy for the FLOCKING composite task. Controllers developed using the adaptive fuzzy behavior hierarchy and composite reinforcement learning had statistically significantly higher performance than those developed using either monolithic or modular reinforcement learning at the 95% confidence level. Furthermore, controllers using the **Small** abstraction level did not exhibit the poor performance previously seen in the single agent tasks. In fact, controllers using the **Small** abstraction level had statistically significantly better performance than all other controllers in the testing set environments at the 99% confidence level as determined by the paired Student's t-test using the Bonferroni adjustment.

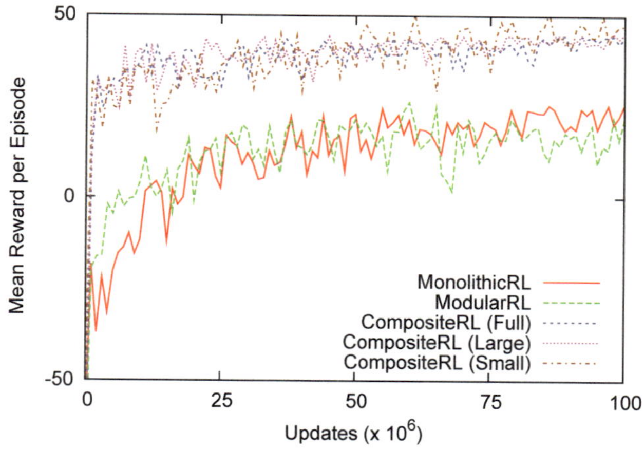

Fig. 10. Reinforcement learning results on the validation set environments for the FLOCKING composite task are shown.

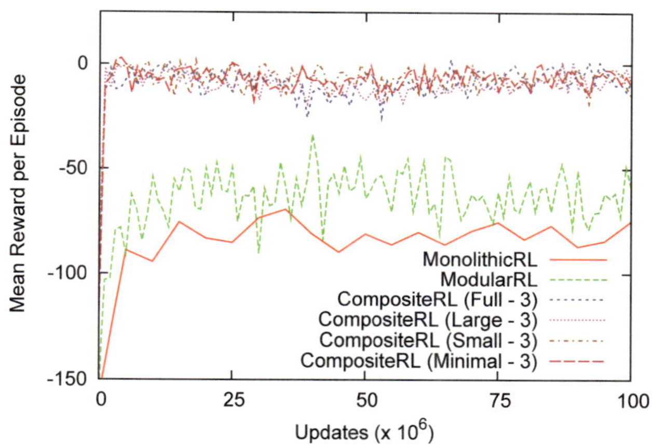

Fig. 11. Reinforcement learning results on the validation set environments for the FLOCKING-CA composite task are shown. Due to storage constraints, results for monolithic reinforcement learning experimental runs used fewer checkpoints than other experimental runs.

Figure 11 depicts the results of using reinforcement learning to learn a policy for the FLOCKING-CA composite task. Again, controllers that used the adaptive fuzzy behavior hierarchy were learned faster than those that didn't use the hierarchy and had higher performance. Note, that these controllers used the three-level hierarchy depicted in Figure 5(c). Controllers developed using modular reinforcement learning performed statistically significantly better than those developed using monolithic reinforcement learning at the 99% confidence level, but were unable to generalize to the full range of environments present in the validation or testing sets.

Not shown in the figure are the results for controllers using a two-level adaptive fuzzy behavior hierarchy. Even with the use of the adaptive fuzzy behavior hierarchy, the significantly

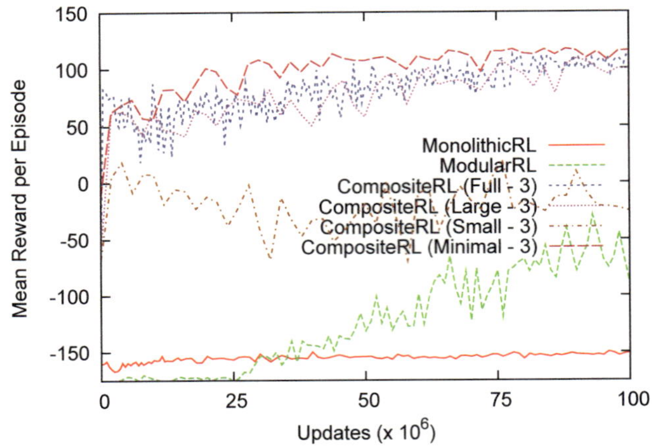

Fig. 12. Reinforcement learning results on the validation set environments for the FLOCKING-CA-GS composite task in two dimensions are shown. The "3" denotes controllers using a three-level behavior hierarchy. The results of controllers using two-level hierarchies are not shown to improve clarity.

larger action space of the 2-level hierarchy negated any benefits that the hierarchy offered. While the hierarchy and the reuse of existing primitive behaviors meant that it did not need to learn the low-level actions needed to accomplish FLOCKING-CA, the size of the state-action space was simply too large to quickly find an effective policy. Furthermore, the increased complexity resulted in almost a four-fold increase in the wall-clock time required to learn and update Q-values for the two-level hierarchies over that of the three-level hierarchies.

Figure 12 depicts the results of using reinforcement learning to learn a policy for the FLOCKING-CA-GS composite task. Just as in the previous experiments, controllers learned using composite reinforcement learning and using the adaptive fuzzy behavior hierarchy had a statistically significantly higher "best-of-run" performance than monolithic reinforcement learning at the 99% confidence level as monolithic reinforcement learning was even unable to learn how to simply avoid a collision. Controllers developed using modular reinforcement learning were able to gain some traction in learning an effective controller, but were unable to converge to an effective policy. Note that just as in the single-agent composite tasks, controllers developed using the **Small** abstraction level performed statistically significantly worse than other controllers developed using the adaptive fuzzy behavior hierarchy, including those using the **Minimal** abstraction level which also uses adaptive priorities.

This is the first set of results in which a difference between controllers using the different abstraction levels can be observed. Results of two-way randomized ANOVA tests show that controllers using the **Minimal** abstraction level were able to more statistically significantly achieve consistently higher performance than controllers using the other abstraction levels at the 95% confidence level. However, controllers using the **Full** abstraction level were able to learn a policy at some point during learning that had statistically significantly better performance than controllers using the **Minimal** abstraction level at the 99% confidence level.

Figure 13 depicts the results of using reinforcement learning to learn a policy for the FLOCKING-CA-GS-RA composite task. These results detail, for the first time, a clear separation in the performance of controllers using the various abstraction levels. Randomized two-

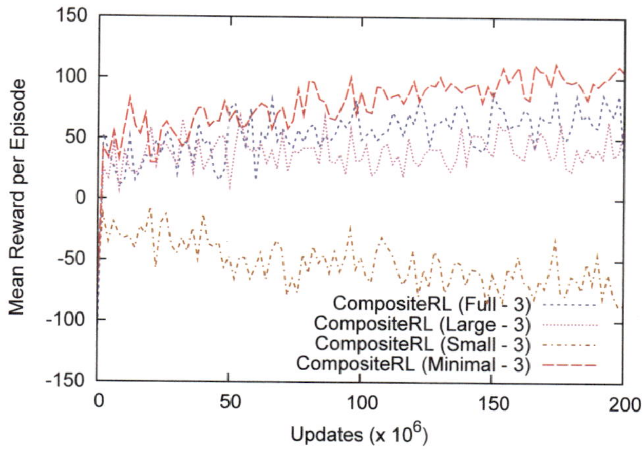

Fig. 13. Reinforcement learning results on the validation set environments for the FLOCKING-CA-GS-RA composite task in two dimensions are shown.

way ANOVA tests show that, like the FLOCKING-CA-GS composite task, controllers using the **Minimal** abstraction level were able to more statistically significantly achieve consistently higher performance than controllers using the other abstraction levels at the 95% confidence level, but there was no statistically significant difference in the "best-of-run" testing fitness between controllers using the different abstraction levels. Controllers using the **Full** abstraction level had a higher mean reward per episode than controllers using the **Small** abstraction level at the 95% confidence level. Monolithic and modular reinforcement learning were not used to learn controllers due to their consistent poor performance in the simpler, multi-agent composite tasks.

6.3 Analysis

These results demonstrate that controllers using adaptive fuzzy behavior hierarchies significantly outperformed controllers with other architectures in terms of performance, rate of development, or both. While there are many reasons for this improvement, we believe that the central reason for this improvement is the action abstraction that adaptive fuzzy behavior hierarchies provide. Note that in the CA-GS-RA task, the action space for monolithic controllers consisted of only two variables: the change in speed and the change of direction. However, for controllers using composite behaviors, the action space of the composite behavior consisted of three variables: the weights for the COLLISIONAVOIDANCE, GOALSEEK, and RUNAWAY primitive behaviors. Despite this increased action space, controllers using composite behaviors were developed significantly faster and with significantly better performance. This is due to the fact that although the action space of the composite behavior was larger, it consisted of high-level, abstracted "meta-actions" instead of the more complex, low-level control actions. As has been previously discussed, although other approaches also use the concept of "meta-actions," the action abstraction used in this chapter is fundamentally different since the primitive tasks used were, in general, concurrent, interfering, and non-episodic.

We can conclude that action abstraction is more useful than state abstraction by comparing the performance of controllers used for the complex, multi-agent composite tasks. In these tasks, the controller could be designed with a hierarchy that used a single composite behavior or a hierarchy that made use of multiple composite behaviors in different hierarchical levels. An example is the three alternatives for implementing the FLOCKING-CA-GS composite behavior shown in Figure 5. Results show that even with significant state abstraction, controllers using the two-level hierarchy shown in Figure 5(a) were only able to achieve mediocre performance due to the sheer size of the action space. However, effective controllers using the three-level hierarchy shown in Figure 5(c) were able to be developed without any abstraction of the agent's state. It is important to also note that using reinforcement learning to learn controllers using the two-level hierarchy in the FLOCKING-CA-GS task took significantly more computational time than those using the three-level hierarchy. This is due to the fact that in the Sarsa algorithm, the Q-value for each of the 3,125 possible actions must be calculated at each time step. Over the course of the entire experimental run, this resulted in almost a four fold increase in the wall clock time required to develop controllers using a two-level hierarchy over those using a three-level hierarchy.

A surprising result is that for many of the composite tasks evaluated, there was no statistically significant difference between controllers using the various state abstraction levels with the exception of the **Small** abstraction level. While the use of abstraction can significantly reduce the size of the state space, the possibility of over-abstracting the state space and negatively impacting the controller's performance exists. However, in general, this was not observed.

Not reflected in these results is the computational effort required to develop the primitive behaviors used by the controllers using adaptive fuzzy behavior hierarchies. The primitive behaviors used in these experiments were manually developed and were designed to be effective, but not optimal. Since the primitive tasks associated with these behaviors are relatively simple, the process of manually creating these rulesets was straightforward. However, if manually creating the behaviors is impractical, results show that effective policies for the single-agent behaviors can be easily learned. Even when the the computational effort of creating the primitive behaviors is included, developing controllers that use adaptive fuzzy behavior hierarchies is still far more beneficial and practical than the other approaches evaluated.

The performance of controllers developed with composite reinforcement learning and using the **Small** abstraction level are of particular interest as it may indicate that we have over-abstracted the state space. In many of the tasks used, an effective policy could be learned using the **Small** abstraction level, but reinforcement learning was unable to *converge* to an effective policy. While there are a number of potential reasons for this lack of convergence, we do not believe this is an inherent problem with the dynamic priorities used by the **Small** abstraction level since reinforcement learning converged to effective policies for the FLOCKING task using the **Small** abstraction level. There were a number of composite tasks for which controllers using the **Small** abstraction level provided effective control. We believe the root cause of the problem lies with the dynamic priority generated for the GOALSEEK primitive task. In each composite task using GOALSEEK, the development of controllers using the **Small** abstraction level was unable to converge.

To evaluate our hypothesis, we altered the **Small** abstraction level by replacing the GOALSEEK adaptive priority with the GOALSEEK state information from the **Full** abstraction level (i.e., the arrival time at and direction to the goal location) and performed a number of the experiments again. The results of these experiments using the altered **Small** abstraction level were compared to the results using the original **Small** abstraction level. The results for the single-agent composite tasks are shown in Figure 14. Controllers that did not use the GOALSEEK adaptive priority were learned faster, had higher performance, or both when compared to controllers which did use the priority. Although not shown, the performance of controllers

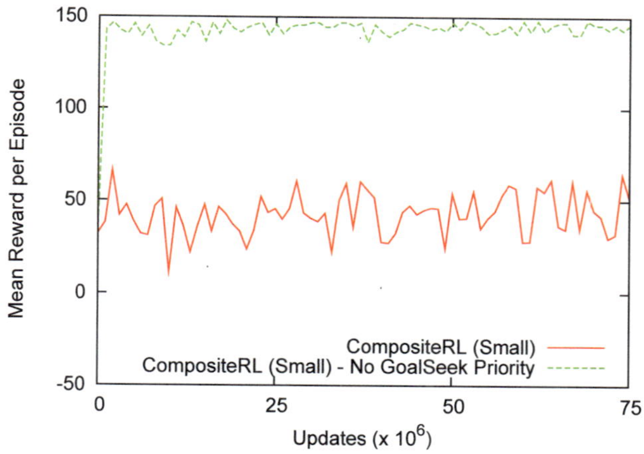

(a) CA-GS

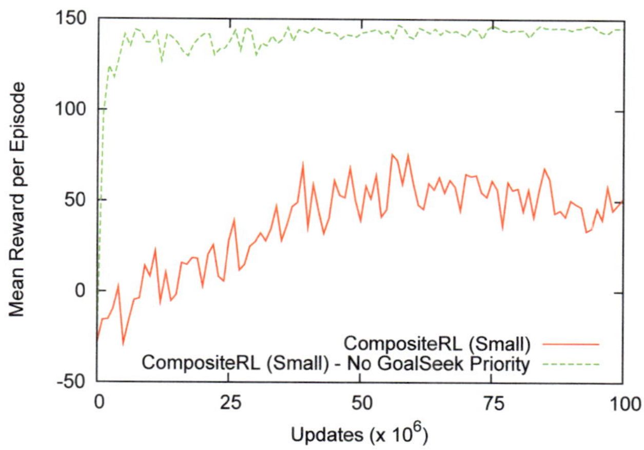

(b) CA-GS-RA

Fig. 14. Results on the validation set environments for the CA-GS and CA-GS-RA composite tasks comparing different approaches for the **Small** abstraction level.

using the modified **Small** abstraction level were comparable to the performance of the controllers learned using the other abstraction levels. This indicates that the GOALSEEK adaptive priority was somehow the contributing factor to the low performance in the previous experiments. Exactly why the GOALSEEK adaptive priority causes such problems is unknown and worthy of future investigation.

6.4 Discussion

As these results demonstrate, neither monolithic or modular reinforcement learning produce effective controllers as the complexity of the composite task increases. For monolithic reinforcement learning, the reason for this inability to gain traction on the problem is that it simply cannot cope with the complexity of the state space. However, this simple explanation does not work for modular reinforcement learning since it was explicitly designed to handle such complexity. While the exact reason for modular reinforcement learning's inability to produce effective control policies is unknown and the subject of future research, our work has illuminated a number of problem areas that could affect its use in developing controllers for the type of tasks under study in this chapter.

First, modular reinforcement learning makes the implicit assumption that rewards are consistent across all the primitive tasks which complicates the process of learning the policies for the primitive tasks (Bhat et al., 2006). While the construction of the composite task's reward function is designed to promote specific traits in the composite task's policy (e.g., a risk-averse policy versus a risk-taking policy), the unintended consequence is that the policies of the primitive tasks show the effects of these traits. This is due to the fact that, in modular reinforcement learning, all learning takes place in the policies of the primitive tasks. As a result, the policy for a given primitive task could potentially only be useful in the composite task for which it was originally learned.

A further potential problem, as modular reinforcement learning is currently implemented, is that it requires that the policies for primitive tasks provide the learned Q-value for a given action. Therefore, it is unable to reuse polices developed using methods other than reinforcement learning. While it is possible, in general, to learn the Q-values for an existing policy offline, this method can produce the same bias in the Q-values that the use of Q-learning produces since the Q-values must reflect the shared control of the agent. Even though alternative methods could be used to provide utility values without the use of Q-values (Pirjanian & Matarić, 2001), modular reinforcement learning still depends on control decisions flowing up from the low-level policies. As a result, there is no scaling advantage to extending beyond a two-level hierarchy where learning occurs at the lowest level since the top level merely uses a simple heuristic to combine the lower-level results.

In light of these difficulties, the success of composite reinforcement learning in these experiments is even more significant. It was the only approach which was consistently able to produce effective controllers. Furthermore, it was the only approach which was able to produce effective controllers for the complex FLOCKING-CA-GS-RA task.

7. Conclusion

The most significant result of these experiments is that, in the problem domains used in this chapter, the abstraction of an agent's action space provided more tangible benefits in the development of agent controllers than abstraction of an agent's state space. In a direct comparison, controllers that used significant action abstraction and no state abstraction had higher performance and were developed faster than controllers that made extensive use of state abstraction and moderate action abstraction. This is due to the fact that action abstraction changed the focus of the controller from one of low-level control to one of high-level coordination. This change in focus not only made the development of controllers for complex composite tasks more practical, but in many of the tasks, it also allowed the controller to have higher performance.

One aspect that is fundamental to the improved performance and rate of development of controllers using adaptive fuzzy behavior hierarchies was the ability to reuse existing primitive and composite behaviors. The ability to reuse, without modification, behaviors developed for one task in another task allowed for the development of controllers in individual pieces. The benefits of this approach are apparent when compared to the other approaches evaluated in these experiments which attempted to develop a controller all at once. As a result of this

reuse, controllers for complex composite tasks that were once impractical to develop can now be developed with reasonable effort.
The results of the experiments shown in this work demonstrate that while the use of modular reinforcement learning has been successful in more constrained problem domains, it was unable to consistently produce effective control policies in the problem domains used here. For the problem domains used, the prospect of simultaneously learning effective policies for each primitive task proved to be too complicated. In contrast, composite reinforcement learning was the only approach that was consistently able to produce effective control policies. As discussed above, we believe that this was due to the use of action abstraction and the ability to reuse existing primitive behaviors, regardless of their implementation.
The most immediate opportunity for future work is a more in-depth investigation of the erratic behavior of using the **Small** abstraction level with the GOALSEEK primitive task. The next opportunity for future work is to use fuzzy reinforcement learning to learn composite behavior policies instead of the discrete Sarsa approach (Jouffe, 1998). The use of fuzzy reinforcement learning offers the potential for faster learning since the agent's state is no longer confined to a single discrete value. Lastly, the results of the current work can be used to develop more complex controllers in a variety of ways. One way is to directly use adaptive fuzzy behavior hierarchies to create far more complicated behavior hierarchies. Since our ultimate focus is in the development of agent controllers for use in complex, multi-agent tasks, the results of this work provide significant contributions in making the development of such controllers practical.

Acknowledgements

We would like to thank all the members of the AI research group at the University of Oklahoma for their contributions. We would like to especially thank to John Antonio, Sesh Commuri, Andrew Fagg, and Amy McGovern for their input and insights. Some of the computing for this project was performed at the OU Supercomputing Center for Education & Research (OSCER) at the University of Oklahoma.

8. References

Berenji, H. R. (1992). A reinforcement learning–based architecture for fuzzy logic control, *International Journal of Approximate Reasoning* **6**(2): 267–292.

Bhat, S., Isbell Jr., C. L. & Mateas, M. (2006). On the difficulty of modular reinforcement learning for real-world partial programming, *National Conference on Artificial Intelligence (AAAI)*, Vol. 21, AAAI Press, pp. 318–325.

Claus, C. & Boutilier, C. (1998). The dynamics of reinforcement learning in cooperative multi-agent systems, *National Conference on Artificial Intelligence (AAAI)*, pp. 746–752.

Cohen, P. R. (1995). *Empirical Methods for Artificial Intelligence*, MIT Press, Cambridge, MA, USA.

Crites, R. H. & Barto, A. G. (1998). Elevator group control using multiple reinforcement learning agents, *Machine Learning* **33**(2): 235–262.

de Oliveira, L. S., Sabourin, R., Bortolozzi, F. & Suen, C. Y. (2003). A methodology for feature selection using multiobjective genetic algorithms for handwritten digit string recognition, *International Journal of Pattern Recognition and Artificial Intelligence* **17**(6): 903–929.

Dietterich, T. G. (2000). An overview of MAXQ hierarchical reinforcement learning, *International Symposium on Abstraction, Reformulation, and Approximation*, Springer-Verlag London, UK, pp. 26–44.

Driankov, D., Hellendoorn, H. & Reinfrank, M. (1996). *An Introduction to Fuzzy Control*, second edn, Springer-Verlag.

Er, M. J. & Zhou, Y. (2006). A novel reinforcement learning approach for automatic generation of fuzzy inference systems, *IEEE International Conference on Fuzzy Systems*, Vancouver, BC, pp. 100–105.

Eskridge, B. E. & Hougen, D. F. (2006). Prioritizing fuzzy behaviors in multi-robot pursuit teams, *IEEE International Conference on Fuzzy Systems*, pp. 1119–1125.

Eskridge, B. E. & Hougen, D. F. (2009). Extending adaptive fuzzy behavior hierarchies to multiple levels, *Technical Report TR-OU-REAL-09-001*, Department of Computer Science, University of Oklahoma, Norman, OK.

Glorennec, P. Y. & Jouffe, L. (1997). Fuzzy Q-learning, *IEEE International Conference on Fuzzy Systems*, Vol. 2, pp. 659–662.

Guyon, I. & Elisseeff, A. (2003). An introduction to variable and feature selection, *Journal of Machine Learning Research* **3**: 1157–1182.

Guyon, I., Gunn, S., Nikravesh, M. & Zadeh, L. A. (2006). *Feature Extraction: Foundations and Applications*, Studies in Fuzziness and Soft Computing, Springer-Verlag, Secaucus, NJ, USA.

Humphrys, M. (1996). Action selection methods using reinforcement learning, *From Animals to Animats 4: Proceedings of the Fourth International Conference on Simulation of Adaptive Behavior*, MIT Press, Bradford Books, pp. 135–144.

Jouffe, L. (1998). Fuzzy inference system learning by reinforcement methods, *IEEE Transactions on Systems, Man and Cybernetics, Part C* **28**(3): 338–355.

Karlsson, J. (1997). *Learning to Solve Multiple Goals*, PhD thesis, University of Rochester, Rochester, NY, USA.

Konidaris, G. & Barto, A. G. (2007). Building portable options: Skill transfer in reinforcement learning, *International Joint Conference on Artificial Intelligence*, pp. 895–900.

Lin, L.-J. (1993). Scaling up reinforcement learning for robot control, *International Conference on Machine Learning*, Morgan Kaufmann, pp. 182–189.

Matarić, M. J. (1997). Reinforcement learning in the multi-robot domain, *Autonomous Robots* **4**(1): 73–83.

Pirjanian, P. & Matarić, M. J. (2001). Multiple objective vs. fuzzy behavior coordination, *Fuzzy Logic Techniques for Autonomous Vehicle Navigation*, Vol. 61 of *Studies in Fuzziness and Soft Computing*, Springer-Phisica Verlag, chapter 10, pp. 235–253.

Raymer, M. L., Punch, W. F., Goodman, E. D., Kuhn, L. A. & Jain, A. K. (2000). Dimensionality reduction using genetic algorithms, *IEEE Transactions on Evolutionary Computation* **4**(2): 164–171.

Reynolds, C. W. (1987). Flocks, herds, and schools: A distributed behavioral model, *Computer Graphics* **21**(4): 25–34.

Reynolds, C. W. (1999). Steering behaviors for autonomous characters, *Proceedings of the Game Developers Conference*, pp. 763–782.

Rohanimanesh, K., Jr., R. P., Mahadevan, S. & Grupen, R. A. (2004). Coarticulation in Markov decision processes, *Conference on Neural Information Processing Systems*, pp. 1137–1144.

Rohanimanesh, K. & Mahadevan, S. (2002). Learning to take concurrent actions, *Conference on Neural Information Processing Systems*, MIT Press, pp. 1619–1626.

Rummery, G. A. & Niranjan, M. (1994). On-line Q-learning using connectionist systems, *Technical Report CUED/F-INFENG/TR166*, Cambridge University.

Russell, S. J. & Zimdars, A. (2003). Q-decomposition for reinforcement learning agents, *International Conference on Machine Learning*, AAAI Press, pp. 656–663.

Smart, W. D. & Kaelbling, L. P. (2002). Effective reinforcement learning for mobile robots, *International Conference on Robotics and Automation*, Vol. 4, IEEE, pp. 3404–3410.

Sprague, N. & Ballard, D. H. (2003). Multiple-goal reinforcement learning with modular Sarsa(0), *International Joint Conference on Artificial Intelligence*, pp. 1445–1447.

Sutton, R. S. & Barto, A. G. (1998). *Reinforcement Learning: An Introduction*, MIT Press.

Tan, M. (1993). Multi-agent reinforcement learning: Independent versus cooperative agents, *International Conference on Machine Learning*, pp. 330–337.

Tunstel, E. (1999). Fuzzy-behavior modulation with threshold activation for autonomous vehicle navigation, *18th International Conference of the North American Fuzzy Information Procesing Society (NAFIPS)*, New York, NY, pp. 776–780.

Tunstel, E. (2001). Fuzzy-behavior synthesis, coordination, and evolution in an adaptive behavior hierarchy, *Fuzzy Logic Techniques for Autonomous Vehicle Navigation*, Vol. 61 of *Studies in Fuzziness and Soft Computing*, Springer-Phisica Verlag, chapter 9, pp. 205–234.

Watkins, C. J. & Dayan, P. (1992). Q-learning, *Machine Learning* **8**(3-4): 279–292.

Whitehead, S. D. (1992). *Reinforcement Learning for the Adaptive Control of Perception and Action*, PhD thesis, University of Rochester.

Yang, J. & Honavar, V. (1998). Feature subset selection using a genetic algorithm, *IEEE Intelligent Systems and Their Applications* **13**(2): 44–49.

2

Graph Laplacian Based Transfer Learning Methods in Reinforcement Learning

Yi-Ting Tsao, Ke-Ting Xiao, Von-Wun Soo and Chung-Cheng Chiu
Department of Computer Science, National Tsing Hua University
HsinChu, Taiwan

1. Introduction

In the real world, people often reuse their knowledge in dealing with daily life problems. They can observe facts in an environment and recall similar experience in the past to deal with new situations. This phenomenon implies that there must be some features for people to compare the similarity between two environments. For example, toilet papers are usually placed nearby cashiers in different marts in Taiwan as shown in Fig. 1. In these two photos, orange ovals represent features for cashiers and red ovals represent features for toilet papers. The features which allow people to recognize the fact "Toilet papers are usually placed nearby cashiers." are the kinds of experience which could be reused.

Fig. 1. Two different marts in Taiwan

One of disadvantages in reinforcement learning (Kimberly & Mahadevan) (Sutton & Barto, 1998) is that two different tasks with different initial states and goal states must be learned to acquire good policies separately. It would waste time to simply learn twice in two different tasks if they share some similar subtasks. Transfer learning is an approach to improve the performance of cross tasks by avoiding redundancy. Some previous work show that transferring knowledge between two tasks could speed up learning (Matthew E. Taylor, Stone, & Liu, 2005). In reinforcement learning, the value function provides a guideline for

action selection in a given state. In other words, the value function could be converted to the corresponding policy, which guides action selection. Therefore, transferring the value function is an intuitive approach in reinforcement learning.
The aim of transfer learning is to reuse learned knowledge from a source task to accelerate learning in a related target task. Many transfer methods which are based on different features, such as the value function or the policy, have been proposed (Hessling & Goel, 2005; Liu & Stone, 2006; Matthew E. Taylor & Stone, 2007; Mattew E. Taylor, Whiteson, & Stone, 2007). Some researchers propose a rule transfer method which is based on case-based reasoning. They acquire some rules by approximating the policy in a source task and then translate them into corresponding rules, which could be used as the policy for a target task (Hessling & Goel, 2005). In more details, they train a decision tree as rules with respect to the value function in a source task and then reuse the decision tree in the target task. In order to transfer, they assume that two tasks have similar descriptions. In addition, some researchers represent the policy as a neural network in a source task and transfer it to a target task (Mattew E. Taylor et al., 2007). However, it requires some hand-coded translation functions. Some researchers represent states and actions as qualitative dynamic Bayes networks (QDBNs) and find their mapping between a source task and a target task (Liu & Stone, 2006). However, finding the mapping needs a lot of efforts. The major problem of the above methods is the use of translation functions that are problem dependent and thus difficult to be defined, even by an expert.
A novel transfer method which is based on proto-value functions has been proposed (Kimberly & Mahadevan, 2006; Mahadevan, 2005; Mahadevan & Maggioni, 2006, 2007). Proto-value functions, which are derived from spectral graph theory, harmonic analysis, and Riemannian manifold, could be used to represent a set of basis functions to approximate a function. This method reuses proto-value functions from a source task and just learns their weights in composing the value function for a target task. Therefore, an advantage of this method is that it transfers from a source task to a target task without any translation function. However, it needs some exploring trials in a target task to acquire accurate weights for proto-value functions.
Reusing learned knowledge could save some time by avoiding redundant learning. Transfer learning is an approach to achieve it. In this chapter, we propose transfer methods to obtain a better prior policy from a source task to reduce learning time in a target task without hand-coded translation functions by graph Laplacian. Graph Laplacian, which is constructed by the topology of the state space, are problem independent, so it is helpful for transfer. In the following sections, we will introduce our transfer methods step-by-step. In section 2, we introduce some background knowledge such as Markov decision process (MDP), reinforcement learning, graph Laplacian, and etc. In section 3, we illustrate our transfer methods in detail. In section 4, we show experimental results on our transfer methods. In section 5, we conclude and discuss future work.

2. Background

2.1 Markov Decision Process

Markov decision process (Puterman, 2005) is a specification of a sequential decision problem with a Markovian transition model and additive rewards. Markov decision process is defined by 4-tuple $(S, A, P^a_{ss'}, R^a_{ss'})$, where S denotes a finite set of states, A denotes a finite set of actions, $P^a_{ss'}$ denotes the transition probability of taking action a from state s to state s', and $R^a_{ss'}$ denotes the reward for transiting from state s to state s' with action a. A function which determines an agent's action in any state on Markov decision process is called a policy π. In other words, a policy is a mapping from a state to a unique action. A value function V_π maps each state to its expected reward with respect to a policy π as shown in (1), where γ denotes a discount factor and $\pi(s,a)$ denotes the corresponding probability of taking action a in state s. The equation (1) is also called Bellman equation.

$$V_\pi(s) = \sum_a \pi(s,a) \sum_{s'} P^a_{ss'}(R^a_{ss'} + \gamma V_\pi(s')) \quad (1)$$

An optimal policy π^* maps each state to a specific action to maximize the expected total discounted reward and an optimal value function V_{π^*} corresponds to the optimal policy π^* as shown in (2).

$$V_{\pi^*}(s) = \max_a \sum_{s'} P^a_{ss'}(R^a_{ss'} + \gamma V_\pi(s')) \quad (2)$$

The value function could be represented in tabular form with one output for each input tuple. However, some state space in the real world is too huge to memorize the tabular form of the value function. Approximating the value function in terms of a linear combination of a set of basis functions as shown in (3) is an apporach to deal with this problem. For each i, v_i denotes a basis function and w_i denotes a corresponding weight.

$$V_\pi = w_1 v_1 + \ldots + w_n v_n \quad (3)$$

Represneting a function by a linear combination of basis functions could save a lot of memory. However, different sets of basis functions might affect the performance of functional approximation and the preformance directly impacts an agent's behavior. In other words, a suitable set of basis functions plays an important role for an agent's behavior on Markov decision process.

2.2 Reinforcement Learning

Reinforcement learning (Sutton & Barto, 1998) is about learning from interaction to achieve the goal. A reinforcement learning problem is based on Markov decision process. In other words, a reinforcement learning problem which satisfies the Markov property[1] is called Markov decision process. Some reinforcement learning problems do not satisfy the Markov property in the real world, but they still could be approximated by the Markov assumption. Most reinforcement learning methods are based on estimating the value function[2] by

---

[1] Roughly speaking, if deciding a next state only requires using current information, it satisfies the Markov property.

[2] The value function includes two types: the state-value function and the action-value function. In this paper, we focus on the state-value function.

approximately solving the Bellman equation. Some other learning methods are also based on estimating the value function. A major difference is that the reinforcement learning methods put more efforts into learning to make good decisions for frequently encountered states and less efforts for infrequently encountered states.

Temporal-difference (TD) learning, which combines the Monte Carlo method and dynamic programming, is a central concept in reinforcement learning. Temporal-difference learning estimates the value function of one state from the next state without waiting for an actual final outcome as shown in (4), where V denotes the value function, s denotes the current state, s' denotes the next state, $R^{a}_{ss'}$ denotes the reward for transiting from state s to state s' with action a, α denotes the learning rate, and γ denotes the discount factor.

$$V(s) = V(s) + \alpha[R^{a}_{ss'} + \gamma V(s') - V(s)] \tag{4}$$

The value function guides an agent's behavior on Markov decision process and reinforcement learning learns the value function by continuously updating. Therefore, the updating method plays an important role in an agent's performance.

2.3 Graph Laplacian

The Fourier analysis is to decompose a function in terms of a sum of trigonometric functions with different frequencies. In other words, the trigonometric functions could be combined together to represent the function. In addition, each frequency of trigonometric functions is inversely proportional to its importance as representing more features of the function. If two functions are similar, their trigonometric functions tend to be the same at low frequencies and the difference at high frequencies.

Graph Laplacian can be defined as the combinatorial Laplacian or the normalized Laplacian (Chung, 1997). The combinatorial Laplacian of an undirected unweighted graph G is defined as an operator $L = D - A$, where A is the adjacency matrix and D is a diagonal matrix whose entries are the row sums of A. In other words, the combinatorial Laplacian could represent the connection (undirected) or the transition (directed) between two vertices u and v as shown in (5), where d_v denotes the degree of vertex v without the self loop. In problem solving, states are represented as vertices and connections or transitions between states are represented as edges.

$$L(u,v) = \begin{cases} d_v & \text{if } u = v \\ -1 & \text{if } u \text{ and } v \text{ are adjacent} \\ 0 & \text{otherwise} \end{cases} \tag{5}$$

Let f denote a function mapping each vertex u in a graph into a real number. The combinatorial Laplacian L acts on a function f as shown in (6), where $u \sim v$ denotes vertex u and vertex v are adjacent. To minimize the equation $\sum_{u \sim v}(f(u)-f(v))^2$ [3] subject to f with condition, which f is a unit vector, is equivalent to solving the eigenproblem of L as shown in (7), where λ denotes the eigenvalue and f denotes the eigenfunction. By the spectral theorem (Chung, 1997), eigenfunctions with respect to smaller eigenvalues are smoother. In other words, the smoothness of eigenfunctions is inversely proportional to their eigenvalues.

$$Lf(u) = \sum_{u \sim v}(f(u) - f(v)) \tag{6}$$

$$Lf = \lambda f \tag{7}$$

Furthermore, the normalized Laplacian $\tilde{L}$ of a graph is defined as $\tilde{L} = D^{-1/2} L D^{-1/2}$ and each eigenfunction of $\tilde{L}$ is defined as $g = D^{-1/2} f$, where f denotes each eigenfunction of L. The difference between the combinatorial Laplacian L and the normalized Laplacian $\tilde{L}$ is that the normalized Laplacian models the degree of a vertex as a local measure.

The spectral analysis of graph Laplacian operator provides an orthonormal set of basis functions that can approximate any square-integrable functions on a graph (Chung, 1997). These basis functions, which are a set of eigenfunctions of L or $\tilde{L}$, are called as proto-value functions (Kimberly & Mahadevan, 2006; Mahadevan, 2005; Mahadevan & Maggioni, 2006, 2007). Proto-value functions construct a global smooth approximation of a function on a graph. In other words, a function on a graph could be decomposed into a linear combination of proto-value functions.

Therefore, the notion of the spectral analysis on graph Laplacian is similar to the Fourier analysis. Basis functions of graph Laplacian corresponding to the smaller eigenvalues represent more features and are more important. It also implies that if two graphs are similar, their features tend to be the same at low-order basis functions and the difference at high-order basis functions.

2.4 Transfer Types

In previous work (Kimberly & Mahadevan, 2006), the authors have proposed three transfer types: task transfer, topological domain transfer, and scaling domain transfer as shown in Fig. 2. The task transfer problem means that the size of states and the transition model does not change but the rewards change. For example, tranferring from Fig. 2(a) to Fig. 2(b) is a task transfer problem and vice versa. The domain transfer problem means that the size of states or the transition model changes but the rewards are still the same. In detail, the scaling domain transfer problem is the change of the size of states and the topological domain transfer problem is the change of a transition model. For example, tranferring from

---

[3] Minimizing the equation $\sum_{u \sim v}(f(u)-f(v))$ has the same result as minimizing the equation $\sum_{u \sim v}(f(u)-f(v))^2$.

Fig. 2(a) to Fig. 2(c) is a topological domain transfer problem and from Fig. 2(a) to Fig. 2(d) is a scaling domain transfer problem. These three transfer types are symmetric which means that if transferring from graph G^S to graph G^T is one of transfer types, transferring from graph G^T to graph G^S is the same transfer type. Notice that R denotes a reward in a state, but rewards could be gained after any state transition in general case.

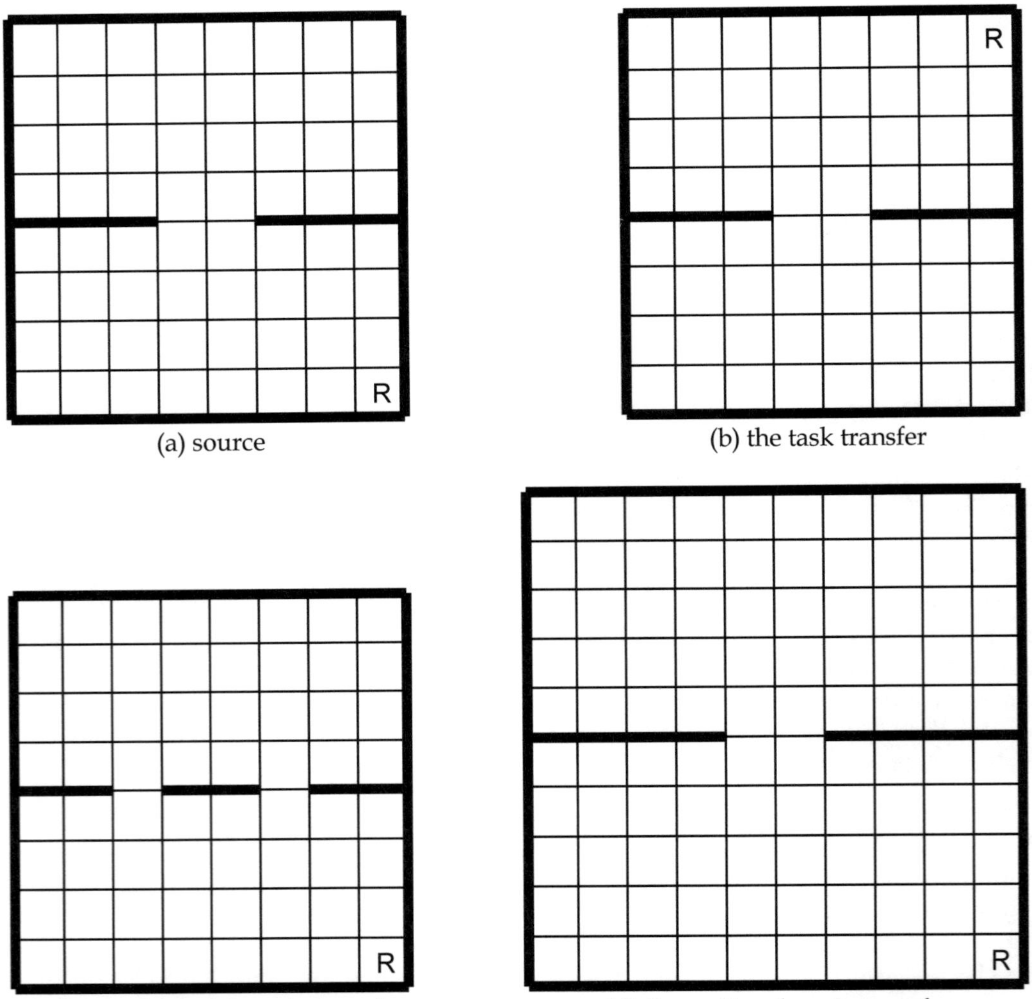

(a) source

(b) the task transfer

(c) the topological domain transfer

(d) the scaling domain transfer

Fig. 2. Examples of transfer types

3. Methodology

3.1 An Example

Before we describe how to transfer, we show a simple example for the combinatorial Laplacian and a simple scenario for the transfer problem. A 3x3 grid world and its corresponding state transitioin graph are shown in Fig. 3(a) and Fig. 3(c). A state is defined as an agent at one of cells in the grid world and the state transition graph shows the possible transitions from one state to another. By definitioin in section 2.2, we could derive the combinatorial Laplacian as shown in Fig. 3(b). The diagonal terms denote the degree of states and the others denote the connection. Notice that the combinatorial Laplacian does not only describe the grid world problems, but also others. For example, the task of putting on a pair of shoes (Russell & Norvig, 2003) is defined as an agent who wants to put on shoes with a condition of putting on socks before shoes. The state transition graph of this problem is shown in Fig. 3(d). By camparing Fig. 3(c) and Fig. 3(d), we could find that the two graphs are the same. It means that their combinatorial Laplacians are also the same. Therefore, we could do the domain transfer between these two tasks.

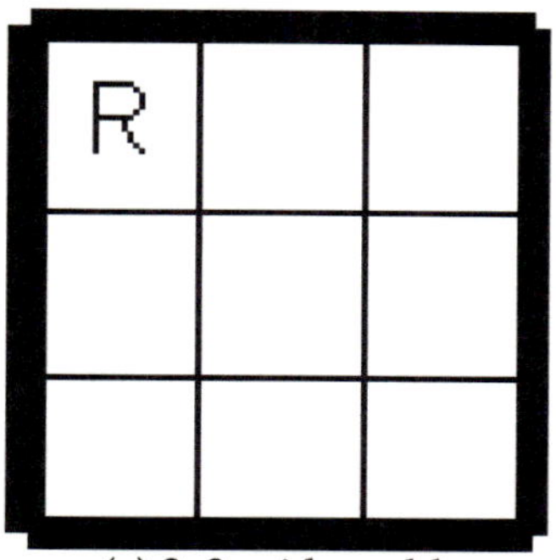

(a) 3x3 grid world

$$\begin{bmatrix} 2 & -1 & 0 & -1 & 0 & 0 & 0 & 0 & 0 \\ -1 & 3 & -1 & 0 & -1 & 0 & 0 & 0 & 0 \\ 0 & -1 & 2 & 0 & 0 & -1 & 0 & 0 & 0 \\ -1 & 0 & 0 & 3 & -1 & 0 & -1 & 0 & 0 \\ 0 & -1 & 0 & -1 & 4 & -1 & 0 & -1 & 0 \\ 0 & 0 & -1 & 0 & -1 & 3 & 0 & 0 & -1 \\ 0 & 0 & 0 & -1 & 0 & 0 & 2 & -1 & 0 \\ 0 & 0 & 0 & 0 & -1 & 0 & -1 & 3 & -1 \\ 0 & 0 & 0 & 0 & 0 & -1 & 0 & -1 & 2 \end{bmatrix}$$

(b) the combinatorial Laplacian

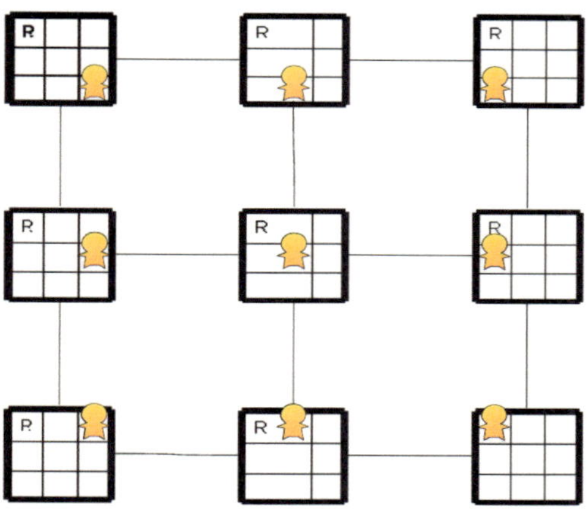

(c) the state transition graph of (a)

(d) the state transition graph of the problem of putting on a pair of shoes

Fig. 3. A simple example

3.2 A Simple Transfer Method

In this section, we describe a simple transfer method which is based on transferring the value function. We represent the value function by a linear combination of basis functions and the idea is transferring the weights between two similar tasks whose details are described in Fig. 4. The first step is to collect the knowledge of state transitions in both tasks.

The second step is to construct the normalized Laplacian by the collected state transitions. The third step is to compute the corresponding basis functions of the normalized Laplacians. The fourth step is to obtain the weights of the source basis functions by approximating the source value function. The fifth step is to approximate the target value function in terms of the target basis functions and the obtained weights. The last step is to acquire the target policy through the approximated target value function.

1. Perform N-steps random walk to obtain M trials on a source task and a target task respectively.
2. Construct the normalized Laplacians $\widetilde{L}^S$, by the undirected graphs G^S, G^T which are obtained by the trials.
3. Solve the eigenproblems of $\widetilde{L}^S$, $\widetilde{L}^T$ to obtain the basis functions $\{v_i^S\}$, $\{v_i^T\}$ which are ordered by the ascending eigenvalues.
4. Approximate the source value function $V_{\pi^*}^S$ to obtain the weights $\{w_i^S\}$ corresponding to $\{v_i^S\}$ by the least-square error fit method.
5. Transfer the weight $\{w_i^S\}$ from $\{v_i^S\}$ to the corresponding target basis functions $\{v_i^T\}$.
$$V_{\pi'}^T = \sum_i w_i \cdot v_i^T$$
6. Convert the approximation target value function $V_{\pi^*}^T$ to the target policy π'.

Fig. 4. A simple transfer method

The reason why the simple transfer method works is that basis functions of both tasks with the same order play the same important role for both value functions. Therefore, we transfer the obtained weights from a source task to a target task. If two tasks are similar, two sets of basis functions tend to be similar. Notice that it does not imply that numeric values are similar but the structure is similar as shown in Fig. 5. On the one hand, a small difference between two tasks cannot affect the global smooth structure so the both low-order basis functions tend to be the same. On the other hand, the high-order basis functions are affected by a small change so the target policy could obtain from the similar low-order basis functions and the different high-order basis functions. For example, the basis functions in Fig. 5 are the lower-order ones and the basis functions in Fig. 6 are the high-order ones.

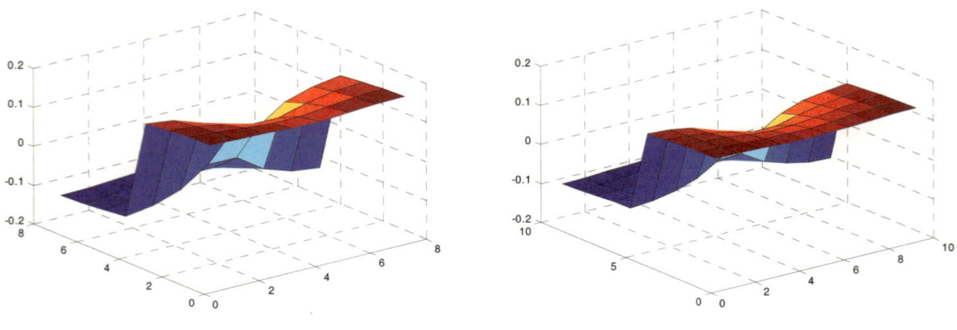

Fig. 5. The similar structure of the basis functions of Fig. 2(a) and Fig. 2(d)

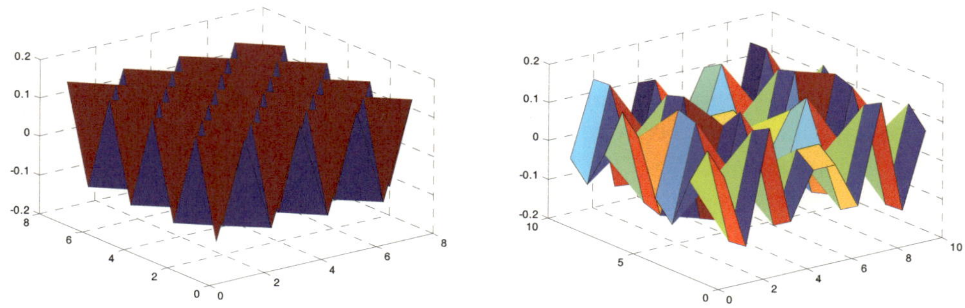

Fig. 6. The different structures of the basis functions of Fig. 2(a) and Fig. 2(d)

3.3 Modified Graph Laplacian

In section 2.3, we introduce the graph Laplacian and the smoothness property of its corresponding eigenfunction. In this section, we assume that each state transition is bidirectional and a positive circular reward does not exist for every task, which means that both edges, $u \sim v$ and $v \sim u$, have positive rewards. Then, the modified graph Laplacian L' of a directed graph is defined in (8), where S_v denotes the entry sum of the v-th row. Roughly speaking, the modified graph Laplacian treats the state with a positive reward as a termination.

$$L'(u,v) = \begin{cases} -S_v & \text{if } u = v \\ -1 & u \sim v \text{ and } v \sim u \text{ without a positive reward} \\ 0 & \text{otherwise} \end{cases} \tag{8}$$

Let f denote a function mapping each vertex u in a graph into a real number and the modified graph Laplacian L' acts on f as shown in (9), where $u \approx v$ denotes $u \sim v$ and $v \sim u$ without a positive reward. To minimize the equation (9) subject to f with the condition which f is a unit vector is equivalent to solving the eigenproblem of L'. It is similar to the graph Laplacian case.

$$L' f(u) = \sum_{u \approx v} (f(u) - f(v)) \tag{9}$$

Because the graph Laplacian L is a positive semidefinite matrix, the eigenvalues of L are non-negative real numbers. To analyze the eigenvalues of the modified graph Laplacian L' we observe the characteristic equation of the modified graph Laplacian L' as shown in (10), where $\hat{L}$ denotes the combinatorial Laplacian L without i-th row and column, which $L'(i,i)$ is equivalent to zero. By the definition, $\hat{L}$ is a possible graph Laplacian. Therfore, $\hat{L}$ is a positive semidefinite matrix and its eigenvalues are non-negtaive numbers. Furthermore, we could derive that the eigenvalues of L' are still non-negative and the normalized version $\widetilde{L}' = D'^{-1/2} L' D'^{-1/2}$, where D' denotes a matrix with diagonal terms of L'.

$$\det(L' - \lambda I) = (-\lambda)^k \cdot \det(\hat{L} - \lambda I) \tag{10}$$

The eigenfunctions with respect to different eigenvalues represent different levels of smoothness. Therefore, the eigenfunction with respect to the first nonzero eigenvalue on the modified graph Laplacian is the smoothest. In most cases, the value function tends to be smooth. By the observation, we find the eigenfunction with respect to the first nonzero eigenvalue have the similar behavior tendency as its value function. An simple task and its value function are shown in Fig. 7, where R denotes a reward to illustrate the tendency. In this grid world task, an agent in each cell represents a state and its topology represents the possible state transitions. An agent reaches the state with R to obtain a reward $+1$ and terminate, otherwise a penalty -0.04 . By the definition, we construct the modified graph Laplacian as shown in (11). Then, we compute the eigenfunction with respect to the first nonzero eigenvalue as shown in Fig. 8. Because the eigenfunction is a vector, it have two possible directions. For convenience, if all values are non-negative, it is called the positive eigenfunction, otherwise the negative eigenfunction. By the definition (Sutton & Barto, 1998), the value of a terminal state in value function is zero and the value of the state which is adjacent to a positive reward is close to the value of the reward. Therefore, we could expect the value function and the negative eigenfunction with respect to the first nonzero eigenvalue to be similar and thus we could transfer the value function by the negative eigenfunction with respect to the first nonzero eigenvalue.

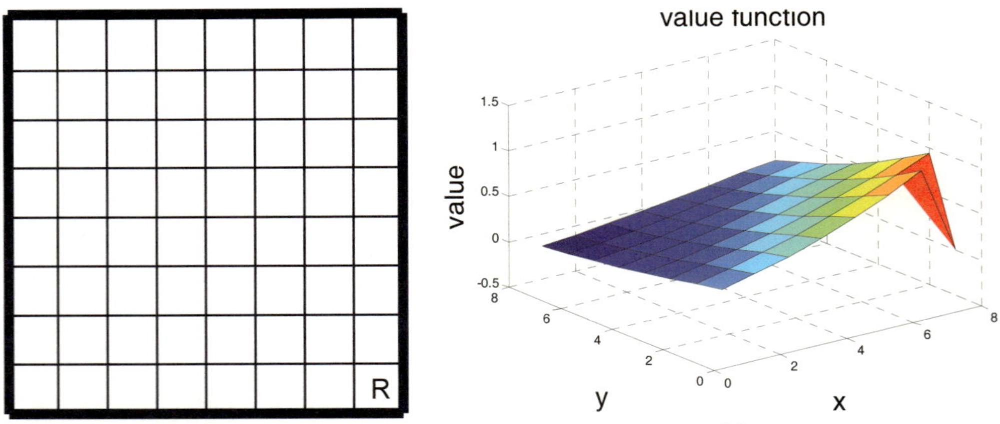

(a) (b)

Fig. 7. A 8x8 grid world task and its optimal value function

$$\begin{array}{c} \downarrow \text{state with } R \\ \begin{bmatrix} 2 & -1 & \cdots & 0 & 0 \\ -1 & 3 & \cdots & 0 & 0 \\ \vdots & \vdots & \ddots & \vdots & \vdots \\ 0 & 0 & \cdots & 3 & -1 \\ 0 & 0 & \cdots & 0 & 0 \end{bmatrix} \leftarrow \text{state with } R \end{array} \tag{11}$$

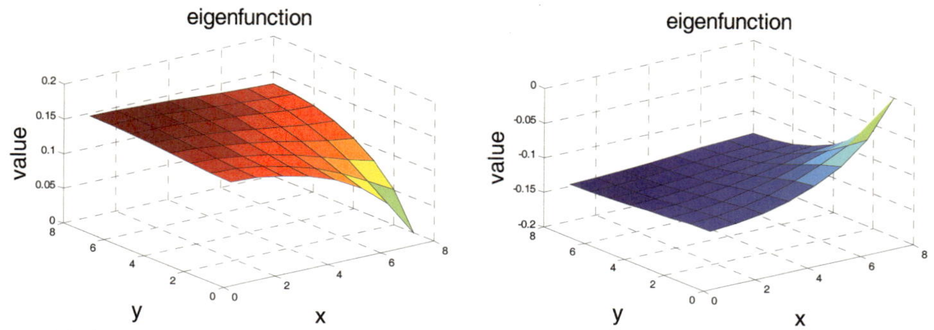

(a) the positive eigenfunction (b) the negative eigenfunction

Fig. 8. The eigenfunctions of the 8x8 grid world in Fig. 7(a) with respect to the first nonzero eigenvalue

3.4 Transfer Method

In this section, we describe a transfer method which is based on the tendency of the eigenfunction with respect to the first nonzero eigenvalue of the modified graph Laplacian. The detail of the transfer method is shown in Fig. 9. The first step is to collect the knowledge of state transitions in both tasks. The second step is to construct the normalized modified Laplacian by the collected state transitions. The third step is to compute the corresponding negative eigenfunctions with respect to the first nonzero eigenvalue of the normalized modified Laplacians. The fourth step is to sort the eigenfunctions in descending order respectively to obtain the one-to-one state mappings which map states in the source task to the corresponding ones in the target task. The fifth step is to map the values of states in the source task to the corresponding ones in the target task. The last step applies only for the case with different state sizes. If the number of states in the target task is bigger than in the source task, some states do not obtain the mapping states in the step 4. Therefore, the extrapolated method is used to estimate their value in terms of the negative eigenfunction in the target task and the value function in the source task. If the number of states in the target task is smaller than in the source task, all states in the target task can find the mapping states in the source task and some states in the source task are useless.

1. Perform N-steps random walk to obtain M trials on a source task and a target task respectively.
2. Construct the normalized modified Laplacians $\widetilde{L}'^S$, $\widetilde{L}'^T$ by the directed graphs G^S, G^T, which are obtained by the trials.
3. Solve the eigenproblems of $\widetilde{L}^S$, $\widetilde{L}^T$ to obtain the negative eigenfunctions with respect the first nonzero eigenvalue v_1^S, v_1^T.
4. Sort the negative eigenfunctions v_1^S, v_1^T in descending order respectively to obtain the one-to-one state mappings.
5. Map the values of the source value function to the values of the corresponding states in the target task.
6. (optional) If the number of states in the target task is bigger than that in the source task, an extrapolated method is used to estimate the rest of states.

Fig. 9. The transfer method

4. Experiments

4.1 Setting

These experiments investigate the effects of the simpler transfer method and the transfer methods by three transfer types. The transition model is shown in Fig. 10. It means that when an agent takes an action in a state, the consequence is not deterministic. For example, if an agent goes forward in a state, the possible next states can be the forward state, the left state and the right state. Notice that the symbol R denotes a terminal state with reward $+1$ and any state transitions could not reach the terminal state with a penalty -0.04 . We compare the results by an ε -greedy TD learning agent which means that the agent takes an action which is not according to the policy with probability ε . We set $\varepsilon = 0.1$, the learning rate $\alpha = 0.1$ and the discount factor $\gamma = 0.9$.

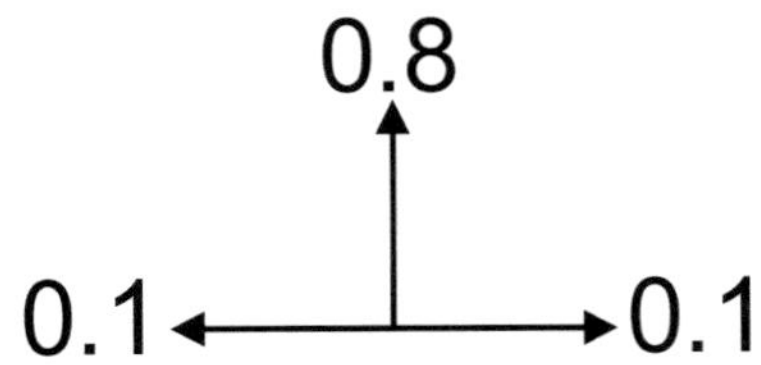

Fig. 10. The transition model in the experiments

The goal of these experiments is to understand the performance and the accelerated effects. To calculate the steps we assume that the upper left corner is the start state. In the domain transfer cases, we compare the steps of reaching the reward of a random policy, the simple transferred policy, the transferred policy and the optimal one as the performance evaluations. In the task transfer cases, we compare the steps of reaching the reward of a random policy and the transferred policy to evaluate the performance. In addition, to show the accelerated effects, we compare the convergence using a random initial policy and the transferred initial policy for all cases.

4.2 Scaling Domain Transfer

To investigate the performance of the simple transferred policy we separate the scaling domain transfer into two cases: the up-scaling case and the down-scaling case. The topology of the task is the same as Fig. 2(a). In the up-scaling case, we choose the 6x6 grid world as a source task and 8x8, 10x10, 12x12, 14x14, 16x16, 18x18, and 20x20 grid world as target tasks. In down-scaling case, we choose the 20x20 grid world as a source task and 6x6, 8x8, 10x10, 12x12, 14x14, 16x16, and 18x18 grid world as target tasks. The results are shown in Fig. 11, where the simple transferred policy is derived from the simple transfer method and the transferred policy is derived from the transfer method. We could discover that regardless of the size is changed in a target task, the simple transferred policy still performs very close to the optimal policy and the transferred policy doe not always perform well. Therefore, we investigate the accelerated effect of the transfer method with different topologies in the up-scaling case as shown in Fig. 2(a) and Fig. 7(a). The results are shown in Fig. 12. We could discover that different topologies have different effects and the transfer method is not always good for the scaling domain transfer.

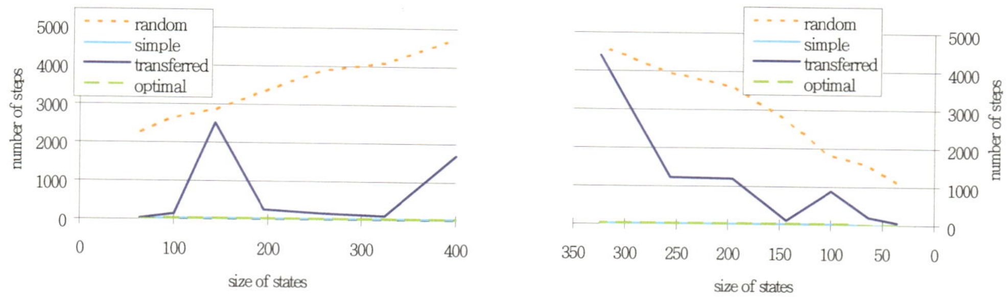

(a) the up-scaling case (b) the down-scaling case

Fig. 11. The performance of transferred policies in the scaling domain transfer

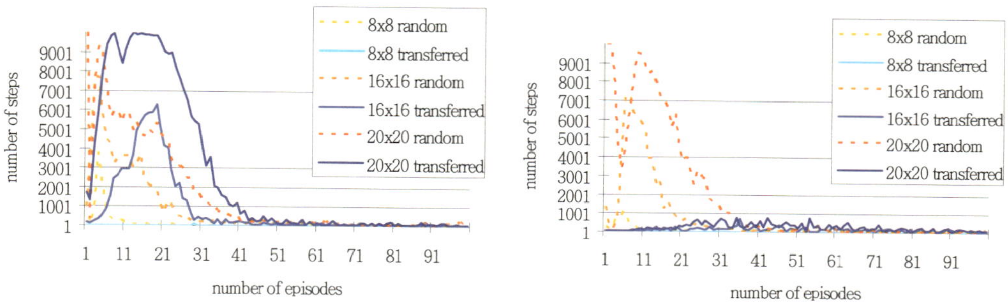

(a) corresponding to Fig. 2(a) (b) corresponding to Fig. 7(a)

Fig. 12. The accelerated effect of the transfer method in the scaling domain transfer

4.3 Topological Domain Transfer

The source task is shown in Fig. 2(a) and the target tasks are shown in Fig. 13. Fig. 13(a) represents that the door is separated into two doors and the distances between each door and the center is equal to a unit. Fig. 13(b) represents that the size of the door is increased. We investigate the topological domain transfer in different sizes as follows: 6x6, 8x8, 10x10, 12x12, 14x14, 16x16, 18x18, 20x20. The performance of the transferred policies is shown in Fig. 14. We could discover that different transfer methods are good for different topological domain transfer tasks. Although sometimes the transferred policy is not as good as the optimal policy, if the convergence is good enough, it is still a pretty good transfer. That is one of reasons why we take the accelerated effect into consideration. Another reason is that even though a policy is acceptable so far, it is possible to have a bad performance in a bigger task. The accelerated effect of the transfer method is shown in Fig. 15. We discover that the convergence of the transferred policy is faster than the random policy in both cases.

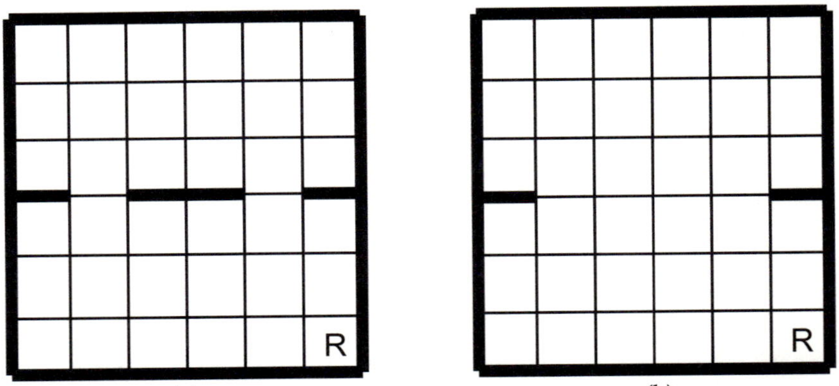

(a) (b)

Fig. 13. The target tasks of the topological domain transfer

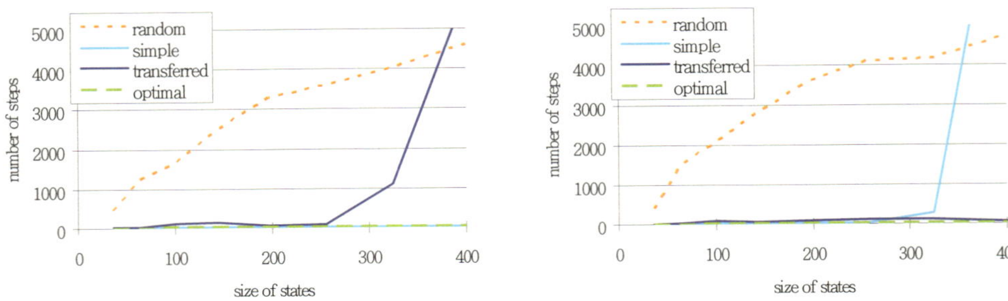

Fig. 14. The performance of transferred policies in the topological domain transfer

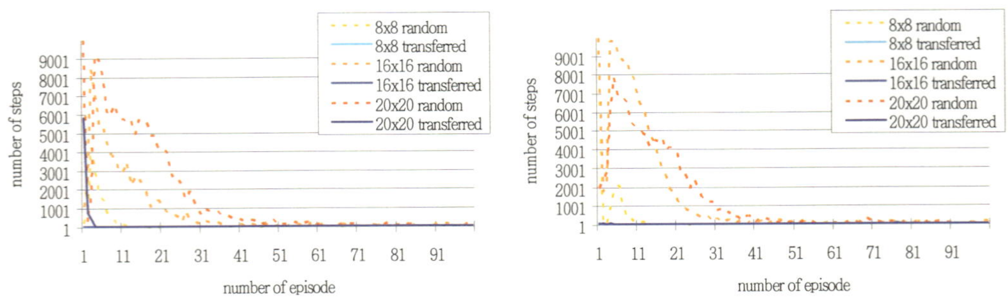

Fig. 15. The accelerated effect of the transfer method in the topological domain transfer

4.4 Task Transfer

So far, we compare only the simple transfer method and the transfer method in the domain transfer cases. In this section, we investigate the transfer method in the task transfer. The reason why we do not discuss the simple transfer method is that it could not use in the task transfer because it does not take the reward into consideration. The source task and the target tasks are shown in Fig. 16. Fig. 16(a) represents the source task and the Fig. 16(b), (c), (d), (e) represent the target tasks with different rewards. Notice that we investigate the task transfer in a fixed size 10x10 because we think the task transfer is independent to the size.

The performance of the transfer method is shown in Fig. 17. We could discover that the transferred policy is much better than the random policy. The accelerated effect of the transferred method is shown in Fig. 18. The convergence is obviously much faster than the random policy. In other words, the transfer method could accelerate learning in the task transfer cases.

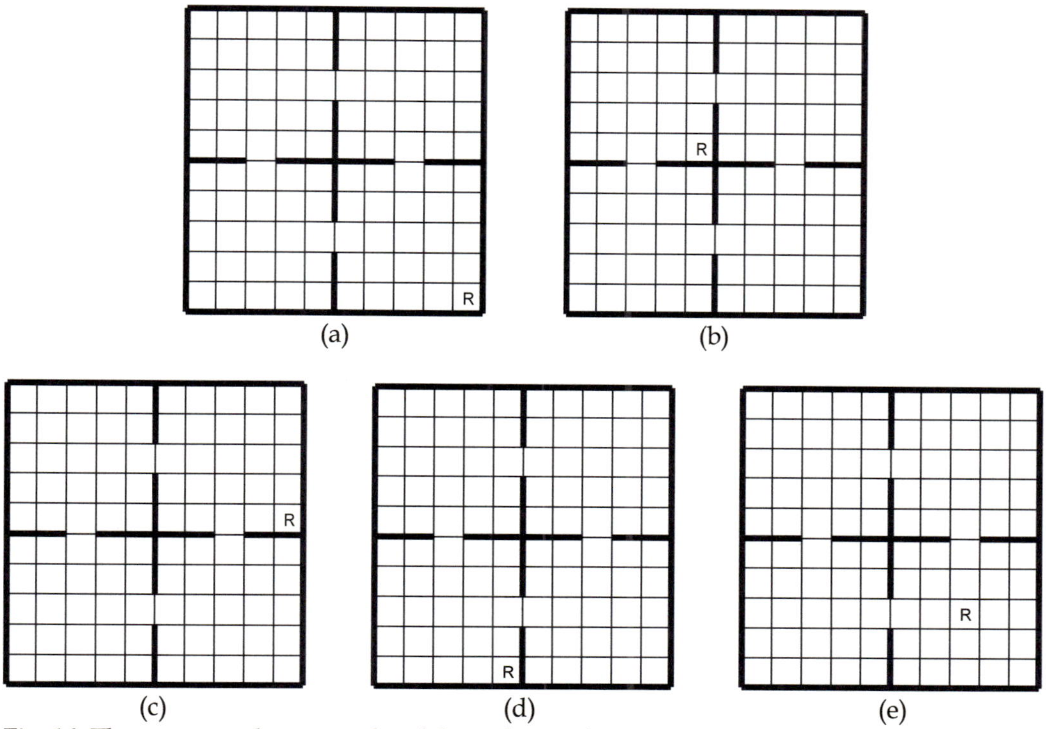

Fig. 16. The source and target tasks of the task transfer

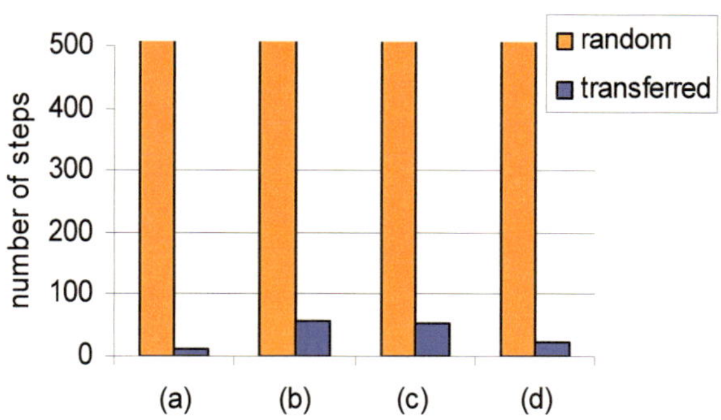

Fig. 17. The performance of the transfer method in the task transfer

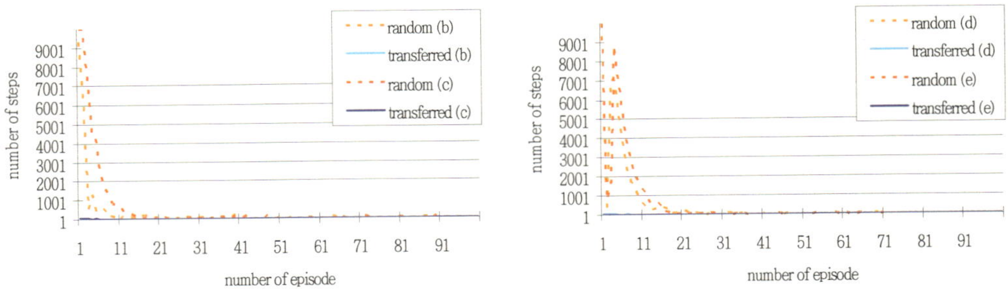

Fig. 18. The accelerated effect of the transfer method in the task transfer

4.5 Synthetic Transfer

In this section, we synthesize the scaling domain transfer, the topological domain transfer and the task transfer to be a synthetic transfer. The synthetic transfer is like transferring a maze to another. The source task and the target tasks are shown in Fig. 19. Notice that these three tasks are randomly generated with the condition that each state could reach the terminal state. The accelerated effects of the transfer method are shown in Fig. 20. The results show that the transfer method is not only used in one of transfer types, but also in the synthetic case. That is the reason why we discuss the transfer method rather than the simple transfer method.

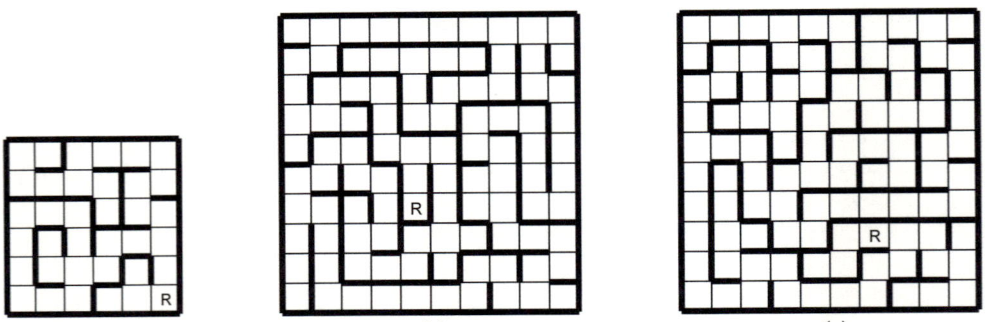

(a) (b) (c)

Fig. 19. The source task (a) and the target tasks (b) and (c) of the synthetic transfer

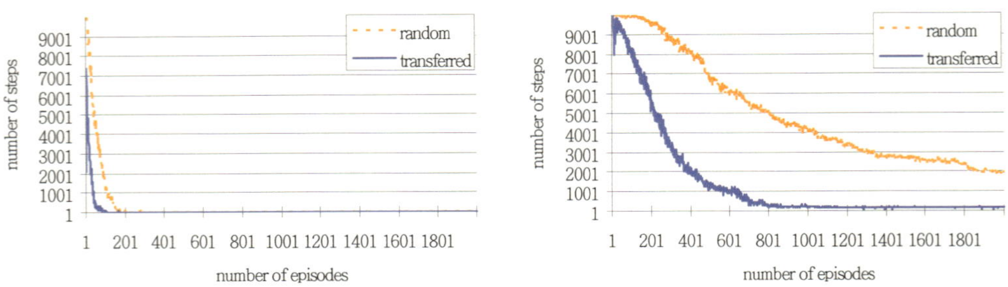

Fig. 20. The accelerated effect of the transfer method in the synthetic transfer

5. Discussions

The theoretical analysis of the simple transfer method is based on the spectral analysis on graph Laplacian. Low-order basis functions of graph Laplacian tend to represent more features of the value functions and high-order basis functions tend to represent fewer features. If low-order basis functions of two tasks are similar, the simple transfer method performs well. In other words, similar tasks tend to keep similar structures in low-order basis functions so transferring weights from one task to another could acquire a good approximate policy. The experimental results show that if two tasks are similar, the transferred policy of the simple transfer method could be very close to the optimal one. However, even though the simple transfer method seems to be good in the domain transfer cases, it could not be used in the task transfer. Furthermore, it still needs more theoretical analysis as to determine if topological similarity is close enough to apply the simple transfer method that ensures the simple transferred policy to be close to the optimal one.

The transfer method could be used in three transfer types: the scaling domain transfer, the topological domain transfer and the task transfer. However, the transfer method is not always better than the simple transfer method. The experimental results show that the transferred policy of the transfer method converges earlier than the random policy. In other words, the evidence demonstrates the accelerated effect of the transfer method. The reason why the transfer method could work in the task transfer is taking rewards into consideration on the modified graph Laplacian. However, how to evaluate the accelerated effect of the transfer method in more objective manner is a challenge because different tasks tend to have different effects.

In this chapter, we have proposed the transfer method based on the topology of state transitions for reinforcement learning. It could be used in three transfer types: the scaling domain transfer, the topological domain transfer and the task transfer. Because the transfer method is transferring the state-value function, we need a perfect transition model to obtain the policy. However, to obtain the perfect transition model sometimes is not easy so extending this idea to the action-value function might be an approach to avoid this problem. Because the transfer method only deals with the discrete tasks, mapping continuous tasks to discrete tasks might be an approach to deal with the transfer in continuous tasks.

6. References

Chung, F. R. K. (1997). *Spectral graph theory*, American Mathematical Society.

Hessling, A. v., & Goel, A. K. (2005). Abstracting reusable cases from reinforcement learning. *Proceedings of the Sixth International Conference on Case-Based Reasoning Workshop*.

Kimberly, F., & Mahadevan, S. (2006). Proto-transfer learning in Markov decision processes using spectral methods. *Proceedings of the Twenty-Third International Conference on Machine Learning Workshop on Structural Knowledge Transfer for Machine Learning*.

Liu, Y., & Stone, P. (2006). Value-function-based transfer for reinforcement learning using structure mapping. *Proceedings of the Twenty-First National Conference on Artificial Intelligence*.

Mahadevan, S. (2005). Proto-value functions: Developmental reinforcement learning. *Proceedings of the Twenty-Second International Conference on Machine Learning*.

Mahadevan, S., & Maggioni, M. (2006). Proto-value functions: A Laplacian framework for learning representation and control in Markov decision processes. *Technical Report.*

Mahadevan, S., & Maggioni, M. (2007). Proto-value functions: A Laplacian framework for learning representation and control in Markov decision processes. *Journal of Machine Learning Research, 8,* 2169-2231.

Puterman, M. L. (2005). *Markov decision processes discrete stochastic dynamic programming,* Wiley.

Russell, S., & Norvig, P. (2003). *Artificial intelligence a modern approach,* Prentice Hall.

Sutton, R. S., & Barto, A. G. (1998). *Reinforcement learning an introduction,* MIT press.

Taylor, M. E., & Stone, P. (2007). Cross-domain transfer for reinforcement learning. *Proceedings of the Twenty-Fourth International Conference on Machine Learning.*

Taylor, M. E.; Stone, P., & Liu, Y. (2005). Value functions for RL-based behavior transfer: A comparative study. *Proceedings of the Twentieth National Conference on Artificial Intelligence.*

Taylor, M. E.; Whiteson, S., & Stone, P. (2007). Transfer via inter-task mappings in policy search reinforcement learning. *Proceedings of the Sixth International Conference on Autonomous Agents and Multiagent Systems.*

3

Tracking behaviours of cooperative robots within multi-agent domains

Fernando Ramos[1] and Huberto Ayanegui[2]
[1]*Tecnologico de Monterrey Campus Cuernavaca*
[2]*Universidad Autónoma de Tlaxcala*
Mexico

1. Introduction

The most important concerns in multi-agent cooperative systems are focused on the construction of models related with the communication, the interaction and the behavior of agents participating in a task. This chapter deals with behavioral aspects of cooperative agents while they are evolving in a task. Behavioral aspects of cooperative agents may give us precious information about individual, relational and functional roles that the agents assume during the different steps of a task. For instance, in competitive domains, such as robotic soccer, teams of agents dispute common resources to reach a goal. The importance of knowing about behavioral aspects of a team of agents under observation could give us valuable information to generate counter strategies or tactics to obtain the resources being disputed.

The behavioral aspects concern strategic and tactical behaviors. The former implies long term actions where the whole team is involved, while the latter is related with short term actions where two or more agents are involved. It is important to point out that tactical behaviors should be submitted to strategic behaviors.

The domains of cooperative agents are commonly complex due to the dynamic conditions and the multiple interactions between agents. Based on the precedent statements, a particular interest in this chapter is focused on the analysis of problems that can difficult the construction of models of behaviors.

Relevant works related with the study of behaviors in multi-agent domains, applied to soccer robotics, are exposed. We aim to illustrate the problematic, the advantages and drawbacks of different approaches that have been proposed to model the behavior of soccer-agents while they are evolving in a task.

Finally, we expose a model able to discover behaviors and tracking patterns in the soccer domains, which was tested in real games extracted from several matches belonging to different Robot-Cup Tournaments. The results obtained by applying this model have shown that it is able to discover satisfactory behaviors of strategic and tactical patterns as well as tracking the behaviors while the robots are evolving in a competitive complex task.

2. Cooperative Agents

Cooperative agents are focused on how a loosely-coupled network of problem solvers can work together to solve problems that are beyond their individual capabilities. Each problem-solving node in the network is capable of sophisticated problem-solving and can work independently, but the problems faced by the nodes cannot be completed without cooperation. Cooperation is necessary because no single node has sufficient expertise, resources, and information to solve a problem, and different nodes might have expertise for solving different parts of the problem (Durfee et al., 1989b).

Multi-agent systems research is concerned with the wider problems of designing societies of autonomous agents, such as why and how agents cooperate (Wooldridge & Jennings, 1994); how agents can recognize and resolve conflicts (Adler et al., 1989; Galliers, 1988b; Galliers, 1990; Klein & Baskin, 1991; Lander et al, 1991); how agents can negotiate or compromise in situations where they are apparently at loggerheads (Ephrati & Rosenschein, 1993; Rosenschein and Zlotkin, 1994); and so on.

An important concern is to design an appropriate organization of a multi-agent system for a particular domain and environment, such as described in the survey by (Horling & Lesser, 2004). In this work, advantages and disadvantages of these organizations are discussed. Such organizations can be hierarchies, holarchies, coalitions, teams, congregations, societies, federations, markets, and matrix organizations.

2.1 Coordination of multi-agent systems

Coordination of tasks is an important aspect directly associated with the success of a plan that supports a strategy and/or tactic. In addition, the coordination plays an important role in the correct execution of cooperative actions, in such a way that conflictive situations could be avoided. In (Chernova & Veloso, 2008) a teacher instructs multiple robots to work together in coordination through a demonstration of the desired behavior, using a communication system and a sharing information system. Another distributed approach that share information, which help to facilitate the coordination and solve problems such as collisions is described in (Jansen & Sturtevant, 2008). One of the most important complex dynamic domains of application of multi-agent systems is the soccer robot systems. In (Candea et al., 2001), aspects of coordination of soccer robots within the framework of RoboCup are treated, doing emphasis in behavior based techniques. The communication and distributed coordination is addressed in this work.

Multi-agent teamwork is critical in a large number of agent applications, including training, education, virtual enterprises and collective robotics (Nair et al., 2004). However, in multi-agent domains, agent interactions become the domain highly complex for the analysis of agent-team behaviors, such is the case of robotic soccer. We consider "complex domains" to be those with enormous state action spaces, dynamic environment, competitive and real time. Obviously, when the multiple interactions of both teams are considered the task of analysis for modeling behaviors is even more complex.

2.2 Behaviors in multi-agent systems

Machine Learning techniques are used to model the robot behaviors from training instances generated during a play by imitating the human behavior derived from the interaction of a human that control a robot soccer agent during a play (Aler et al., 2009). Low-level behaviors take place: looking for the ball, conducting the ball towards the goal or scoring in the presence of opponent players. Lin et al. (2009), uses color features and hybrid systems compose of multi-layer perceptrons and genetic algorithms for the recognition of human behaviors based on trajectory patterns. Social insects provide a rich source of traceable social behavior for testing multi-agent tracking, prediction and modeling algorithms (Balch et al., 2001).

The use of predictive systems for studying agent opponent behaviors driven by the recognition of team actions, such as usual paths performed by an agent, plays performed by two agents or preferences from bid exchanges, can serve to build behavior patterns that can serve as guide to recognize behaviors of several agents participating in a cooperative task. An approach based on HMM serves to determine spatio-temporal behavior agent patterns through the recognition of team actions (Luotsinen & Bölöni, 2008). Meanwhile, Bayesian Networks can be used as learning system to characterize behaviors of the opponent. In particular in (Hindriks & Tykhonov, 2008), Bayesian Networks are used to learn opponent preferences from bid exchanges by making some assumptions about the preference structure and rationality of the bidding process. Based on the observations of agent behaviors the recognition of tactical enemy plans is made in military applications (Mulder & Voorbraak, 2003; Henniger & Madhavan, 2004) compared the performance of three predictive models all developed for the same, well-defined modeling task. Specifically, this paper compares the performance of an Extended Kalman Filter (EKF) based model, a neural network based model and a Newtonian-based dead-reckoning model, all used to predict an agent's trajectory and position.

2.3 Tracking behaviors

Multi-Agent systems, such as soccer robots, change constantly or apparently change due to the dynamic conditions and multiple interactions between agents. Due to this problems, the tracking of agents becomes very difficult and, by the way, the behaviors assumed by the agents risk of being quite different even in similar environment conditions. Tracking behaviors of multi-agent systems is very important in the study of opponent team attitudes in the design of counter strategies in soccer-agents worlds.

Tambe and Rosenbloom enhance the importance of agent tracking (Tambe & Rosenbloom, 1996). They argue that agent tracking is a key capability required for interactions in multi-agent environments. It involves monitoring other agents' observable behaviors and inferring their unobserved behaviors or high-level goals and plans. Their work examines the implications of such an agent tracking capability for agent architectures. It specifically focuses on real-time and dynamic environments, where an intelligent agent is faced with the challenge of tracking the highly flexible mix of goal-driven and reactive behaviors of other agents, in real-time. This support takes the form of an architectural capability to execute the other agent's models, enabling mental simulation of their behaviors. They have implemented an agent architecture, an experimental variant of the Soar integrated architecture, that conforms to all of these requirements. Agents based on this architecture have been implemented to execute two different tasks in a real-time, dynamic, multi-agent domain.

They propose some of the key requirements for agent tracking in real-time, dynamic environments. This analysis is based on tasks in a real-world, multi-agent environment and assumes that an agent is situated in the environment, as it tracks other agents while simultaneously interacting with them. Key requirements revealed by this analysis include:

1. Tracking other agents' highly flexible mix of goal-driven and reactive behaviors.
2. Recursively tracking its own actions from the perspective of other agents, so as to understand their impact on the other agents' behaviors.
3. Tracking groups of other agents, possibly acting in coordination.
4. Simultaneously tracking and reacting to other agents' actions.
5. Tracking other agents' activities in real-time, while resolving ambiguities.

For an illustrative example of agent tracking in pilot agents for a combat simulation environment, consider first the air-to-air combat scenario in Figure 1, involving fighter jets. The pilot agent **L** in the light-shaded aircraft is engaged in a combat with pilot agents **D** and **E** in the dark-shaded aircraft. Since the aircraft are far apart, **L** can only see its opponents' actions on radar (and vice versa). In Figure 1-a, **L** observes its opponents turning their aircraft in a coordinated fashion to a collision course heading, i.e., with this heading, they will collide with **L** at the point shown by **x**. Since the collision course maneuver is often used to approach one's opponent, L infers that its opponents are aware of its (**L**'s) presence, and are trying to get closer. Given a highly hostile environment, **L** may also infer that opponents are closing into fire their missiles. However, **L** has a missile with a longer range, so L reaches first its missile range. **L** then turns its aircraft to point straight at **D**'s aircraft and fires a radar-guided missile at **D** (Figure 1-b). Subsequently, **L** executes a 35° *fpole* turn away from **D**'s aircraft (Figure 1-c), to provide radar guidance to its missile, while slowing its rate of approach to the enemy aircraft.

While neither **D** nor **E** can observe this missile on their radar, they do observe **L**'s pointing turn followed by its fpole turn. They track these to be part of L's missile firing behavior, and infer a missile firing. Therefore, they attempt to evade his missile by executing a 90° beam turn (Figure 1-d). This causes their aircraft to become invisible to **L**'s radar. Deprived of radar guidance, **L**'s missile is rendered harmless. Meanwhile, in Figure 1-d, **L** tracks its opponents' coordinated beam turn (even while not seeing the complete turn). **L** then prepares counter-measures in anticipation of the likely loss of both its missile and radar contact.

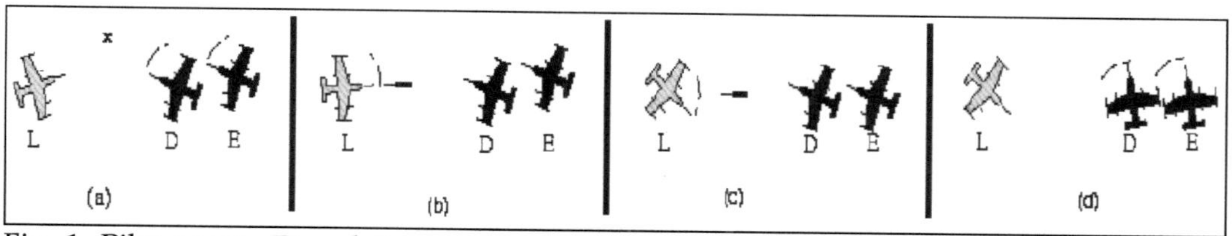

Fig. 1. Pilot agents **D** and **E** are engaged in combat with **L**. An arc on an aircraft's nose shows its turn direction.

Finally, Tambe and Rosenbloom argue that if agents are to successfully inhabit complex, dynamic social worlds, they must obtain architectural support for agent tracking -an important capability required for agent interactions. Their approach has been used in a large-scale operational military exercise (Tambe et al., 1995).

The use of relevant parameters helps to increase the robustness of tracking by using also predictive models. Such is the case of (Muñoz, 2008; Muñoz et al., 2008; Muñoz et al., 2009), where color information associated with clothes of people, and predictive models based on Kalman Filter and Bayesian Networks, has helped to reduce the errors of the tracking system.

The use of classification algorithms, such as K-means, serves to categorize animal tracking data into various classes of behaviors even in the absence of biological factors that should be considered (Schwager et al., 2007). An automatic video tracking system is used to study behaviors, movements and interactions, between insects such as beetles, fruit flies, soil insects, ticks and spiders (Noldus et al., 2002).

Ukita and Matsuyama propose a real time cooperative multi-target tracking based on Active Vision Agents that interact dynamically between them. An architecture compose of three layers that use parallel processes through which the information is exchanged for an effective cooperation (Ukita & Matsuyama, 2005).

Most of the behaviors in soccer agent systems depend on the strategies to be performed. Strategies conditioned also tactical and individual plays. Associated with the strategies specific structures, formations of players, determine importantly the correct execution of strategies and tactics.

2.4 Formations

Formation for multi-agent systems with large population of members is the main concern of the work described in (Xiao et al., 2009), where formation information is divided into two parts: some agents are responsible of global formation information to carry out the navigation of the whole team. Meanwhile, the other agents regulate their positions delaing with local information in distributed manner. In (Porfiri et al., 2007) is described a tracking and formation control for an agent team within a dynamic environment by using shared information to control their trajectories in a cooperative manner.

Most of the research involved in multi-agent modeling is based on building models considering partial aspects and non relevant aspects of the team. Nevertheless, relevant aspects associated with any team should be taken into account in order to model its behaviors. These aspects include: individual actions (individual aspect), relationships between agents (tactical aspect) and formation behaviors (strategy aspect). This chapter emphasizes on the fact of having an expressive representation model which takes into account different aspects exhibited in a team of agents. The adequate representation of these aspects enables the discovery of behavior patterns at different levels of abstraction in a complex domain. Thus, we argue that an expressive representation model at different levels of abstraction facilitates the discovery of behavior patterns in a complex domain such as robotic soccer. Some of the most important behaviors are related with strategic and tactical plays (Ramos & Ayanegui, 2008a) . On the one hand, a team that presumes to play by following certain strategies should play under the context of formations to assure order, discipline and organization during a match (Kuhlmann et al., 2005). On the other hand, tactical plays occur, most of the time, under the context of formations. The discovery of tactical or team behaviors needs the tracking of both the positions of players at any instant of the game and relevant relations able to represent particular interactions between players. Nevertheless, the tracking task becomes very complex because the dynamic conditions of the game brings about drastic changes of positions and interactions between players, which difficult the construction of models capable of recognizing and discovering behaviors of teams playing soccer matches (Lattner et al., 2005). In (Ramos & Ayanegui, 2008b), we proposed a model able to manage the constant changes occurring in the game, which consists in building topological structures based on triangular planar graphs. Thus, based on this model tactical behavior patterns have been discovered and tracked in spite of the dynamic conditions. The test domain for this research was simulated robotic soccer, specifically, the Soccer Server System (Noda & Frank, 1998), used in the Robot World Cup Initiative (Kitano et al., 1997), an international AI and robotics research initiative. A total of 10 matches was analyzed. The results obtained have been shown that the model has been able of recognizing and discovering behaviors satisfactory.

3. Related works with soccer agents

Raines et al. (2000) developed a system called ISAAC, a tool that helps humans to analyze, evaluate and understand agent and multi-agent behavior. ISAAC analyzes soccer games off-line after its end using data from the agents observable behavior traces. An impressive wide range of behaviors of the individual agent, of agent interactions and of team success or failure are analyzed (see Figure 2)

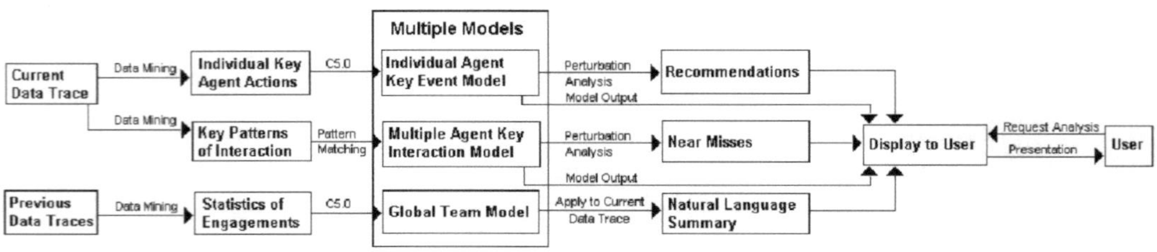

Fig. 2 Flow chart for ISAAC model generation and analysis

Data traces are matched against generic interaction pattern only tofigure out the success or failure of the interaction behavior. This information is statistically processed and presented to the human observer. Authors propose an analysis of the events leading up to key events, such as shots on goal in the case of the RoboCup soccer simulation. ISAAC analyses the situations when the defence of the goal succeeds or fails with respect to a number of variables, such as the distance of the closest defender, the angle of the closest defender with respect to the goal, and the angle of the attacker from the centre of the field, the angle of the shot on goal and the force of the kick. The user is able to do a perturbation analysis to determine which changes in a rule will increase the goal success rate (e.g. changing the angle at goal, increasing the force of the kick). This enables analysing teams to seek improvements. ISAAC produces learned rules to explain the performance of the team as well as predict future outcomes. However, there is no automated way for these learned rules to be used by the agent team; rather, the team designer analyzes the rules and decides how to modify the team.

Without a priori knowledge of current team assignments, the behavior recognition problem is challenging since behaviors are characterized by the aggregate motion of the entire team and cannot generally be determined by observing the movements of a single agent in isolation. To handle this problem, Sukthankar and Sycara (2006) introduce the algorithm STABR (Simultaneous Team Assignment and Behavior Recognition), that generates behavior annotations from spatio-temporal agent traces. STABR completely annotates agent traces with (1) the correct sequence of low-level actions performed by each agent and (2) an assignment of agents to teams over time. Such algorithm employs a randomized search strategy (Fischler & Bolles, 1981) to identify candidate team assignments at selected time steps; these hypotheses are evaluated using dynamic programming to derive a parsimonious explanation for the entire observed spatio-temporal sequence. To prune the number of hypotheses, potential team assignments are fitted to a parameterized team behavior model; poorly-fitting hypotheses are eliminated before the dynamic programming phase. The proposed approach is able to perform accurate team behavior recognition without exhaustive search over the partition set of potential team assignments, as demonstrated on several scenarios of simulated military maneuvers.

3.1 Problem Formulation

The formulation of the problem is: Let $\mathbf{A} = \{ a_0, a_1, \ldots, a_{N-1} \}$ be the set of agents in the scenario. A team consists of a subset of agents, and we require that an agent only participate in one team at any given time; thus a team assignment is a set partition on **A**. An agent that is not currently a member of any team is known as a singleton, and is unrestricted in its motion. By contrast, the agents in a team are constrained to move according to a set of team behaviors, **B**. The subset of behaviors available to a given team is specified by the domain and can depend on the number of agents in the formation and their relative configurations. For instance, the domain could specify that four agents in a square formation may execute a "wheel" (formation advances in an arc by rotating about a corner), but not a "pivot" (formation rotates about its center), which may be restricted to teams of three agents. In the course of a scenario, agents (either singletons or subsets of disbanding teams) can assemble into new teams; similarly, teams can disband to enable their members to form new teams or to operate as singletons. Thus the team assignment is expected to change over time during the course of a scenario. The team assignments over time and the behavior executed by each team are hidden. Assume that the input consists only of a *spatio-temporal traces*, which is a sequence of noisy observations of the 2D position of each agent through time, $a_i(t) \in R^2$.

To illustrate this with an example, Figure 3 shows several frames from a scenario with 16 agents. In Figure 3(a), 12 of the agents are arrayed in three teams of four agents in a square formation, ($\{a_0, \ldots, a_3\}$, $\{a_4, \ldots, a_7\}$, $\{a_8, \ldots, a_{11}\}$), with the remaining four agents as singletons. In Figure 3(b), the squares are converging towards the central area and the formations are starting to interleave. In Figure 3(c), the squares are disbanding and those are regrouping into four groups of three, arrayed as triangles. Finally, in Figure 3(d), the triangles are moving away from the central area.

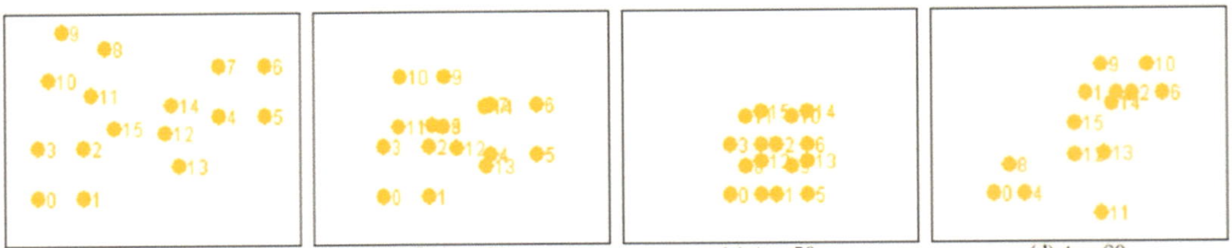

(a) $t = 0$ (b) $t = 24$ (c) $t = 50$ (d) $t = 80$

Fig. 3. (a) An example scenario with three teams of 4 agents, (($\{a_0, \ldots, a_3\}$, $\{a_4, \ldots, a_7\}$, $\{a_8, \ldots, a_{11}\}$) and four singleton agents ($a_{12}, \ldots, a_{15}$); (b) teams maneuver while maintaining formation and converge to central area; (c) the three teams disband and regroup into four teams of 3 agents; (d) the various teams scatter as units. The interleaving of agent formations, the presence of singletons and observation noise (suppressed here) makes the team assignment and behavior recognition challenging.

The goal is to recover a team and a behavior assignment for every agent $a_i \in A$ at every time-step *t*. It is important to note that one cannot, in general, infer the behavior of a team by examining the motion trace of any single agent. Similarly, one cannot assign an agent to a team without confirming that the behavior of the team is legal.

Ideally, one may wish to consider every legal agent-to-team assignment and team-to-behavior assignment at every time-step and then select the sequence that best matches the observed data. However, a straightforward implementation of this idea is computationally infeasible.

STABR analyzes spatio-temporal traces in three stages.

- First, it performs a static analysis of agent positions at each time-step to identify potential agent configurations that may correspond to known formations; these are used as an initial set of agent-to-team assignment hypotheses in later stages. STABR maintains multiple potentially-conflicting assignments for an agent, if there is spatial support.
- Second, STABR examines hypothesized team assignments in isolation and determines whether they have sufficient local spatio-temporal support. Pruning unlikely hypotheses at this stage is crucial since it greatly affects the performance of the last stage. This analysis also enables STABR to determine plausible behavior assignments for each of the surviving hypotheses.

- Third, these agent-to-team hypotheses are used to generate complete partitions over the agents. In the worst case, this state space could be exponential in the number of surviving hypotheses, underscoring the benefits of pruning. STABR then organizes the states (partitions) over the spatio-temporal sequence in the form of a lattice and employs dynamic programming to identify minimal cost solutions. These correspond to agent-to-team and team-to-behavior assignments that are a good fit to the observed sequence.

Experiments on several simulated military maneuvers demonstrated that STABR is accurate at both team assignment and behavior recognition.

Riley used a set of predefined movement models and compare these with the actual movement of the players in set play situation (Riley et al., 2002). In new set play situations the coach then uses the gathered information to predict the opponent agent's behavior and to generate a plan for his own players. The main drawback of Riley's model is that it is built based on individual movements of players without taking into account the relationships between agents. Raines and colleagues (Nair et al., 2004) presented a system called ISAAC which analyzes a game in mode off-line to generate rules about the success of players. ISAAC used the individual and relational models in an independent way. It tries to discover patterns in each level based on events that affect directly the result of the game. Two key differences between ISAAC and our approach are: we build a model of a team based on behavior patterns, independently of success or failures events; ISAAC is unable to discover the strategic behavior of a team. Bezek and colleagues (Bezek et al., 2006) presented a method to discover pass patterns incorporating domain knowledge and providing a graphic representation for detected strategies. Although their approach obtains tactical behavior patterns, they only consider the players involved in the passes without taking into account the notion of team behaviors. Visser and colleagues (Visser et al., 2001) recognized the formation of the opponent team using a neural networks model. The output was a predefined set of formations. The main difference with our approach is that Visser and colleagues did not represent relations between players. As Visser mentioned in his work, his approach is unable of tracking the changes of formations. This is because the lack of structures due to the absence of relations between players.

4. Multi-Level representation model

We emphasize on the fact of having an expressive representation model which takes into account different aspects exhibited in a team of agents. The adequate representation of these aspects enables the discovering behavior patterns at different levels of abstraction in a complex domain. In this work, we present an expressive representation model able to discover behavior patterns by taking into account various aspects such as individual aspects about agents, relationships between agents (tactical aspect) and formation behaviors (strategy aspect). In order to facilitate the discovery of behavior patterns, we need to have a representation model able to express relevant aspects at different abstraction levels. Such model should endow a reasoning system, through an expressive representation model, with the capacity of discovering strategic, tactical and individual behavior patterns.

The different levels of abstraction, each one representing a different aspect of the team, are built in a bottom-up mode, that is, higher levels are constructed based on lower levels. For instance, the representation of formations of a team is based on the relational level, which is composed of relations between zones. At the same time, each zone represents a relationship between individuals (players). As an example, the formation 4:3:3 represents four defenders, three midfielders and three forwards. The proposed multi-layered representation model is shown in Figure 4.

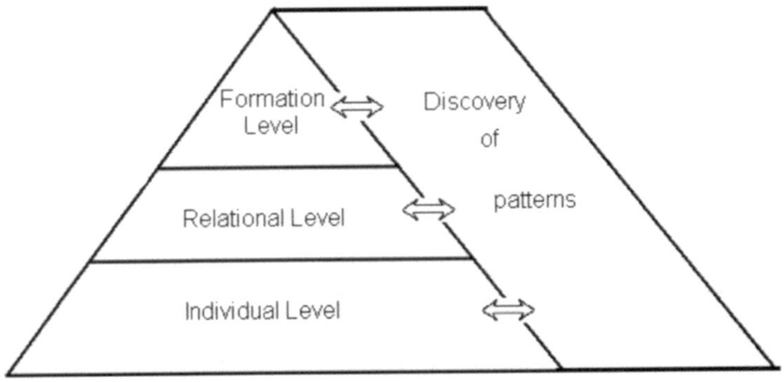

Fig. 4. Representation Model

Individual level. It represents the individual information of the objects in the field, such as players and ball. Such information can be acquired from the Soccer Simulator System directly.

Relational level. It represents the relationship between players.

Formation level. A formation represents the relation among defenses, midfielders and forwards of a team. The formation reveals part of the general strategy of a team. Formations are the way a soccer team lines up its defense, midfield, and attack line during a match. When talking about formations, defenders are listed first and then midfielders and forwards. For example, a code 5:3:2 represents a formation composed by five defenders, three midfielders, and two forwards (see Figure 5). As in the real soccer game, the goalkeeper is not considered as part of the formation. Usually, teams playing in strategic and organized ways search for respecting predefined structures or formations.

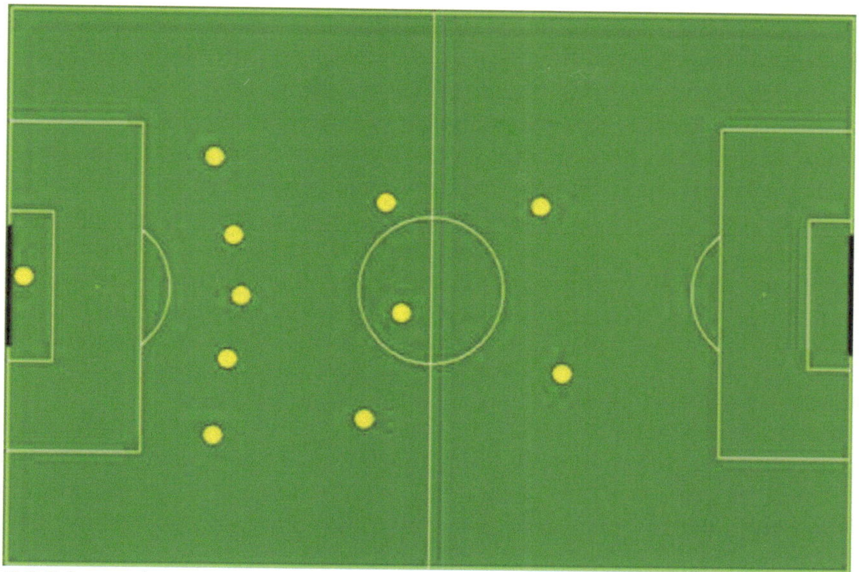

Fig. 5. A 5:3:2 formation

4.1 Recognition of formations

The focus of this work is on teams that play following patterns of high level of abstraction (formations) based on a distribution of zones named Defensive (D), Middle (M) and Attack (A), as in classic soccer game. These patterns will be represented as follows: D:M:A. Due to the dynamic conditions of the soccer game, the players are in constant movement and temporally breaking the alignment of players belonging to a zone. To handle the constant changes without an expressive representation of the relations between players can result in an inefficient way of recognizing formations submitted to a dynamic environment. In the next section will be explained how the zones and the players belonging to them are recognized in this work

4.1.1 Recognition of team zones

As in human soccer domains the players in robotic soccer should tend to be organized. That is, each player has a strategic position that defines its movement range in the soccer field. The role of a player is quite related with a predefined area within which an individual player can play basically in the field. Any behaviors of a player depend on its current role. According to the position of the player, roles in robotic soccer can be divided into four types: goalkeeper, defenders, midfielders and forwards. Different roles are associated with different positions and different behaviors that players assume. However, due to the dynamic changing conditions of a match, a defender could become a forward temporarily as his team is trying to attack. So the roles of a player are dynamically changing. Consequently, the recognition of formation patterns is difficult due to the dynamic and real time conditions of the environment. In a first step, we will discover what players belong to what zone. For this, the clustering algorithm, K-means (MacQueen, 1967), is applied. K-means classifies a given data set through a certain number of clusters (assume *k* clusters) fixed a priori. In this work, k=3 such that three zones will be defined: defensive, middle and attack zones. From the log file (game film), the data from one team is extracted and K-means is applied in each simulation cycle of the game. The positions of each player, with respect to the x axis, are taken as the input of the clustering algorithm and the output of clustering is the classification, according to their x position, of all players of the team in the three clusters. Clustering algorithm is useful to determine the three zones of a team but it is not able to represent the multiple relations between players of each zone. Given that patterns of formations are based on relations that determine structures then an additional model is crucial for the recognition of formation patterns. The next section describes an adequate representation model able to facilitate the recognition of formation patterns.

4.2 Topological Structure Model

A formation is represented by a set of relations between players. Thus, the relations represent the structure that supports a formation. So, a change of relations between players entails a change of formation. It is needed at least the change of one relation to transform one structure into another one. Constant changes of relations could occur because the multiple relations in a formation and the dynamic nature of a match. Figure 6(a) illustrates the relations of each one of the players with the rest of their teammates. A total of 90 relations are obtained by $n(n-1)$, where n represents the number of players. This formula considers two relations by each pair of players. Thus, one relation is represented by the link from player A to player B and the second one from player B to player A. For practical reasons, just one of these relations is considered. Thus, the total of relations is 45. Figure 6(b) illustrates these 45 relations.

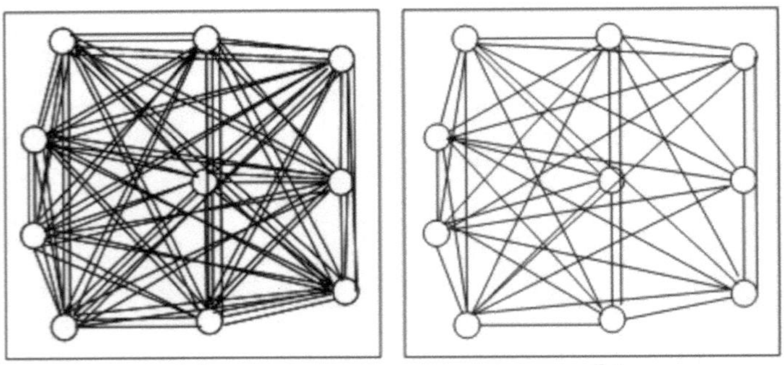

(a) (b)

Fig. 6. All possible relations between players of a soccer team. (a) 90 relations and (b) 45 relations.

On the one hand, the control of such number of relations becomes very difficult to be managed because any change of relations would produce a change of structure. In addition, it could happen that several changes of relations occur at the same time then the problem of detecting what relations are provoking changes of structures becomes much more difficult to be managed. On the other hand, the 45 relations are not relevant in a real match, because a relevant relation is the one in which a player uses to exchange passes and positions in a strategic way. In this work, the goal is to build a simple but robust structure based on relevant relations modeled by a planar graph.

A graph G is planar if it can be represented on a plane in such a way that the nodes represent different points and two edges should be encountered only at their ends. The intersection of two edges out of their ends breaks the planar property of the graph G. This graph G is also named as planar topological graph (Berge, 1983). Two or more graphs are topologically the same if they can be transformed by elastic deformations until their form coincides.

The relevant relations used to build the topological structure are related with the notion of neighborhood. Thus, an agent remains related with his closer neighbor belonging to his zone (defensive (D), medium (M) or attack (A)), and his closer neighbor belonging to the neighbor zone as illustrated in Figure 7(a) and Figure 7(b). Figure 7(c) shows the integration of both kinds of relations for a 4:3:3 formation.

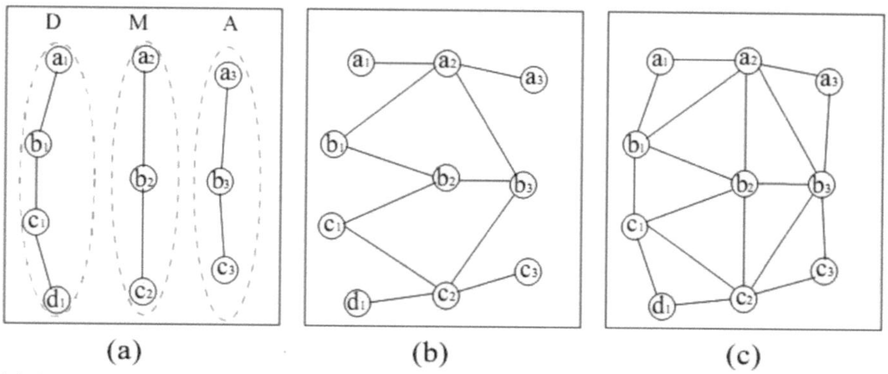

Fig. 7. (a) Step 1. Neighbor nodes of the same zone are linked. (b) Step 2. Neighbor nodes of neighbor zones are linked. (c) Planar graph obtained from step 1 and step 2.

Figure 7(c) shows the planar graph represented by triangular sub-graphs as result of applying the previous two steps. The total number of relations of a graph, which has been built based on the method described above, is given by N_m +15; where N_m is the number of nodes of the middle zone (Due to the lack of space the deduction of this formula is not described in this work). For instance, for a formation 4:4:2, the number of relations will be 19, because $N_m = 4$. The advantages of this method that the number of relations has been reduced from 45 to 19 for the formation 4:4:2. Then, 26 relations have been eliminated. Triangular graphs are able to assume a topological behavior (Ramos & Ayanegui, 2008a). That is, even if a structure is deformed because positional changes of nodes, the topological property of the triangular graphs helps to preserve the structure.

4.3 Pattern Recognition Process

Figure 8 shows the process to recognize patterns of formations and changes of structures that support the formations. The first module serves to determine the zones by using a clustering algorithm; the second module builds the multiple relations which are expressed by a topological graph and finally in the third module the changes of structures are detected if topological properties of a defined structure have been broken.

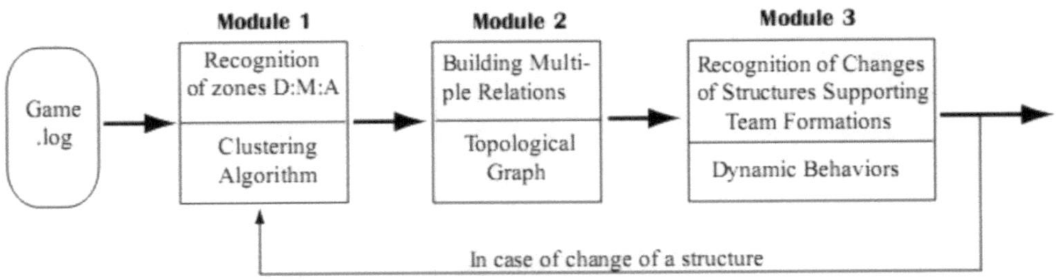

Fig. 8. Process to recognize pattern formations

Module 1. *Recognition of team zones.* The algorithm of clustering is performed during the first cycles of the match and it is stopped until the number of players in each group does not change. In this way, the three zones of a team, defensive, middle and attack zones are recognized.

Module 2. *Building multiple relations and a topological graph.* Based on the three zones recognized by the clustering algorithm and relevant multiple relations a topological planar graph is built.

Module 3. *Recognition of Changes of Structures that support Team Formations.* Changes of structures are detected if topological properties of a defined structure have been broken. A topological graph is, by definition, a planar graph (Berge, 1983). In a planar graph any pair of nodes belonging to the graph can be linked without any intersection of links. Otherwise, if the topological property of the graph has been broken then another structure supporting a formation should be built. Intersections occur when players change their roles in order to build a new formation or due to reactive behavior in response to the opponent. If intersections of links occur, clustering algorithm should redefine the zones and a new topological graph should be built.

5. Discovering of Tactical Behaviour Patterns

The process to discover tactical behavior patterns is illustrated in Figure 9. The following six steps describe such process:

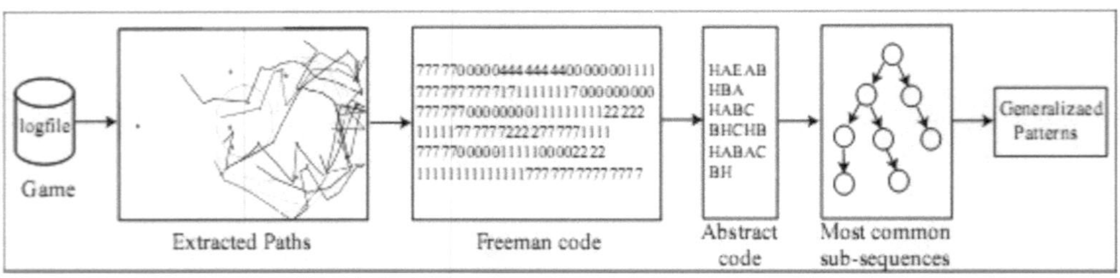

Fig. 9. The steps to discover the tactical behavior patterns

Step 1. Read *logfile*. Input data mainly related with players and ball positions;

Step 2. Extraction of similar paths. A set of ball's paths occurring under similar contexts are extracted. The extracted paths in Figure9 shows paths starting from the middle zone of the field and then distributed either to the right or to the left side until ball reach a zone close to the goal;

Step 3. First Freeman codification. The set of extracted paths are coded to be represented by a sequence of orientations using a Freeman codification (Freeman, 1973) which is composed of eight orientations.

Step 4. Second Freeman codification. The sequence of step 3 is recoded to obtain a more abstract code. Let A,B,...,H be the new abstract segments where each one represents a freeman code sequence with the same orientation, such that, A represents the sequence of 0's, B represents the sequence of 1's, and so on. Thus, a path coded as 7-7-7-1-1-1 can be represented by the code HB;

Step 5. Identification of most frequent sub-sequences. A method based on a generalization of a tree is applied to discover the general behavior patterns representing the paths of tactical plays. For instance, let's take two paths: BAH and ABA. Let's suppose that the trie is empty. It will first insert BAH into it. It will then insert the two remaining suffixes of BAH: {AH, H}. Next, it will then insert the next path and its suffixes: {ABA, BA, A}, into the trie. The most common single sub-sequence is A, the most common two subsequences is BA.

Finally, the players and zones are associated to the generalized paths. The topological structures used to track formations have been a very good support to determine the players participating in tactical plays, as well as the zones through which the plays have taken place. Thanks to the topological graph, we are able to know at each instant of the game the players and their relations participating in a play.

6. Experimental Results

In this section, important experimental results are analyzed. They are derived from two teams: The TsinghuAeolus soccer team, who won the Simulation RoboCup Championship in 2002. It is presented an analysis of the match between TsinguAeolus vs. Everest; and theWrightEagle team, who won the second place in the same competition that held in 2007. The model has been proven in nine matches, but for the relevance of the teams, we present the analysis of results of two matches, one for the TsinguAeolus and one for the WrightEagle. Figure 10 shows a sequence simulation cycles that represent the structures involving the soccer-agents in a path of a tactical play. Because of the lack of space it is shown some of the sub-graphs that compose the total sequence of sub-graphs representing the path (in fact, there are approximately 50 sub-graphs for this tactical play). As can be seen, the shadowed sub-graphs contain the soccer agents involved in the tactical plays. They are in this case: the middle center, the right middle, the right forward, the center forward and the left forward.

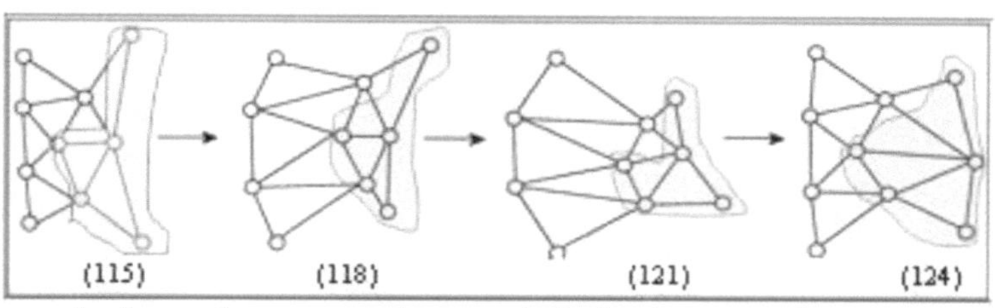

Fig. 10. Sequence of sub-graphs representing a tactical play incorporating agents and field zones

As first step, the paths of the ball were extracted to be analyzed and coded by the code of Freeman. In this way the set of paths can be compared numerically by measuring the similarity between them. Another advantage of this codification is that we can have an idea about how long the paths are. However, what is interesting in this analysis is not exactly how long a path is, but, from the point of view of behavior, the form adopted by the path and obviously the properties associated with the intention or purpose of it, in this case to get close to a position of shooting to the goal. Due to these reasons, it is proposed in this work a more abstract representation. Then the paths coded by the code of Freeman have been recoded to obtain a more abstract code. The paths represented by abstract codes have facilitated the application of the model to discover behavior patterns related with tactical plays. It is important to point out that similar paths are not necessary those to end in a goal, but those that assume a similar behavior from the start of the path to the final objective. Figure 11 illustrates two shapes of generalized paths of tactical behaviors played through the right and left side of the terrain. These generalized paths correspond to the TsinghuAeolus team.

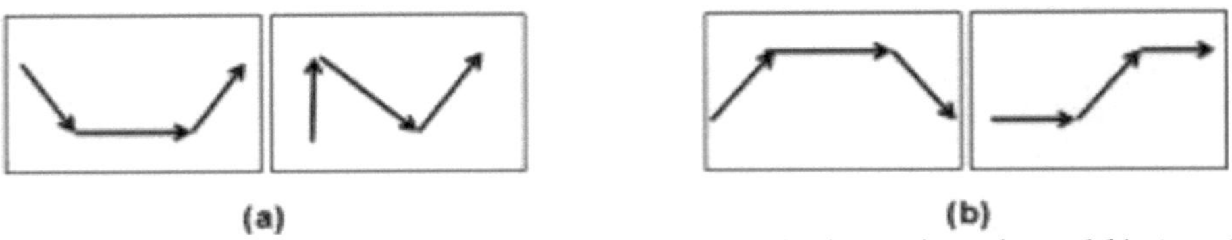

Fig. 11. Generalized paths of tactical behaviors: a) Attacks by right side and b) Attacks by left side

For the case of the WrightEagle team, they played in the right side, Figure 12 shows the extracted paths that get close to the opposite goal and Figure 13 shows two shapes of discovered generalized paths. Based on the results obtained, it is observed that the model to obtain the paths representing the tactical plays do not depend on the analyzed team. The topological structures used to track formations have been a very good support to determine the players participating in tactical plays, as well as the zones through which the plays have taken place.

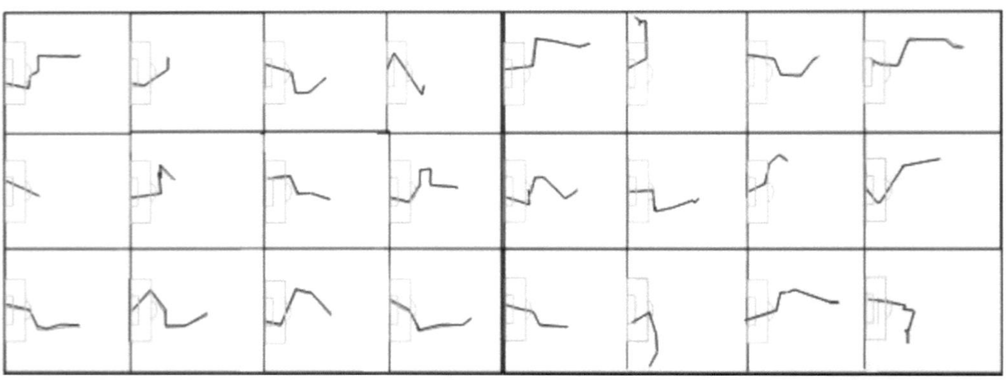
Fig. 12. Extracted paths that get close to the opposite goal. The team is attacking from left to right side.

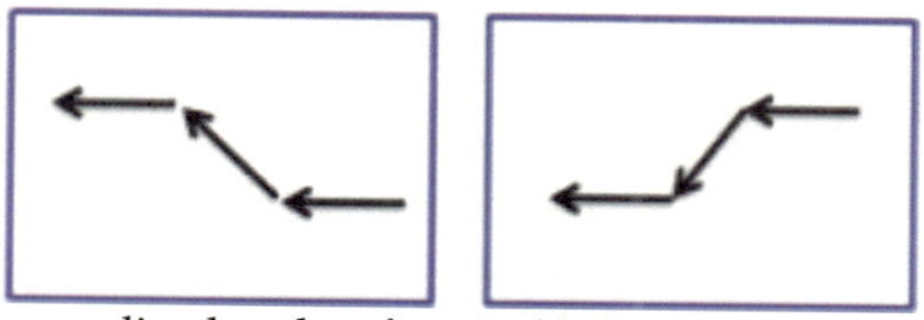

Fig. 13. Two shapes of generalized paths of tactical behaviors

7. Conclusions

This chapter has been focused on the analysis of relevant aspects related with interaction and behavior models of cooperative multi-agent systems participating in a task. Our main interest in these aspects concerns the models of tracking of multi-agent behaviors. Along with the concept of tracking and behaviors, the concepts of coordination, prediction and opponent models have been revised in order to have a general panorama around of this important area in multi-agent systems applied to soccer agent robotics.

Behavioral aspects of cooperative agents may give us precious information about individual, relational and functional roles that the agents assume during the different steps of a task. The discovery of tactical plays and the recognition of formations supporting strategies of team represent relevant information to implement counter strategies or tactics to reduce the performance of the opposite team or, in the best of cases, to beat it. Nevertheless, the dynamic nature of soccer matches along with the multiple interactions between players difficult enormously the task of discovery. The model based on topological graphs has contributed importantly to manage the difficulties due to the dynamic nature of the soccer game. It can facilitate the tracking of formations. In addition, it provided the algorithm of discovery tactical plays with important information concerning the players participating in such plays.

An original idea described in this chapter is related with the double codification of the paths, which has facilitated the interpretation of paths to implement the algorithm described in section 4.3. The discovered paths can be considered as generalized because they were obtained from a set of paths by applying the generalization algorithm described in section 4.3. This chapter dealt with offensive actions to be modeled as an opponent model. However, a richer spectrum of team behaviors should take into account also defensive strategies and tactics, which is an important line of research.

8. References

Nair, R.; Tambe, M.; Marsella S.; Raines, T. (2004). Automated assistants for analyzing team behaviors, *Journal of Autonomous Agents and Multi-Agent Systems*, 8(1).

Ramos, F. & Ayanegui, H. (2008a): Discovering Tactical Behavior Patterns Supported by Topological Structures in Soccer-Agent Domains. In Proceedings of the *7th International Joint Conference on Autonomous Agents and Multi-agent Systems*, Padgham, Parkes, Muller and Parson (eds.), May 12-16, Estoril, Portugal, pp. 1421-1424.

Kuhlmann, G.; Stone, P.; Lallinger, J. (2005). The ut austin villa 2003 champion simulator coach: A machine learning approach. In *RoboCup 2004,* Nardi, D., Riedmiller, M., Sammut, C.,Santos-Victor, J. (eds.). LNCS (LNAI), vol. 3276, pp. 636–644. Springer, Heidelberg.

Lattner, A., D.; Miene, A.; Visser, U. & Herzog, O. (2005). Sequential pattern mining for situation and behavior prediction in simulated robotic soccer. In *RoboCup 2005,* A. Bredenfeld, A. Jacoff editors, volume 4020 of LNCS, pages 118–129. Springer, Heidelberg.

Noda, I. & Frank, I. (1998). Investigating the complex with virtual soccer. In Heudin, J.-C., editor, *Virtual Worlds,* volume 1434 of Lecture Notes in Computer Science, pages 241–253. Springer.

Kitano, H.; Tambe, M.; Stone, P. & Veloso, M. (1997). The robocup synthetic agent challenge 97. In Kitano, H., editor, *RoboCup 1997,* volume 1395 of LNCS, pages 62–73. Springer.

Riley, P.; Veloso, M. & Kaminka, G. (2002). An empírical study of coaching. *On proceedings of Distribuited Autonomous Robotic Systems* 6, Spring-Verlag.

Bezek, A.; Gams, M. & Bratko, I. (2006). Multi-agent strategic modeling in a robotic soccer domain. In Nakashima, H., Wellman, M.P., Weiss, G., Stone, P. (eds.) *Autonomous Agents and Multi-Agent Systems,* pp. 457–464. ACM Press, New York

Visser, U.; Drcker, C.; Hbner, S.; Schmidt, E. & Weland, H.-G. (2001). Recognizing formations in opponent teams. In Stone, P., Balch, T.R., Kraetzschmar, G.K. (eds.) *RoboCup 2000.* LNCS (LNAI), vol. 2019, pp. 391–396. Springer, Heidelberg

MacQueen, J.B. (1967). Some Methods for classification and Analysis of Multivariate Observations. In *Proceedings of 5th Berkeley Symposium on Mathematical Statistics and Probability,* Berkeley, vol. 1, pp. 281–29. University of California Press (1967).

Berge, C. (1983). Graphes. *Guathier-Villars.*

Freeman, H. (1973). On the encoding of arbitrary geometric configurations. *IRE Transactions.*

Durfee, E. H,. Lesser, V.R. and Corkill, D.D. (1989b). Trends in cooperative distributed problem solveing. IEEE Trnsactions on Knowledge and Data Engineering, 1(1), 63-83.

Wooldrige, M. & Jennings, N.R. (1994). Formalizing the cooperative problem solving process. In Proceedings of the 13th International Workshop on Distributed Artificial Intelligence (IWDAI-94), Lake Quinalt, WA, pp. 403-417. Reprinted in Huhns and Singh (1998).

Adler, M.R. et al. (1989). Conflict resolution strategies for non hierarchical distributed agents. In Distributed Artificial Intelligence (eds. L. Gasser and M. Huhns), Volume 2, pp. 139-162. Pitman, London and Morgan Kaufmann, San Mateo, Ca.

Galliers, J.R. (1988b). A theoretical frameqork for computer models of cooperative dialogue, acknowledging multi-agent conflict. PhD thesis, The Open University, UK

Galliers, J.R. (1990). The positive role of conflict in cooperative multi-agent systems. In Descentralized A.I. Proceedings of the First European Workshop Modelling Autonomous Agents in a Multi-Agent World (MAAMAW-89) (eds. Y. Demazeau and J.P. Miller), pp-33-48. Elsevier, Amsterdam.

Klein, M. & Baskin, A.B. (1991). A computational model for conflict resolution in cooperative design systems. In CKBS-90. Proceedings of the International Working Conference on Cooperative Knowledge Based Systems (ed. S.M. Deen), pp. 201-222. Springer, Berlin.

Lander, S., Lesser, V.R. & Connel, M.E. (1991). Conflict resolution strategies for cooperating expert agents. In CKBS-90. Proceedings of the International Working Conference on Cooperating Knowledge Based Systems (ed. S.M. Deen), pp. 183-200. Springer, Berlin.

Ephrati, E. & Rosenschein, J.S. (1993). Multi-agent planning as a dynamic search for social consensus. Proceedings of the International Joint Conference on Artificial Intelligence (IJCAI-93). Chambéry, France, pp. 423-429.

Rosenschein, J.S. and Zlotkin, G. (1994). Rules of Encounter: Designing Conventions for Automated Negotiation among Computers. MIT Press, Cambridge, MA.

Horling, B. & Lesser, V. (2004). A survey of multi-agent organizational paradigms. *Knowledge Engineering Review,* Vol. 19, Issue 4, pp. 281-316., ISSN: 0269-8889. Cambridge University Press, New York, NY, USA.

Chernova, S. & Veloso, M. (2008). Teaching multi-robot coordination using demonstration of communication and state sharing. In *Proceedings of the 7th international Joint Conference on Autonomous Agents and Multi-agent Systems - Volume 3* (Estoril, Portugal). International Conference on Autonomous Agents. International Foundation for Autonomous Agents and Multi-agent Systems, Richland, SC, 1183-1186.

Jansen, R. & Sturtevant, N. 2008. A new approach to cooperative pathfinding. In *Proceedings of the 7th international Joint Conference on Autonomous Agents and Multi-agent Systems - Volume 3* (Estoril, Portugal). International Conference on Autonomous Agents. International Foundation for Autonomous Agents and Multi-agent Systems, Richland, SC, 1401-1404.

Candea, C.; Hu, H.; Iocchi, L.; Nardi, D. & Piaggio, M. (2001). Coordination in Multi-Agent RoboCup Teams. In *Robotics and Autonomous Systems* , Vol. 36 (2001) , p. 67-86.

Aler, R.; Valls, J.; Camacho, D. & Lopez, A. (2009). Programming Robosoccer agents by modeling human behavior. *Expert Systems with Applications,* Volume 36, Issue 2, Part 1, pp. 1850-1859.

Lin, L., Seo, Y., Gen, M., and Cheng, R. (2009). Unusual human behavior recognition using evolutionary technique. *Computers & Industrial Engineering, Volume 56, Issue 3, April 2009, pp. 1137-1153.*

Balch, T.; Khan, Z. & Veloso, M. (2001). Automatically Tracking and Analyzing the Behavior of Live Insect Colonies. *AGENTS'01, May 28-June 1, 2001, Montreal, Quebec, Canada.*

Luotsinen, L. J. & Bölöni, L. (2008). Role-based teamwork activity recognition in observations of embodied agent actions. In *Proceedings of the 7th international Joint Conference on Autonomous Agents and Multi-agent Systems - Volume 2* (Estoril, Portugal, May 12 - 16, 2008). International Conference on Autonomous Agents. International Foundation for Autonomous Agents and Multi-agent Systems, Richland, SC, 567-574.

Hindriks, K. & Tykhonov, D. (2008). Opponent modelling in automated multi-issue negotiation using Bayesian learning. In *Proceedings of the 7th international Joint Conference on Autonomous Agents and Multi-agent Systems - Volume 1* (Estoril, Portugal, May 12 - 16, 2008). International Conference on Autonomous Agents. International Foundation for Autonomous Agents and Multi-agent Systems, Richland, SC, 331-338.

Mulder, F. & Voorbraak, F. (2003). A formal description of tactical plan recognition. *Information Fusion*, Volume 4, Issue 1, March 2003, pp. 47-61.

Henniger & Madhavan. (2004). *Robotics and Autonomous Systems*, Volume 49, Issues 1-2, 30 November 2004, pp. 91-103.

Tambe, M. & Rosenbloom, P.S. (1996). Architectures for Agents that Track Other Agents in Multi-agent Worlds, *Intelligent Agents II*, Springer Verlag Lecture Notes in Artificial Intelligence, LNAI 1037.

Tambe, M.; Johnson, W. L.; Jones, R.; Koss, F.; Laird, J. E.; Ronsenbloom, P.S. & Schwamb, K. (1995). Intelligent agents for interactive simulation environment. *AI Magazine (16) 1,* Spring 1995.

Muñoz, R. (2008). A Bayesian plan-view map based approach for multiple-person detection and tracking. *Pattern Recognition, Volume 41, Issue 12, December 2008, Pages 3665-3676.*

Muñoz, R.; García, M. & Medina, R. (2008). Adaptive multi-modal stereo people tracking without background modelling. *Journal of Visual Communication and Image Representation*, Volume 19, Issue 2, February 2008, Pages 75-91.

Muñoz, R.; Aguirre, E.; García, M. (2007). People detection and tracking using stereo vision and color. *Image and Vision Computing,* Volume 25, Issue 6, 1 June 2007, pp. 995-1007.

Schwager, M.; Anderson, D. M.; Butler, Z. & Rus, D. (2007). Robust classification of animal tracking data. *Computers and Electronics in Agriculture*, Volume 56, Issue 1, March 2007, pp. 46-59.

Noldus, L.; Spink, A. & Tegelenbosch, R. (2002). Computerised video tracking, movement analysis and behavior recognition in insects. *Computers and Electronics in Agriculture*, Volume 35, Issues 2-3, August 2002, pp. 201-227.

Ukita, N. & Matsuyama, T. (2005). Real-time cooperative multi-target tracking by communicating active vision agents. *Computer Vision and Image Understanding,* Volume 97, Issue 2, February 2005, pp. 137-179.

Xiao, F.; Wang, L.; Chen, J. & Gao, Y. (2009). Finite-time formation control for multi-agent systems. *Automatica*, In Press, Corrected Proof, Available online 19 August 2009.

Porfiri, M.; Roberson, G. & Stilwell, D. (2007). Tracking and formation control of multiple autonomous agents: A two-level consensus approach. *Automatica*, Volume 43, Issue 8, August 2007, pp. 1318-1328.

Ramos, F. & Ayanegui, H. (2008b). Discovering Behavior Patterns in Muti-agent Teams. In *Agent and Multi-Agent Systems: Technologies and Applications,* Second KES International Symposium, KES-AMSTA 2008, Incheon, Korea, March 26-28, 2008. pp. 391-400.

Raines, T.; Tambe, M. & Marsella, S. (2000). Automated assistant to aid humans in understanding team behaviors. In *Agents-2000.*

Sukthankar, G. & Sycara, K. (2006). Simultaneous team assignment and behavior recognition from spatio-temporal agent traces. In *Proceedings of 21st national conference on artificial intelligence AAAI 2006.*

Fischler, M. & Bolles, R. (1981). Random sample consensus: A paradigm for model fitting with application to image analysis and automated cartography. *Communications of the ACM* 24 (6).

Petri Net Robotic Task Plan Representation: Modelling, Analysis and Execution

Hugo Costelha
Institute for Systems and Robotics, Instituto Superior Técnico
Superior School of Technology and Management, Polytechnic Institute of Leiria
Portugal

Pedro Lima
Institute for Systems and Robotics, Instituto Superior Técnico
Portugal

1. Introduction

As the usage of robots in everyday tasks increases, there is a need to improve our knowledge concerning the execution of those robotic tasks. Robotic task models are usually not based on formal approaches but tailored to the task at hand. Applying discrete event system concepts to model robotic tasks provides a systematic approach to modelling, analysis and design, scaling up to realistic applications, and enabling analysis of formal properties, as well as design from specifications.

Most of the work found on the literature concerning the design of robotic tasks using Discrete Event Systems is based on Finite State Automata for code generation (Dominguez-Brito et al., 2000), qualitative specifications (Kosecka et al., 1997), some quantitative specifications (Espiau et al., 1995), modularisation (Kosecka et al., 1997) and even to model multi-robot systems (Damas & Lima, 2004). Work using Petri nets to design robotic tasks under temporal requirements, focusing also on the generation of real-time, error-free code can be found in (Montano et al., 2000). Petri net Plans were introduced in (Ziparo & Iocchi, 2006) for design and execution of task plans. However, these do not close the loop, i.e., do not consider the actual implications of the actions on the environment, focusing mostly on the design.

In this chapter we describe a Petri net based framework which allows a systematic approach for modelling, analysis and execution of robotic tasks. This framework is divided in three layers: task plan models, action models and environment models. The models range from the robot decision-making algorithms (task plan models) to the environment dynamics, due to physics and/or actions of other agents (environment models).

In the proposed models, Petri net places represent tasks, primitive actions and logic predicates set by sensor readings. These logic predicates provide and abstraction of the world relevant features. By composing these models, and applying analysis techniques, important a priori information can be obtained regarding the properties of the task. The models are based on Marked Ordinary Petri Nets and Generalised Stochastic Petri Nets (Murata, 1989), allowing

for transitions to be immediate or stochastic, and leading to both the retrieval of logical properties, such as deadlocks and resource conservation, and (probabilistic) performance properties, such as probability or average time to reach a desired state.
Given the action and environment models, different task plans can be quickly evaluated using the analysis techniques, allowing for a priori quality/performance based decisions. Furthermore, due to the introduced abstractions and inherent Petri net restrictions, the state space is reduced.
By introducing comunication models we further extend the framework to model cooperative robotic tasks, namely those involving the coordination of two or more robots, which require the exchange of synchronisation messages, either using explicit (e.g., wireless) or implicit (e.g., vision-based observation of teammates) communication. Different communication models allow the analysis of different scenarios, such as perfect communication, delayed communication or absence of communication.
Extensive tests were done using a robotic soccer scenario under full observability.

2. Petri Nets

Petri nets (Petri, 1966) are a widely used formalism for modelling Discrete Event Dynamic Systems (DEDS). They allow modelling important aspects such as synchronisation, resources availability, concurrency, parallelism and decision making, providing at the same time a high degree of modularity, making them suitable to model robotic tasks.
Petri nets are preferred to Finite State Automata (FSA) due to their larger modelling power and because one can model the same state space with a smaller graph. Moreover, although composition of Petri nets usually leads to an exponential growth in the state space (as for FSA), graphically the growth is linear in the size of the composed graphs given that the state is distributed. This makes the design process simpler for the task designer, and helps managing the display of the tasks both for monitoring and designing purposes. Moreover, we use Marked Ordinary Petri Nets (MOPN) and Generalised Stochastic Petri Nets (GSPN) (Murata, 1989), allowing the retrieval of logical and (probabilistic) performance properties.
Modularity in Petri nets is achieved since each resource can be modeled separately and then composed with others. Although composition operators exist for FSA, Petri nets can model subsystems with input and output places, so that they can be connected as in a circuit.

2.1 Marked Ordinary Petri Nets

The simplest models we use are Marked Ordinary Petri nets:

Definition 2.1. *A marked ordinary Petri net is a five-tuple* $PN = \langle P, T, I, O, \mathcal{M}_0 \rangle$*, where:*

- $P = \{p_1, p_2, \dots, p_n\}$ *is a finite, not empty, set of places;*
- $T = \{t_1, t_2, \dots, t_m\}$ *is a finite set of transitions;*
- $I = P \times T$ *represents the arc connections from places to transitions, such that* $i_{lj} = 1$ *if, and only if, there is an arc from* p_l *to* t_j*, and* $i_{lj} = 0$ *otherwise;*
- $O = T \times P$ *represent the arc connections from transition to places, such that* $o_{lj} = 1$ *if, and only if, there is an arc from* t_l *to* p_j*, and* $o_{lj} = 0$ *otherwise;*
- $\mathcal{M}(j) = [m_1(j), \dots, m_n(j)]$ *is the state of the net, and represents the marking of the net at time* j*, where* $m_n(j) = q$ *means there are* q *tokens in place* p_n *at time instant* j*.* $\mathcal{M}(0)$ *is the initial marking of the net.*

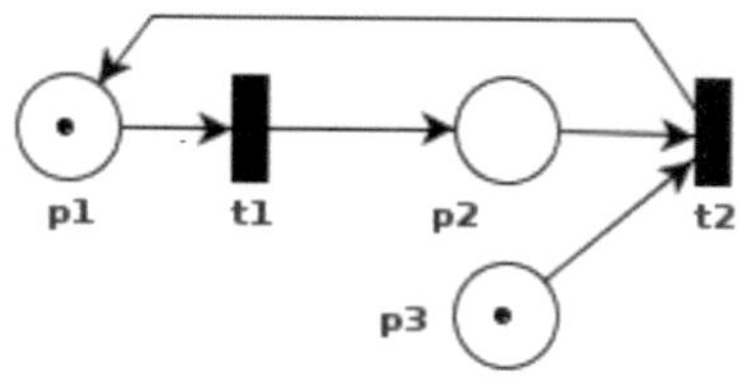

Fig. 1. A simple Petri net.

A simple MOPN is depicted in Fig. 1. Basically we have two types of nodes: places, represented by circles, and transitions, represented by filled rectangles. The places can contain any number of tokens, represented by the number of dots (or a number) inside the place. For instance, in the Petri net shown in Fig. 1 place p_1 and place p_3 both have one token, while place p_2 has zero tokens.
The state of the net is given by the marking of the net, which in turn is given by the number of tokens in the places. For instance, the initial marking of the Petri net from Fig. 1 is given by $\mathcal{M}_0 = [1,0,1]$.
In this class of Petri nets, all the transitions are *immediate* (have zero firing time), i.e., once they are enabled and fired, the new marking is instantly reached.
When referring to input or output nodes of a particular node, we are referring to the nodes connected to or from that node. For instance, transition t_3 has places p_2 and p_3 as its input places, while it has only one output place, p_1.

2.2 Generalised Stochastic Petri Nets

MOPNs are suited for qualitative analysis, but not for performance analysis. For this purpose, one uses generalised stochastic Petri nets.

Definition 2.2. *A standard GSPN is an eight-tuple* $PN = \langle P, T, I, O, \mathcal{M}_0, R, S \rangle$, *where:*

- $P, T, I, O, \mathcal{M}_0$ *are as defined in 2.1;*
- T *is partitioned in two sets:* T_I *of immediate transitions and* T_E *of exponential transitions;*
- R *is a function from the set of transitions* T_E *to the set of real numbers,* $R\left(t_{E_j}\right) = \mu_j$, *where* μ_j *is called the firing rate of* t_{E_j};
- S *is a set of* random switches, *which associate probability distributions to subsets of conflicting immediate transitions.*

Stochastic (exponential) transitions, once enabled, fire only when an exponentially distributed time d_j has elapsed. This definition of GSPNs includes also the possibility of associating a probability distribution to conflicting immediate transitions, by the use of the *random switches*. These random switches can be static (invariant to the marking of the net) or dynamic (dependent on the marking of the net).
We use a particular implementation of random switches, by associating weights to the immediate transitions, as described in Definition 2.3.

Definition 2.3. *A GSPN is an eight-tuple* $PN = \langle P, T, I, O, \mathcal{M}_0, R, W \rangle$, *where:*

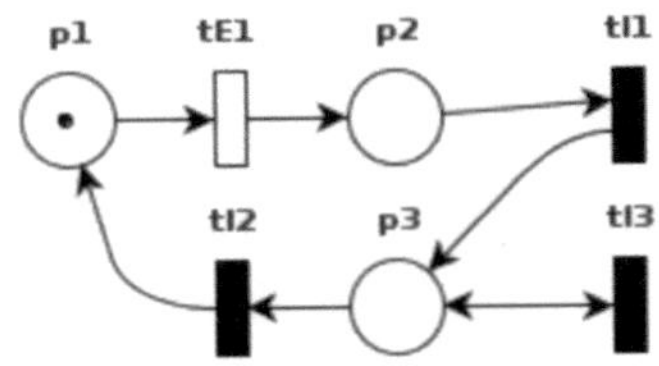

Fig. 2. Generalised stochastic Petri net.

- *$P, T, I, O, \mathcal{M}_0, R$ are as defined in 2.2;*
- *W is a function from the immediate transitions set T_I to a set of real numbers, $W\left(t_{I_j}\right) = w_j$, where w_j is the weight associated with immediate transition t_{I_j};*
- *For any given marking, the probability of firing an enabled transition t_i is equal to $w_i/\mathcal{W}$, where $\mathcal{W}$ is the sum of the weights of all enabled transitions for the given marking.*

Consider the GSPN model depicted in Fig. 2. In this example, t_{E_1} is an exponential timed transition (drawn with a unfilled rectangle), while t_{I_1}, t_{I_2} and t_{I_3} are immediate transitions with associated weights. Initially t_1 is enabled, since p_1 has tokens, and will fire after an exponentially distributed time with rate μ_1 has elapsed. The token flows from p_1 to p_2 and, since t_{I_1} is an immediate transition, it will immediately flow from p_2 to p_3, reaching marking $\mathcal{M}_3 = [0, 0, 1]$. In this marking t_{I_2} and t_{I_3} form a set of conflicting transitions, whereas only one will fire, according to the following probabilities:

$$P_f\left(t_{I_2}\right) = \frac{w_2}{w_2 + w_3} \qquad P_f\left(t_{I_3}\right) = \frac{w_3}{w_2 + w_3}$$

If t_{I_3} is fired, the marking remains the same, if t_{I_2} is fired, the net returns to the initial marking. The GSPN marking is a semi-Markov process with a discrete state space given by the reachability graph of the net for an initial marking (Murata, 1989; Viswanadham & Narahari, 1992). A Markov chain can be obtained from the marking process, and the transition probability matrix computed by using the firing rates of the exponential timed transitions and the probabilities associated with the random switches. This enables the use of tools already available to analyse Markov chains directly from the GSPN, instead of relying on, e.g., Monte Carlo simulation.

2.3 Additional Specifications

In our framework, we embody the Petri net models with some additional building blocks, namely macro places, and make use of the place labels to distinguish between different types of places, such as: *action macro places*, *predicate places* and *regular* (or *memory*) *places*. These different types of places do not introduce any change regarding the execution of the Petri nets, but are key in the analysis process explained later.
Regular (or memory) places are normal Petri net places, without any special properties. The remaining types of places are described in the following sections.

Fig. 3. Representation of predicate by a set of places.

2.3.1 Predicate Places

Predicate places are used to represent logic predicates, having always one or zero tokens. Although Predicate Petri nets exist in the literature (Röck & Kresman, 2006), the tools available to work with this type of Petri nets are very scarce. As such, we use regular places to represent predicates, as explained next.

Definition 2.4. *A predicate place p is a place associated with the predicate P, described by $p \models P$, such that:*

- $\forall_j, P_j = true \Leftrightarrow m_p(j) = 1$
- $\forall_j, P_j = false \Leftrightarrow m_p(j) = 0,$

where P_j is the predicate P at time step j.

Basically, a place representing a predicate has one token if that predicate is true and zero tokens otherwise.

Definition 2.5. *A Petri net model of a predicate is a MOPN where:*

- $P = \{\neg p, p\}$, *where and $\neg p$ and p are predicate places associated with predicates $\neg P()$ and $P()$ respectively;*
- $I = \emptyset$;
- $O = \emptyset$;
- $\forall_j \mathcal{M}_j = [0,1] \vee [1,0]$.

Although we could achieve the same results by using just one place for representing a predicate, that would lead to the use of inhibitor arcs. Once again we rather maintain the use of the base Petri nets, with minimal extensions added, so as to be able to use a larger set of available Petri tools. Furthemore, although it increases the number of places, it does not increase the state space, and provides a cleaner interface to the user.
As an example, a Petri net model representing the predicate `SeeBall` is depicted in Figure 3. Note the usage of the *predicate.* (or, alternatively, *p.*) prefix to denote that the place is a predicate place, and the *NOT_* prefix to denote the negated predicate.

2.3.2 Macro Places

Macros, albeit not always using the same definition, are used to create hierarchical Petri nets (Bernardinello & Cindio, 1992), leading to a higher degree of modularity. The use of macro places allows the drawing of entire Petri net models from lower layers has single places in higher layers, providing for cleaner and reusable models.
Places associated with macros will also have a particular prefix in the place label. Furthermore, since macro places represent entire Petri nets, we need to have expansion algorithms when obtaining one single Petri net without macro places. These details will be given later in Section 4.1.

3. Modelling Single-Robot Tasks using Petri Nets

The base framework used throughout this work was developed aiming at:

Modularity - fostering the reuse of developed components;

Design - providing an intuitive, and possibly graphical, task design solution;

Analysis - providing means to analyse a robotic task both before and after its execution;

Execution - keeping the models suitable for execution, taking into account that its implementation would have to follow the framework theoretical foundations.

To achieve these goals, a Petri net based solution was developed, using four different layers, as depicted in Figure 4.

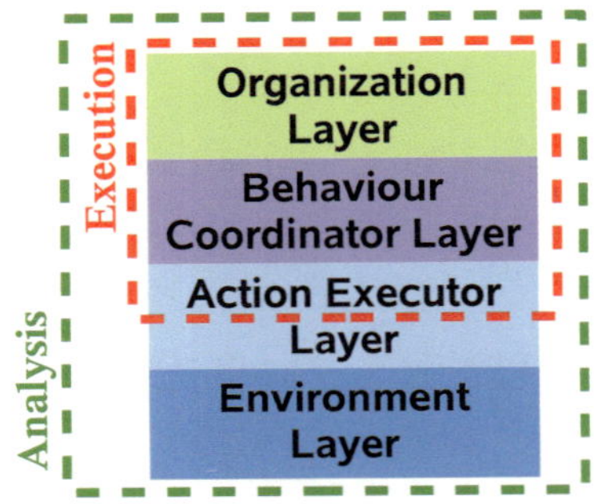

Fig. 4. Models Hierarchy.

Each layer is formed by a set of Petri net models which represent different granularity levels, being the Environment layer the bottom one, and the Organisation layer the top one. The meaning of each layer is as follows:

Environment Layer Petri net models at this level represent changes made by other agents (such as other robots) or even physics (such as the braking of a free rolling ball);

Action Executor Layer At this level we find Petri net models of the actions, representing the changes performed in the environment by these actions, and the conditions under which these changes can occur;

Action Coordinator Layer Here lies the Petri net based task plan models, which basically consist of compositions of actions;

Organisation Layer This layer is where higher decision models appear, such as goal selection, thus consisting of compositions of Action Coordinator Layer models.

As can be seen in Figure 4, all models are used in the analysis process, but only the two higher layers and, partially, the Action Executor layer models will be used for execution. This will be further explained in the following sections. Note that, currently, we have not implemented the Organisation layer yet.

3.1 Environment Layer

To better understand how the Environment models are designed, consider a free rolling ball. In this case, due to friction on the floor, it is expected that the ball will stop after some time. To model this process using a GSPN model under our framework, we must first discretise it, such that we can describe it through the use of logic predicates. In this example, we could consider that the ball could be moving fast, slowly or be stopped, and that the ball will, with time, pass from the fastest movement to the stopped state. With this discretisation, we can model the free ball movement with the Petri net model depicted in Figure 5.

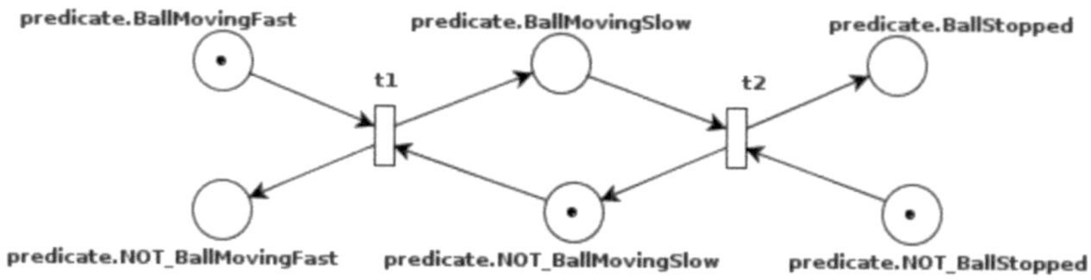

Fig. 5. Petri net model of a moving ball.

If, for instance, one also wanted to model the fact that some other agent could increase the ball speed, we could add transitions in the opposite direction, albeit with different associated rates, considering the probability of that occurrence. Furthermore, it is also possible to include several transitions with different rates associated with the same state change, as in the example depicted in Figure 6. In this example, the rate at which the ball slows down depends on the weather conditions.

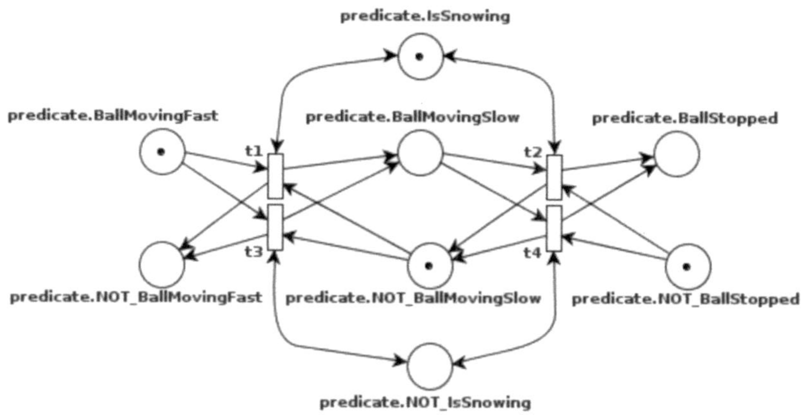

Fig. 6. Petri net model of a moving ball considering thee weather conditions.

3.2 Action Executor Layer

Each action Petri net model is a GSPN which represents how the action impacts the environment and under which conditions. As such, each action model consists on a set of transitions representing the environment changes, which can be associated to the success or failure of the action, following the rules described in Definition 3.1. The general model of an action is depicted in Figure 7.

Definition 3.1. *A Petri net model of an action is a GSPN, where:*

1. $P = P_E \cup P_R$ *contains only predicate places, where*

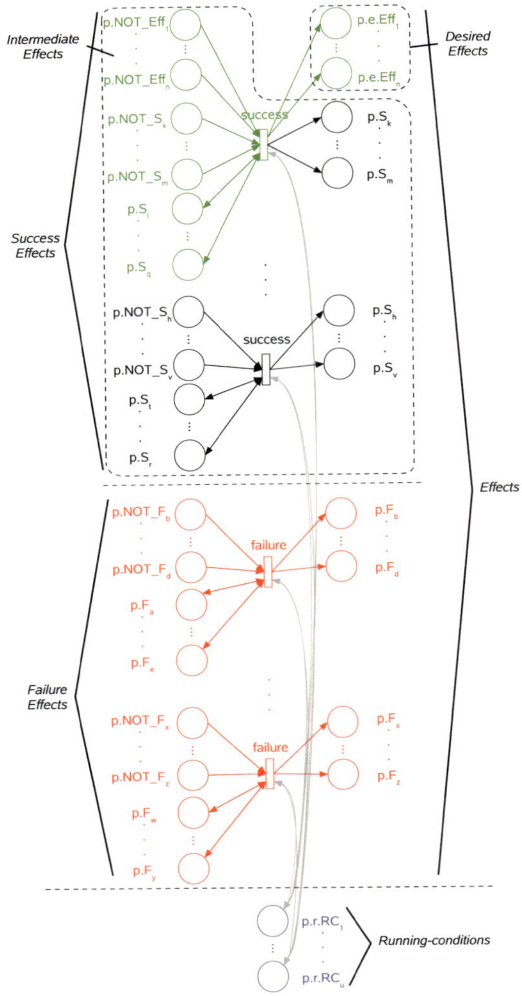

Fig. 7. General action model.

P_E *is the effects place set;*

P_R *is the running-conditions place set;*

2. *All places in* P_R *have "*`r.`*" after the "*`predicate.`*" prefix;*
3. $P_E = P_{E_S} \cup P_{E_F}$, *where* P_{E_S} *and* P_{E_F} *are designated respectively* success places set *and* failure places set.
4. $P_{E_S} = P_{E_{S_I}} \cup P_{E_{S_D}}$, *where* $P_{E_{S_I}}$ *and* $P_{E_{S_D}}$ *are designated respectively* intermediate effects place set *and* desired effects place set.
5. *All places in* $P_{E_{S_D}}$ *have "*`e.`*" after the "*`predicate.`*" prefix;*
6. $T = T_S \cup T_F$ *with* $T_S \cap T_F = \emptyset$, *where:*

   T_S *is the set of transitions associated with successful impact of the action;*

T_F *is the set of transitions associated with failure impact of the action;*

7. *If there is an arc from place* p_n*, associated to predicate* $\mathcal{P}$*, to transition* t_j*, then there is an arc from* t_j *to place* p_m*, associated to predicate* $\neg\mathcal{P}$*, or an arc back to* p_n*;*
8. *All transitions have one input arc from each running-condition;*
9. *If a desired effect place is an output place of a transition, then all the desired effects places are also output places of that transition;*
10. *All transitions* t_j *in* T_S *have the label* $\texttt{success}_j$ *or* $\texttt{s}_j$*;*
11. *All transitions* t_j *in* T_F *have the label* $\texttt{failure}_j$ *or* $\texttt{f}_j$*;*

Having the *running-conditions* as input places of all transitions models the fact that the action can only cause any impact on the environment if these conditions are met. Given that all places are predicate places, rule 7 implies that the action model maintains the predicates Definition 2.5, resulting in a safe Petri net (has at most one token per place for all markings).
As an example, consider an action named `CatchBall`, where the purpose of the robot is to catch a ball. It would be expected that the robot could only catch the ball if it were near the ball and if it could see the ball, meaning its *running-conditions* would be `CloseToBall` and `SeeBall`. Furthermore, the *desired-effects* of this action would be catching the ball, i.e., getting the predicate `HasBall` to true. This results in the Petri net model show in Figure 8.

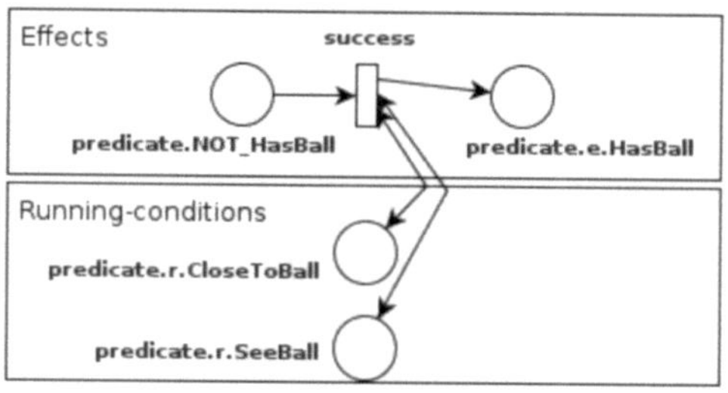

Fig. 8. Petri net model of action `CatchBall`.

Failures were not explicitely included in this model. Although including them is possible, and even expected in many situations, these are already implicitely present, since this model will be composed with the environment model, which models changes performed by others.
For execution purposes the Action Executor models are used partially, by using only the *running-conditions* and *desired-effects* to prevent using each action outside their scope.

3.3 Action Coordinator Layer

The Action Coordinator layer contains Petri net models of the task plans. A Petri net model of a task plan consists of a MOPN where places are associated with actions. Places associated with actions are referred to as *action places*, and correspond to action macro places.
To better explain this topic, we will follow an example of a soccer playing robot. In this example, the robot uses actions `Move2Ball`, `CatchBall`, `Dribble2Goal`, `Aim2Score` and `Kick2Goal`, resulting in the task plan Petri net model depicted in Figure 9.

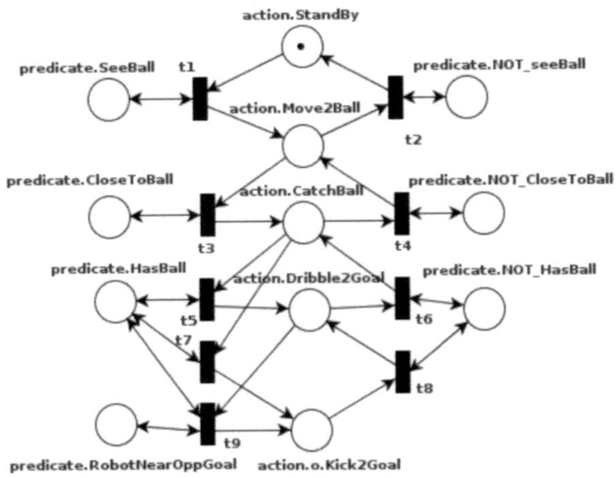

Fig. 9. Petri net model of the `Score_Goal` task.

Note that we use "`action.`" in the labels prefixes to denote action places. The label "`o.`" is used to denote which places should be marked in the desired final state of a given task model, denoting them as *output places*. Although this knowledge is not used yet, it will allow us to determine a task *desired-effects* in the future. There is no need to mark the places which are marked in the initial state, since this information is already given by the initial marking of the task model.

4. Analysis of Single-Robot Tasks

Given that all layers are modelled using Petri nets, we can compose all these models together in a single Petri net model. This single Petri net model represents the overall task, which we can analyse a priori. This analysis can be both for logical (e.g. deadlocks) and probabilistic performance properties (e.g. probability of reaching a given state).

Furthermore, there are a number of properties that must be met during design time, which allow for some error detection at an early stage of development. As an example consider the boundedness of the net. Given that we are using predicate places, they can have only one or zero tokens. If one detects more than one token in a predicate place at design time, or that the sum of tokens in the two places associated with a predicate is not always one, it means that there is an error in the models. In the predicate places case, this translates to a simple design rule which states that if a given predicate p is an input place of a transition t, then one, and only one, of predicate places NOT_p or p must be an output place of transition t. If additionally one requires macro places to have at most one token, it results in a safe net requirement (i.e., have at most one token for all places, for all possible markings). Having the total number of tokens in the two places associated with a predicate equal to one is referred in Petri nets as a place invariant (Murata, 1989), which can also be determined from a priori analysis.

Having the modelling and analysis processes integrated under the same framework allows for a design process based on a continuous loop of design-analysis-design. This loop guides the development of the tasks in a structured way, leading to improved task plans even before gathering results from the execution process.

Furthermore, data also can also be extracted from the execution process in order to analyse the task a posteriori, and to further improve the models.

4.1 Expansion Process

The *Expansion Process* enables us to obtain the single Petri net for analysis by merging all the environment, action and task Petri net models. The place labels play an important role in this process, since these allow us to distinguish between the different types of places.
The expansion process is performed using Algorithm 4.1 while obeying the following set of rules:

- Predicate places with the same label are considered the same place;
- Macro places are always different places, regardless of their label;
- All transitions are different, regardless of their label.

The action macro places function as enabling places of all transitions on the associated models, i.e., if there is a token in the action macro place, then the transitions of the associated Petri net model are enabled (as long as the *running-conditions* and remaining input predicate places are true).

Algorithm 4.1: Full task Petri net model generation algorithm.

Input: Environment, task and action Petri net models
Output: Full Petri net model of the task

```
begin
    Create an empty Petri Net, denoting it full-net;
    foreach environment model do
        Add the environment model to full-net;
        Prefix all added transitions with the name of the model;
    end
    Add the task model to full-net;
    foreach action macro place in full-net do
        Add the Petri net model of the action associated with the action macro place to
        full-net;
        Add an arc from the action macro place to all transitions in the added Petri net
        model;
        Add an arc from all transitions in the added Petri net model to the action macro
        place;
        Prefix the action macro place label with an "e" to denote that this is no longer a
        macro place, i.e., it has been expanded;
        Prefix the labels of all added transitions with the name of the action;
    end
    Remove the tokens from all predicate places;
end
```

Prefixing the transitions with the model names during the expansion algorithm enables us to distinguish them while performing the analysis of the final model.
After having obtained the single Petri net, one needs to choose an initial state for the task by setting the number of tokens in the predicate places. Having set the initial marking of the net,

one can use available tools such as PIPE (Akharware, 2005) or TimeNET (Zimmermann, 2001) to study the task properties.

5. Execution of Single-Robot Tasks

In order to be able to execute the task plans developed within the framework, one needs to have a Petri net execution framework. In our case we have implemented such a framework in the decision layer of our MeRMaID middleware (Barbosa et al., 2007).

In MeRMaID, the sensorial part of the implementation keeps the predicates up to date (at least all the predicates that are revelant at any given state). Given a Petri net based task plan model, the *Petri net Executor* checks which transitions are enabled, considering the current selected actions and enabled predicates, and fires them accordingly. All actions that have tokens at any given moment are the actions that will be enabled. We have also taken advantage of part of the information provided at the Action Executor level, namely the *running-conditions*, so as to prevent running an action at the lower level when these are not satisfied.

The execution of the tasks can be monitored in order to assert and compare experimental results with the theoretical ones, allowing to check the models for errors or needed improvements.

6. Single-robot Task Example

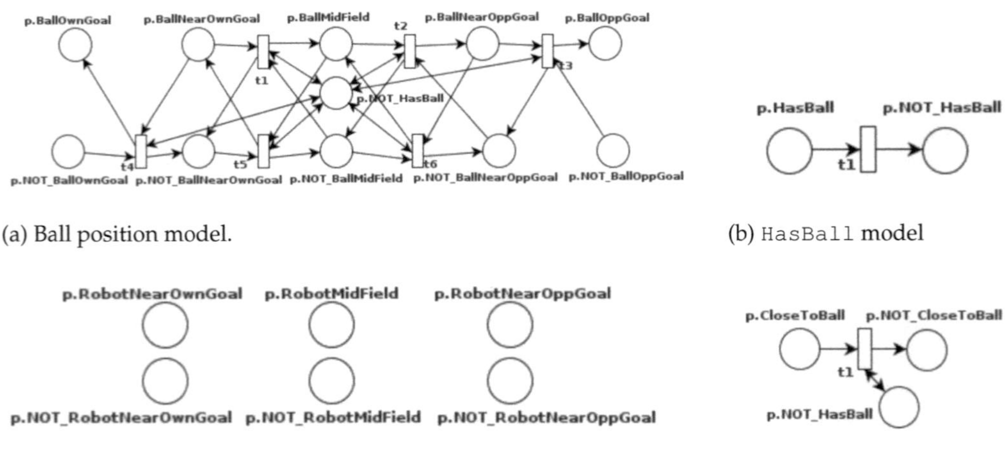

(a) Ball position model. (b) `HasBall` model

(c) Robot Position model. (d) `CloseToBall` model

Fig. 10. Environment models for task `Score_Goal`.

To illustrate the framework application, we will detail a robotic soccer example using the single-robot task plan depicted in Figure 9. In this task we use the following predicates:

Ball position: `BallOwnGoal`, `BallNearOwnGoal`, `BallMidField`, `BallNearOppGoal`, `BallOppGoal`;

Robot position: `RobotNearOwnGoal`, `RobotMidField`, `RobotNearOppGoal`;

Other: `SeeBall`, `HasBall`, `CloseToBall`.

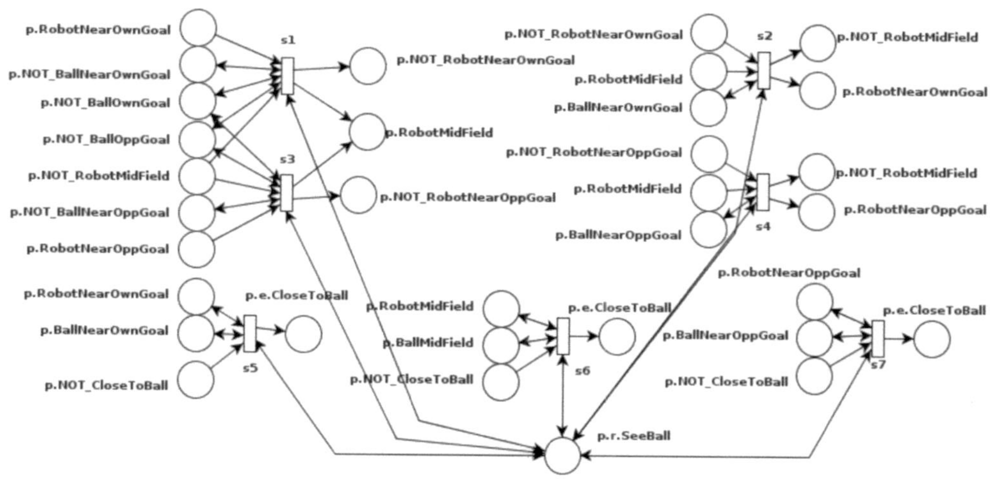

(a) Move2Ball model.

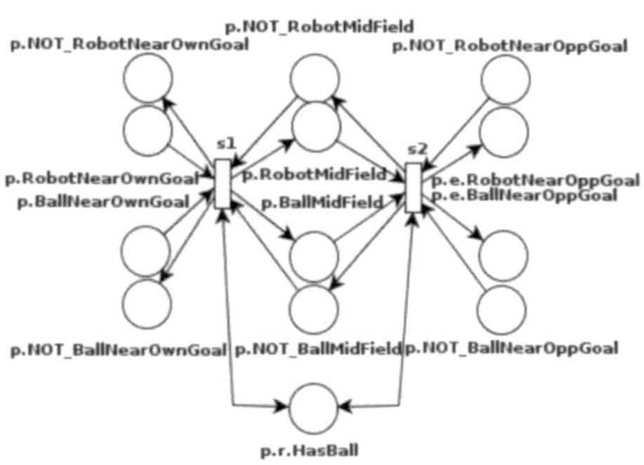

(b) Dribble2Goal model.

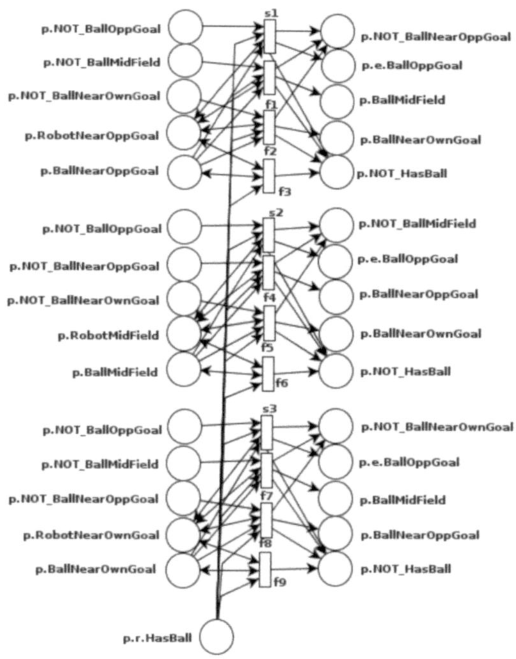

(c) Kick2Goal model.

Fig. 11. Action models

Predicate HasBall is true when the robot has posession of the ball, while CloseToBall is true when the robot is near the ball. The soccer field was divided in three regions, leading to the ball and robot position models, plus predicates BallOwnGoal and BallOppGoal, which are true when a goal is scored in our goal or in the opponent goal, respectively.

The environment models for this task are depicted in Figure 10. As can be seen from the models, we considered that the ball can be moved without being a direct result of the robot actions, or leave the proximity of the robot, as long as the robot does not hold the ball (Figure 10a and Figure 10d, respectively). The Petri net model in Figure 10b models the fact that the robot will eventually loose the ball posession. Furthermore, we considered that the robot could always see the ball, meaning predicate `SeeBall` is always true.
The actions used in this task are `StandBy`, `Move2Ball`, `CatchBall` (see Figure 8), `Dribble2Goal` and `Kick2Goal`, with the models being depicted in Figure 11. Note that we used labels s_n for success transitions, and f_n for failure transitions. The `StandBy` model is not shown because it is an empty model, i.e, since it does not perform changes in the environment, it does not contain any transition.
Table 1 gives a summary of the actions *running-conditions* and *desired-effects*. Recall that this information is available in the predicate labels of the action models, as explained in Section 3.2.

Action	Running-conditions	Desired-effects
`StandBy`	-	-
`Move2Ball`	`SeeBall`	`CloseToBall`
`CatchBall`	`SeeBall,Close2Ball`	`HasBall`
`Dribble2Goal`	`HasBall`	`RobotNearOppGoal,BallNearOppGoal`
`Kick2Goal`	`HasBall`	`BallOppGoal`

Table 1. Action properties.

The `Move2Ball` action is used by the robot to get near the ball. The model basically makes the robot position predicates change towards the ball position predicate that is true, as long as the robot sees the ball. We include additional tests to avoid the robot moving to the ball when this is inside a goal.
The `CatchBall` action purpose is to grab the ball when the robot is close to the ball. As such, it makes the predicate `HasBall` become true, as long as the robot sees the ball and is near the ball.
The `Dribble2Goal` action is used by the robot to take the ball from its current position to near the opponent goal, thus changing the robot and ball position predicates until `BallNearOppGoal` and `RobotNearOppGoal` become true, as long as the robot has the ball. Action `Kick2Goal` purpose is to score a goal, making the predicate `BallOppGoal` become true, as long as the robot has the ball. While actions `StandBy`, `Move2Ball`, `CatchBall` and `Dribble2Goal` do not explicitely include failures, the `Kick2Goal` action models does so. In action `Kick2Goal` we explicit modelled the fact that the robot can shoot torwards the goal from any place of the field, but the ball can end in any place of the field. Transitions s_i correspond to success transitions, while transitions f_i correspond to failures. By setting an higher rate to transition s_1 then s_2 and s_3, we are setting an higher probably of scoring when closer to the opponent goal. The other actions failures are modelled through the environment models. For instance, the predicate `HasBall` can become false at any time (see Figure 10b), leading to a failure of actions such as `CatchBall` and `Dribble2Goal`.
The rates used in the various models are as follows: 0.1 for the environment model rates except for the `HasBall` model, which we used 0.2; 1.0 for all action success transitions, except for transitions s_2 and s_3 in action `Kick2Goal`, where we used $1/4$ and $1/8$ respectively; for the failure transitions we used $1/4$. Note that since these are theoretical models, we consired

time to be measured in *time units*, meaning that an exponential transition with a rate of 1.0 will fire in average 1.0 times per *time unit* when enabled.

6.1 Results

We performed three transient tests of the task plan model shown in Figure 9 with TimeNET (Zimmermann, 2001), by considering different weights for transitions t_5 and t_7 (the only random switch available):

Shoot_First: by assigning weight 0 to transition t_5 and weight 1 to t_7, t_5 will never fire, meaning the robot goes from action `CatchBall` to action `Kick2Goal` without going through action `Dribble2Goal`, thus kicking to the goal as soon as it grabs the ball;

Shoot_50_50: by assigning weigh 1 to transitions t_5 and t_7, the robot chooses one of `Dribble2Goal` and `Kick2Goal` with probability 0.5, as soon as it grabs the ball while running action `CatchBall`;

Shoot_Later: by assigning weight 1 to transition t_5 and weight 0 to t_7, t_7 never fires, meaning the robot runs action `Kick2Goal` after having run action `Dribble2Goal` successfully. As such, the robot will only kick the ball when it has posession of the ball and it is near the opponent goal;

For each test we placed the robot near its goal and the ball in the field center, resulting in the following initial predicate state: `NOT_BallOwnGoal`, `NOT_BallNearOwnGoal`, `NOT_BallMidField`, `BallMidField`, `NOT_BallNearOppGoal`, `NOT_BallOppGoal`, `RobotNearOwnGoal`, `NOT_RobotMidField`, `NOT_RobotNearOppGoal`, `SeeBall`, `NOT_HasBall` and `NOT_CloseToBall`.

Since none of the actions performs changes on the environment when the ball is inside a goal, one can expect the task to include deadlocks, corresponding to scored goals. Qualitative analysis of the full task model confirmed that expectation, resulting in six deadlock states, corresponding to a goal scored from any of the three field regions into one of the two possible goals. Furthermore, we determined that the task is safe, having at most on token per place.

Each test consisted in analysing the task running from the initial marking until a deadlock occurred (goal scored), computing the number of expected tokens in places `BallOwnGoal` and `BallOppGoal` over time. This measure corresponds to the probability of having a goal scored in our goal or the opponent goal, yielding the results depicted in Figure 12.

The plots confirm that the ball must end in one of the goals, given that the sum of the probabilities of scoring in either goal when the system is already stationary is one.

As expected, kicking as soon as the robot grabs the ball leads to a lower scoring probability in the long term, since the the robot kicks from any position on the field, leading to more failures. However, analysing the initial time instants, depicted in Figure 13, shows that shooting the ball immediately leads to a higher scoring probability in the short term.

This is one example of interesting a priori results one can obtain using this framework. This knowledge can then be used in runtime, for instance, to change the weights of transitions t_5 and t_7 according to the score status and the game time left.

In qualitative terms, we determined that the task is safe, i.e., there is at most one or zero tokens in each place for all markings. Given that the action models are safe (see Definition 3.1), and the task `Score_Goal` is also safe (considering all possible predicate states), this results was expected. Furthermore, we also determined that all two places associated to a predicated formed place invariants wiht a total of 1 tokens, thus fully obeying Definition 2.5, as expected.

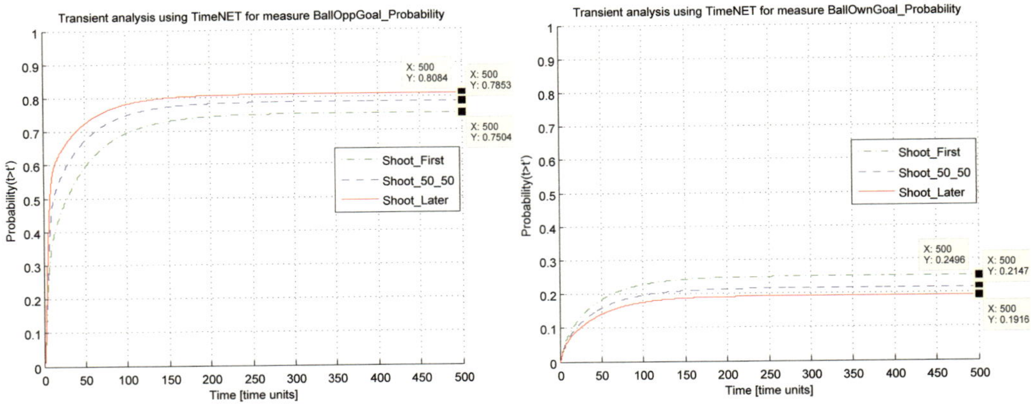

(a) Probability of scoring in the opponent goal. (b) Probability of scoring in our goal.

Fig. 12. Score goal probability evolution.

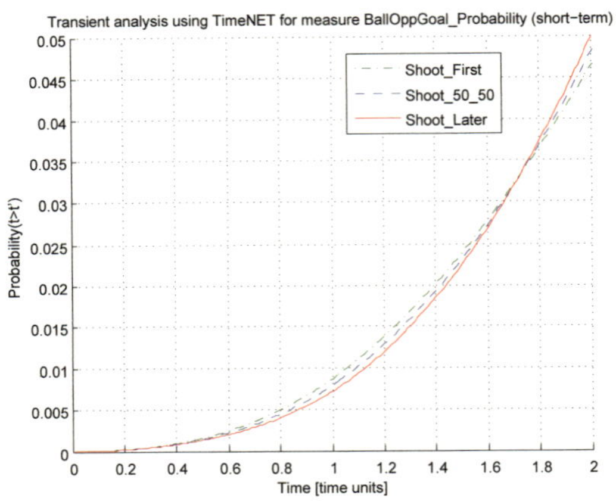

Fig. 13. Probability of scoring in the opponent goal (initial time instants).

7. Modelling Multi-Robot Tasks using Petri Nets

The main difference between individual tasks and cooperative multi-robot tasks, is that some kind of synchronism must occur between the robots during task execution. This synchronism occurs through the use of communication, either explicitly or implicitly. Explicit communication happens when a robot (the sender) sends a message directly to the other robot(s), usually using Ethernet or wireless communications. Implicit communication happens when a robot, or robots, (the receivers) perceive some situation regarding the sender robot. As such, in order to model multi-robot tasks with our Petri Net based framework, we need first to introduce communication models.

7.1 Communication Models

The major problem when using communication is the time information takes to go from the sender to the receiver, which, theoretically, can go from zero time to infinite time (communication failure). To model communication, we considered three different communication models, which cover this time range. The base concept in these models is that a robot has a predicate place at a given value and wishes to transmit that information to a teammate. The teammate, upon receiving the information, gets its predicate updated to the same value as its teammate. The simplest communication model is presented in Figure 14a. Here the communication is considered instantaneous and always successful. Increasing the model complexity by adding a probabilistic arrival time for the communication, results in the model depicted in Figure 14b. In this case, communications are still considered always successful, but the amount of time it takes varies according to an exponential distribution. The full communication model is presented in Figure 14c. Here, we not only include a varying time delay, but also the possibility that the transition never reaches its destination, thus modelling communication failures.

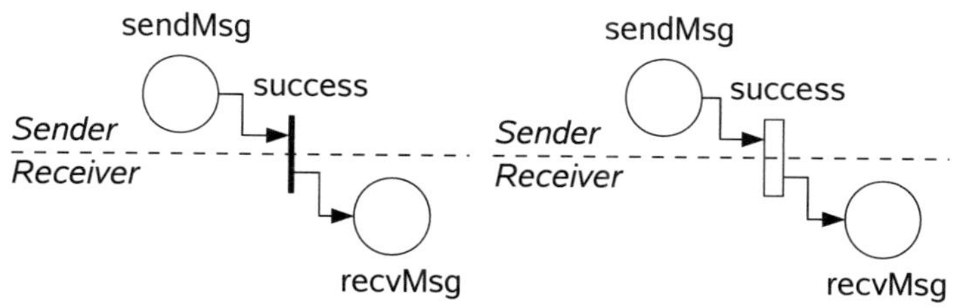

(a) Deterministic communication model without failures.

(b) Communication model with exponentially distributed time and no failures.

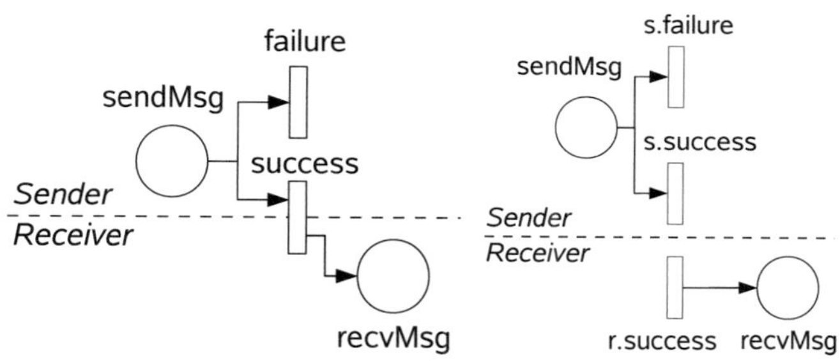

(c) Full communication model with exponentially distributed time and failures.

(d) Separate view of the full communications model.

Fig. 14. Communication models.

Given the various communication models, we can choose which one to use, according to the context where the model is being applied and the properties we wish to analyse. When using the communication models, they will be seen in a distributed way to simplify the graphical view, as depicted in Figure 14d. Note that, when seen distributed, the communication transitions include a prefix to distinguish if the transition belongs to the sender or the receiver.

7.2 Communication Actions

In order to use the communication models to model direct communication between robots during a relational task, we define *Communication Actions*, which will be used to establish the required synchronisation. These actions, besides the specifications already defined for ordinary actions, include an additional reset mechanism. This mechanism is used to model the fact that a communication event, when sent, is only received if the receiving robot, or robots, are expecting it, otherwise the event is ignored. For each sending communication model there will always be a receiving communication action model. As an example, see the Action Executor level models of actions `SendReady2Receive` and `RecvReady2Receive` in Figure 15a and Figure 15b respectively.

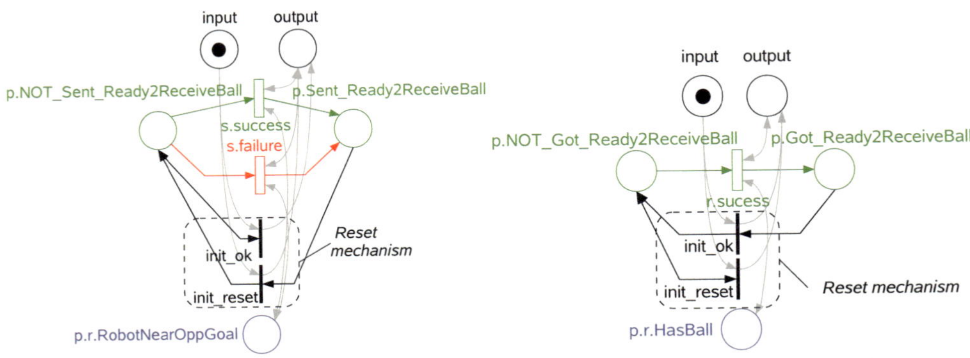

(a) Action `SendReady2Receive` model. (b) Action `RecvReady2Receive` model.

Fig. 15. Communication actions example.

Note that the *running-conditions* cannot be connected to the reset mechanism, as the token must be able to pass from place `input` to place `output` regardless of the current state.
The two depicted actions can be used to synchronise a two-robot behaviour, by running one in each robot.

7.3 Multi-Robot Task Plans

With the introduction of the communication models and communication actions, specifying a multi-robot task is similar to the specification of individual robot tasks. The major difference is that we need to use communication actions to ensure that the behaviours running during a multi-robot task execution are synchronised. For now we are assuming that the choice of running a relational task was already done, and focus on the multi-robot task execution analysis.

7.4 Analysis of Multi-Robot tasks

The analysis of multi-robot tasks in this framework is similar to the individual robot tasks case, adding the introduction of the communication models and actions. The difference relies on the fact that one needs to prefix the place labels identifying the robot they belong to, so as to distinguish between what is running in each robot, and the expansion of the communication actions need an additional step. Since each robot can run the same communication action at different times during the execution of a task plan, and the resulting Petri net used for analysis is static, simply expanding the communication actions would not work. This needed additional step corresponds to the creation of analysis versions of the communication actions, which is implemented through the following items:

1. Move the transition associated with the communication from the receiving action model to the sending action model. The receiving transition is merged back with the successful sending transition, i.e, we obtain a single transition, located in the sending action, by connecting the arcs previously connected to the receiving transition to the successful sending transition;

2. Add the counter `RUNNING_commAction` to the receiving communication action with a token. Counter places have the prefix "c";
3. Make the added counter a *running-condition* of the sending communication action, connected only with the successful transition associated with the communication event.

The introduced counter will indicate the number of instances of receiving actions running in each robot and, most important, it will allow to track if a robot receiving action is running or not. This counter will be treated like a predicate at the expansion phase, i.e., every counter with the same label will be considered the same place.
With these analysis versions, the communicaton actions can be used anywhere in a robot task model, allowing for any receiving action to pair with the associated sending action, independently of where the communication actions appear in the task models. As an example, consider again the communication actions `SendReady2Receive` and `RecvReady2Receive` in a two robot setup, with their analysis versions depicted in Figure 16a and Figure 16b.
Naturally, it should be expected to have always at most one token in the counter, otherwise multiple actions were sending the same message simultaneously. This property can be computed during the analysis phase.

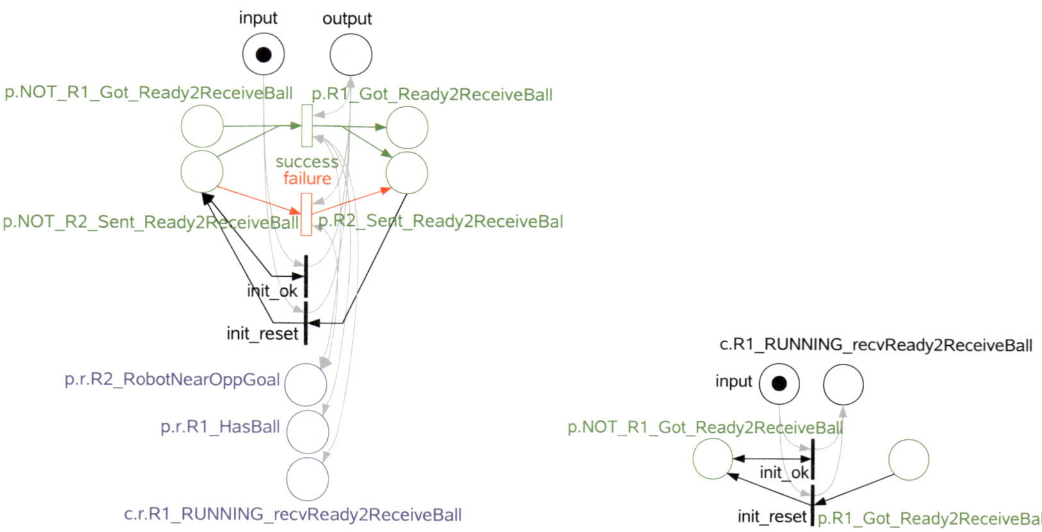

(a) Action `SendReady2Receive` model for analysis.

(b) Action `RecvReady2Receive` model for analysis.

Fig. 16. Communication actions example.

Although the action places are always considered different places, regardless of their label, these are also prefixed with the robot label, since different robots can have different action models. During the expansion of the macro places for analysis, all the communication action macro places are expanded into their analysis version instead of their original version. If we have more than two robots, then a selection mechanism must be used to select to which robot, or robots, the message is to be sent. The user never needs to see the analysis versions of the actions, since these are used only internally for analysis, and are automatically created from their original versions.

7.5 Multi-Robot Task Example

To illustrate the application of the framework to the multi-robot case, we will consider a pass example between two robots, the kicker and the receiver.

Given two tasks, `coordinatedKick`, for the kicker, and `coordinatedReceive`, for the receiver, a two-robot PASS task plan corresponds to a single `coordinatedPass` relational task, which consists of running both individual tasks in parallel, one in each robot. The key here is to make sure that both individual tasks run synchronously, either by implicit or explicit communication.

We assume that some higher level took the decision that the robots should commit with the coordinated pass, and will focus on the task execution analysis, keeping the critical sections synchronised.

For this example, we used the same list of predicates used in the single-robot example (see Section 6), plus predicates `Got_Ready2ReceiveBall` and `Sent_Ready2ReceiveBall`, associated to the communication actions. In terms of environment models we will use a ball position model (Figure 10a) and, per robot, one position model (Figure 10c), a lost ball model (Figure 10b) and a ball proximity model (Figure 10d).

For the PASS relational task plan we used actions `StandBy`, `Move2Ball` (Figure 11a) and `CatchBall` (Figure 8), used previously in the single robot example, plus the following actions:

`Go2KickerPosture`: The robot which has the ball, the kicker, moves to the kicker posture to be ready to pass the ball (Figure 17b), which is always considered to be near its own goal;

`SendReady2Receive`: The receiver acknowledges that it is ready to receive the ball (Figure 15a);

`RecvReady2Receive`: Waits for a communication from the receiver to know it is ready to receive the ball (Figure 15b);

`PassBall`: Passes the ball to another robot. In this case we considered that passes are only done from near its own goal or the midfield to near the opponent goal (Figure 17c);

`Go2ReceiverPosture`: The robot moves to a destination posture, which is good for receiving the ball. We considered the receiving posture to be always near the opponent goal (Figure 17a).

All transitions were removed from the action `Move2Ball` model except transition s_7, so as to allow the robot to be able to capture the ball only when near the opponent goal.

Task `CoordinatedKick` is obtained by running actions `Go2KickerPosture` and `RecvReady2Receive` in parallel, followed by action `PassBall` upon getting predicates `Ready2Pass` and `GotReady2Receive` to true. Task `CoordinatedReceive` is formed by a sequence of actions, starting with `Go2ReceiverPosture`, followed by `SendReady2Receive` when predicate `RobotNearOppGoal` gets true, ending with action `CatchBall` when `SentReady2Receive` gets true. Regarding communication, the relevant actions for the `coordinatedPass` relational task are `RecvReady2Receive` and `SendReady2Receive`, the two communication actions detailed previously. The Petri net models of both tasks are depicted in Figure 18a and Figure 18b.

Given that our focus here is on the analysis of the execution of a multi-robot task, without using yet selection or commitment mechanisms, we consider a scenario where both robots are already set up for the execution of the pass. As such, the pass between the two robots can be obtained through the PASS task plan depicted in Figure 19.

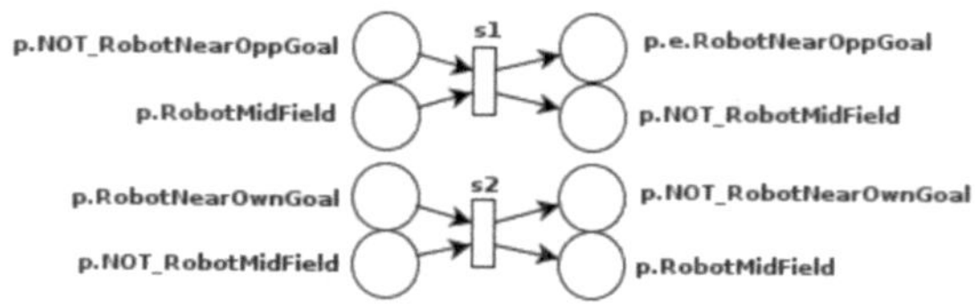

(a) Action `Go2ReceiverPosture` model.

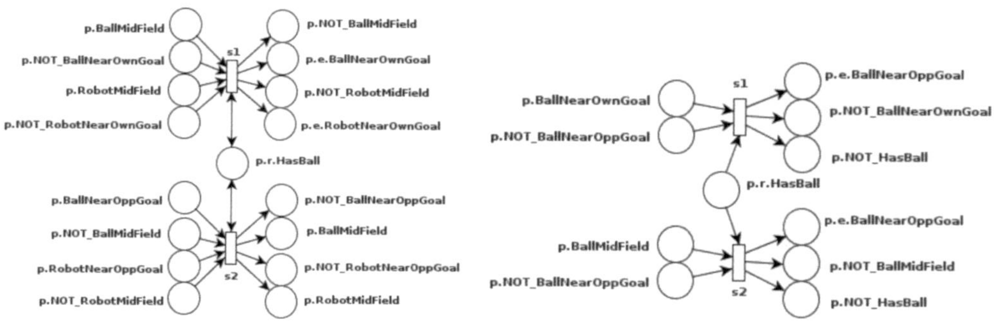

(b) Action `Go2KickerPosture` model. (c) Action `PassBall` model.

Fig. 17. Action models used in the multi-robot example.

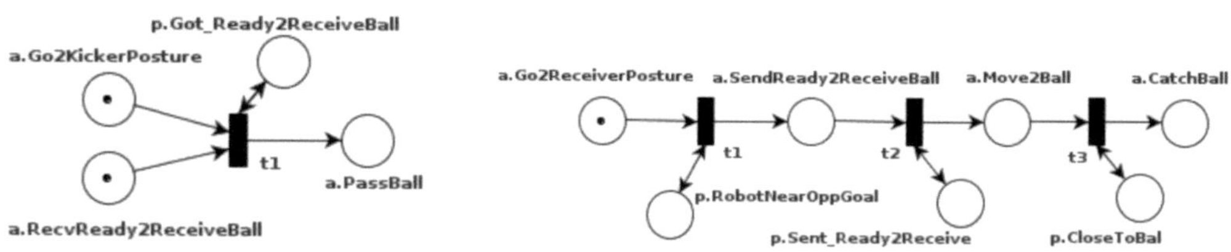

(a) Task `CoordinatedKick` model. (b) Task `CoordinatedReceive` model

Fig. 18. Task models used in the multi-robot example.

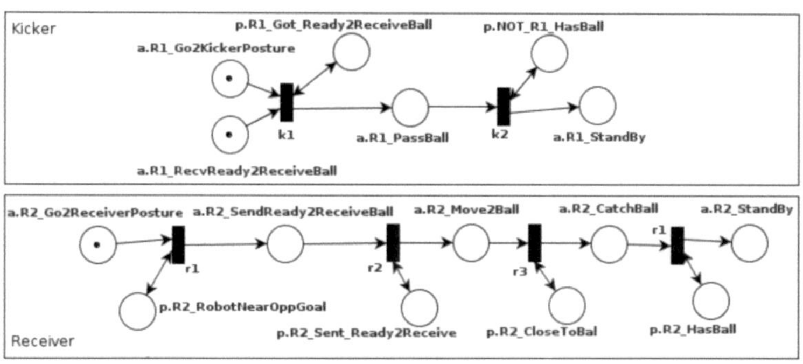

Fig. 19. PASS task plan.

7.6 Results

The setup used for the results consisted on placing both robots in the mid-field area, with robot R1 holding the ball, resulting in the following initial predicate state: `NOT_BallOwnGoal`, `NOT_BallNearOwnGoal`, `BallMidField`, `NOT_BallNearOppGoal`, `NOT_BallOppGoal`, `NOT_R1_RobotNearOwnGoal`, `R1_RobotMidField`, `NOT_R1_RobotNearOppGoal`, `R1_SeeBall`, `R1_HasBall`, `R1_CloseToBall`, `NOT_R1_Got_Ready2ReceiveBall`, `NOT_R2_RobotNearOwnGoal`, `R2_RobotMidField`, `NOT_R2_RobotNearOppGoal`, `R2_SeeBall`, `NOT_R2_HasBall`, `NOT_R2_CloseToBall`, and `NOT_R2_Sent_Ready2ReceiveBall`.

We analysed the PASS task plan success probability by monitoring the number of tokens in place `action.R2_StandBy`. Since robot R2 only reaches action `StandBy` if it was able to successfully receive the ball, reaching this action means the PASS task plan was successful.

The first results were conducted considering a deterministic environment (by removing the stochastic transitions from the environment models). Given that no failures were explicitely included in the action models, the only failure in this case is the communication failure. As such, the plan success probability should depend only on the relation between the communication failure and success rates, yielding:

$$P_{Plan\ success} = \frac{\lambda_{comm\ success}}{\lambda_{comm\ success} + \lambda_{comm\ failure}}$$

Exp. #	Action success rates	Comm. success rates	Comm. failure rates	Plan success probability
1	1	1	1	0.50
2	1	1	10	0.09
3	1	10	1	0.91
4	1	10	10	0.50
5	10	10	10	0.50

Table 2. Plan success probability vs transition rates with deterministic environment.

Table 2 shows the results obtained with different transitions rates for this setup, confirming the above statement. The graph showing the expected number of tokens in place `action.R2_StandBy` over time is shown in Figure 20 for experiments 1, 4 and 5. This graph shows that, although the stationary plan success probability only depends on the communication rates, increasing the success transition rates leads to a performance improvement in the short term.

Next we introduced additional failures by including the full models for `HasBall` and `CloseToBall` environment models for each robot, as shown in Figure 10b and Figure 10d. The ball position model was kept deterministic, without stochastic timed transitions. We tested this setup with different transition rates, obtaining the results show in Table 3.

In this case, increasing the communication success also increases the plan success probability as expected, but only to a certain point, as experiments 5 and 6 show. Only by increasing the remaining action transitions success rate can we further increase the plan success probability. In experiment 7, the success rates are much higher than the failure rates, leading to an almost 100% success probability.

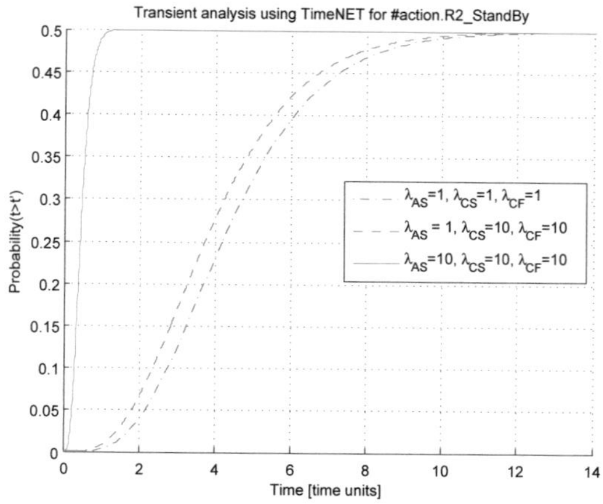

Fig. 20. PASS task plan success probability over time for different transition rates.

Exp. #	Env. rates HasBall	Env. rates CloseToBall	Action success rates	Comm. success rates	Comm. failure rates	Plan success probability
1	0.2	0.1	1	1	1	0.32
2	0.2	0.1	1	1	10	0.06
3	0.2	0.1	1	10	1	0.62
4	0.2	0.1	1	10	10	0.34
5	0.2	0.1	1	100	0.1	0.69
6	0.2	0.1	1	10000	0.0001	0.69
7	0.2	0.1	10	10000	0.0001	0.96

Table 3. Plan success probability vs transition rates with probabilistic environment.

Qualitatively we could determine, like in the single-robot example, that the task is safe, and that the predicate places form place invariants. Furthermore, as expected, both setups end always in deadlock, given that the tasks are sequential.

8. Conclusions and Future Directions

Petri nets provide a practical and intuitive way of modelling robotic tasks and associated components, being also appropriate to monitor the execution of tasks given their graphical nature. The fact that a GSPN is equivalent to a Markov chain brings an additional advantage by allowing the use of currently available tools and techniques to extract important a priori information about a given task.

Being able to model the actions more thoroughly at a lower level allows for mores realistic models, without compromising the analysis possibilities. Furthermore we can create all the models separately and build the task plan by creating a network of actions. This task plan can be ran directly on the robots for execution purposes and, for analysis purposes, we compose all the models that were designed separately onto one single Petri net, and analyse that net.

The introduction of communication models allowed the extension of the framework to multi-robot tasks, enabling a priori extraction of qualitative and quantitative properties of multi-robot tasks. Different communication models enable the study of the impact of a range of communication problems on the task success. We are currently improving the communication

action models to allow modelling broadcast type messages, which will allow for easier multi-robot tasks (with any number of robots) modelling.
Tests were performed using simulated robotic soccer scenarios which showed the applicability of the framework for both single-robot and multi-robot tasks. Qualitative properties, such as deadlock and safeness, and quantitative properties, such success probability over time, of the task were obtained from the full Petri net model.
In order to fully enable the use of the framework for multi-robot tasks, one still needs to implement selection and commitment mechanism. These mechanisms already exist in the literature (Cohen & Levesque, 1991; Palamara et al., 2009; van der Vecht & Lima, 2005) and we are working on incorporating them in our models. When analysing the complete models we will also be able to extract properties concerning the selection and commitment maintenance.
We are currently implementing an identification algorithm which will allow building the action and environment models from real world data, leading to more realistic models. Furthermore, we plan to introduce observation models, allowing the use of the framework under scenarios without full observability.

Acknowledgements

This work was supported by the Portuguese Fundação para a Ciência e Tecnologia under under grant SFRH/BD/ 12707/2003 and ISR/IST pluriannual funding through the PIDDAC Program funds.

9. References

Akharware, N. (2005). *PIPE2: Platform Independent Petri Net Editor*, Master's thesis, Imperial College of Science, Technology and Medicine, University of London.

Barbosa, M., Ramos, N. & Lima, P. (2007). Mermaid - multiple-robot middleware for intelligent decision-making, *IAV2007 - 6th IFAC Symposium on Intelligent Autonomous Vehicles*.

Bernardinello, L. & Cindio, F. D. (1992). A survey of basic net models and modular net classes, *Advances in Petri Nets 1992, The DEMON Project*, Springer, pp. 304–351.

Cohen, P. R. & Levesque, H. J. (1991). Teamwork, *Noûs* **25**(4): 487–512.

Damas, B. D. & Lima, P. U. (2004). Stochastic Discrete Event Model of a Multi-Robot Team Playing an Adversarial Game, *Proceedings of the 5th IFAC/EURON Symposium on Intelligent Autonomous Vehicles*.

Dominguez-Brito, A. C., Andersson, M. & Christensen, H. I. (2000). A Software Architecture for Programming Robotic Systems based on the Discrete Event System Paradigm, *Technical Report CVAP244, ISRN KTH/NA/P–00/13–SE*, Centre for Autonomous Systems, KTH (Royal Institute of Technology).

Espiau, B., Kapellos, K., Jourdan, M. & Simon, D. (1995). On the Validation of Robotics Control Systems Part I: High Level Specification and Formal Verification, *Technical Report 2719*, INRIA.

Kosecka, J., Christensen, H. I. & Bajcsy, R. (1997). Experiments in Behaviour Composition, *Robotics and Autonomous Systems* **19**: 287–298.

Montano, L., García, F. J. & Villaroel, J. L. (2000). Using the Time Petri Net Formalism for Specification, Validation, and Code Generation in Robot-Control Applications, *The International Journal of Robotics Research* **19**(1): 59–76.

Murata, T. (1989). Petri nets: Properties, analysis and applications, *Proceedings of the IEEE* **77**(4): 541–580.

Palamara, P. F., Ziparo, V. A., Iocchi, L., Nardi, D. & Lima, P. (2009). Teamwork design based on petri net plans, pp. 200–211.

Petri, C. A. (1966). Kommunikation mit automaten, *Technical report*. English translation.

Röck, A. & Kresman, R. (2006). On Petri nets and predicate-transition nets, *Proceedings of the International Conference on Software Engineering Research and Practice & Conference on Programming Languages and Compilers, SERP 2006*, pp. 903–909.

van der Vecht, B. & Lima, P. U. (2005). Formulation and Implementation of Relational Behaviours for Multi-robot Cooperative Systems, *Proceedings of RoboCup-2004: Robot Soccer World Cup VIII*, Springer-Verlag, pp. 516–523.

Viswanadham, N. & Narahari, Y. (1992). *Performance Modeling of Automated Manufacturing Systems*, Prentice Hall.

Zimmermann, A. (2001). TIMENET - a software tool for the performability evaluation with stochastic petri nets.

Ziparo, V. A. & Iocchi, L. (2006). Petri net plans, *Proceedings of the Fourth International Workshop on Modelling of Objects, Components, and Agents (MOCA'06)*, pp. 267–290.

Effective Planning for Conflicting Situations for Ubiquitous Sensor Network Environments

Toshiharu Sugawara[1] Satoshi Kurihara[2] Toshio Hirotsu[3]
Kensuke Fukuda[4] and Toshihiro Takada[5]
[1]*Waseda University,*
[2]*Osaka University,*
[3]*Hosei University,*
[4]*National Institute of Informatics,*
[5]*NTT Communication Science Laboratories,*
Japan

1. Introduction

Applications of sensor networks and ubiquitous computing have received attention. They can provide many kinds of important services for supporting daily and social activities in home, schools, offices and public spaces in the future (Kurihara, 2008). However, to realize these kinds of applications, a number of new technologies in AI and multi-agent systems (MAS) are also required because many devices and control programs are concurrently work to achieve their goals in cooperation with other ones. These works arise according to the human requirements based on their individual activities. In order to achieve these required goals, each agent has to create the plan (means-end analysis) and then performs it. However, the plan often conflict with those that are being created, already being scheduled, and executed by other agents because of the limited resources. Furthermore, since the human's activities are usually real-time with deadline, the agent must also be able to complete its planning and resolution of these conflicts within a reasonable time to have an acceptable quality plan. This means that both efficient planning and sophisticated conflict resolution are strongly required.

We adopt hierarchical planning (for example, see (Erol & Nau, 1994; Sacerdoti, 1974) using the decision-theoretic planning approach (Goldwin, & Simmons, 1998) for efficient planning but it is not trivial to apply hierarchical planning to MAS. In hierarchical planning, appropriate (abstract) plans are selected level by level to maximize the utility $U(p)$, where p is the expected final plan comprising a sequence of primitive actions. However, in the MAS context, conflicts between agents affect the efficiency and quality of resulting plans. When a conflict is found at lower levels, an additional sophisticated process for avoiding it (*conflict resolution*) must be invoked and some extra actions (such as waiting for synchronization and detouring) may have to be added to the plan. The conflict resolution process may become costly or fail. Even a single conflict, if it is difficult to resolve, will result in a plan with

considerably lower quality. As a result, in multi-agent systems, the second- or third-best plans may result in better overall performance.
The objective of our research is to enable agents, using reinforcement learning, to predict which tasks in an abstract plan will conflict with other agents' plans at a lower level with higher probability and either involve a costly conflict resolution process and/or result in a low-quality plan after it has been resolved. We emphasize that the appearances of conflicts strongly depend on the resource structures of the environments of the sensor-network applications. This suggests that the learning is mandatory.
Our basic idea is threefold, *conflict patterns, screening level* and *conflict discount*. First, we will introduce *conflict patterns* (*CP*) at a certain abstract level called the *screening level* (*SL*). The screening level is a one of intermediary level of the hierarchical model at which the conflicts of generating plans are predicted. The possible conflicts are stored as conflict patterns to specify the situations where conflicts will occur with high probabilities if the agents refine the current plan to the lower levels. The *conflict discount* is a negative utility that cumulatively predicts the probability of conflicts in the subsequent refinement process, the cost of resolutions, and the quality/performance of the resulting plans on the basis of CPs in the plans at the screening level and past experience. The conflict discount is calculated and updated by using statistically learned expected values or by reinforcement learning, so that the agents select the appropriate refinement at the SL.
Note that we assume that the initial utility is good for selecting plans for single-agent cases. This utility may lead to acceptable but minimum quality plans after conflict resolution in the MAS context. Thus, agents learn the conflict discount appropriate for the environment in order to select better SL plans.
In this chapter, we formally define conflict patterns and discuss the estimation of their conflict discounts. We then introduce the notion of sub-conflict patterns for avoiding redundant calculations of conflict discounts and reducing memory space. We also clarify the distributed version of the planning framework with our conflict estimation, which is an extension of that in (Sugawara et al., 2005). Then we present an experimental evaluation of the efficiency of plans generated by our method for a simulated laboratory room. This chapter is organized as follows: First, we discuss the issue addressed here and the planning framework used in our application systems. We then explain the process of conflict detection and resolution. Following that, we introduce the use of conflict patterns to classify situations involving conflicts with other agents' plans. Then, the experimental results to evaluate our approach are presented. We show that our proposed planning strategy makes agent's planning more efficient in the situation where conflicts are predicted. Finally, we cover related work and offer some concluding remarks.

2. Conflict estimation in hierarchical planning

In hierarchical planning, plans are generated using an abstract hierarchy of the domain model, which includes tasks and resources in an abstract form. Initial states and goals are first described in the most abstract model, and a number of task sequences are generated to achieve these goals. One of the sequences is then selected according to a particular planning strategy (A utility is used in the case of the decision-theoretic planning.[1]), and each task in the sequence is further refined into task sequences in the less-abstract model. This refine-and-select process is iterated until all tasks have been refined to primitive tasks in the lowest model. In general, while abstract (higher-level) models are simple and thus do not contain complete information, they are appropriate for understanding the global and long-term picture of activities. Naturally, the lower-layer models are more informative and complicated, so they are used for detailed descriptions of local and sectional plans.

Let's consider our laboratory room shown in Figure 1 that will be the example environment of the experiments in this paper. In this figure, there are a number of hierarchical models of the room; the model at level 0 is the most abstract and the one at level 3 is the most concrete (so primitive). The plan at a certain level is generated based on the corresponding model. Initial states and goals are first described in the most abstract (or uppermost) model, and a number of task sequences are generated to achieve these goals in this model. (An example of the task hierarchy established in accordance with the model hierarchy is shown in Figure 2.) This plan generation is usually based on the descriptive information represented in the corresponding model. One of the sequences is selected according to a particular planning strategy (the utility is used in the case of DTP), and then each task in the sequence is further refined, that is, the sub-task sequences in the less-abstract model for achieving the task are generated. These sequences are called refinements of the task.

Actual conflicts are identified when all tasks have been expanded into primitive tasks, since the required amount of resources and time needed for executing the plan are precisely determined at this level. This may not prevent an agent from investigating the possibility of conflicts at an abstract level, however. For example, if a certain room is roughly modelled as a single object at an abstract level such as the level-0 model in Figure 1 and two agents have plans to work in this room at the same time, they can resolve this possible conflict by one agent deciding to work at another time. However, this conflict may not occur after the plans have been expanded into primitive ones, because it might turn out that the agents are able to work at different places in the room. In general, the process of conflict detection and resolution in abstract layers is simple because its domain model and related operators are simple. However, it usually results in redundant and inefficient plans.

Normal utilities for making efficient or high-quality plans do not usually take into account possible conflicts with other agents. As a result, although they can create acceptable plans when there is no interference between plans, they might not be able to do so when there is interference. Furthermore, in applications where real-time performance is stipulated, it is preferable that agents predict which conflicts will vanish or be easy or difficult to resolve during the remainder of the planning period. It is important, therefore, to provide another utility for plan selection when there is the possibility of conflict. However, determining what the conflicts are and which tasks easily cause them is a function of the location of scarce or heavily used resources and the type of agent; thus, the outcome strongly depends on the situation and environment where the sensor-network system is deployed. This type

---

[1] An agent selects the plan that may lead to the highest utility. However, the utility value is determined from the primitive task/plan, so the utility of a non-primitive task/plan is expressed as a range calculated according to the possible lower-level refined plans. It has been reported that agents should choose the plan that contains the highest utility and expand it to the next layer for effective planning (Goldwin & Simmons, 1998).

of information cannot be provided *a priori* during the design time. Therefore, agents have to learn an additional utility for MAS contexts.

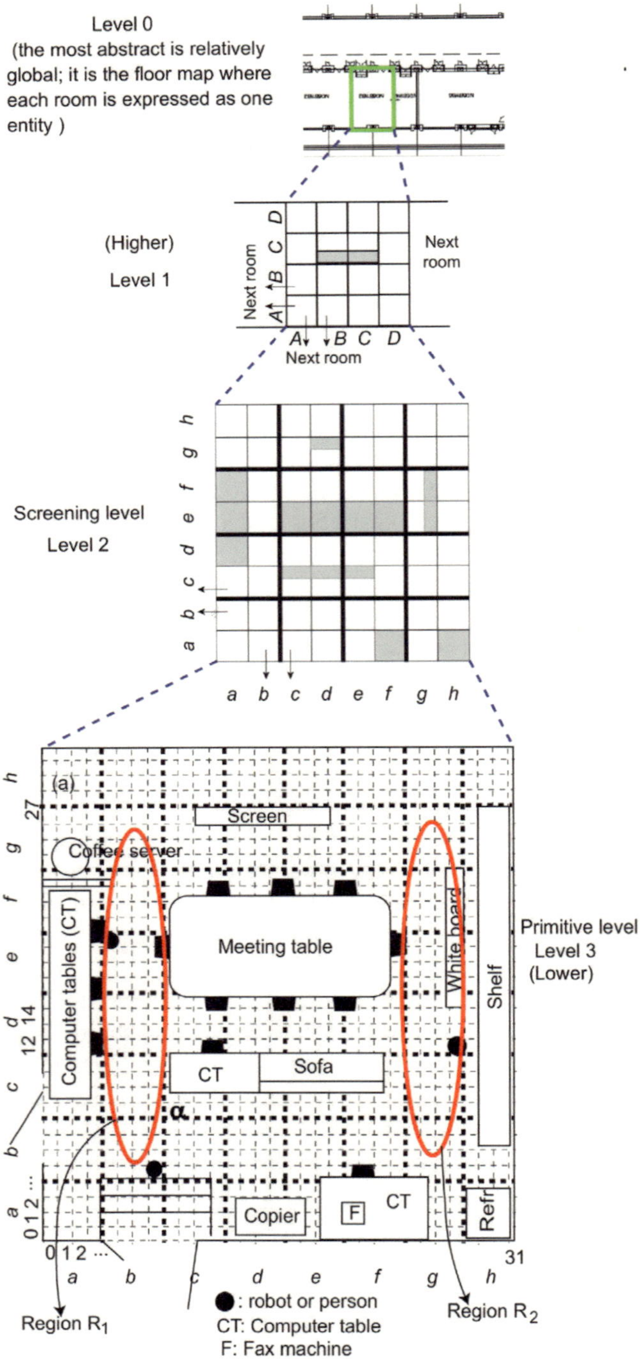

Fig. 1. Example of a hierarchical description.

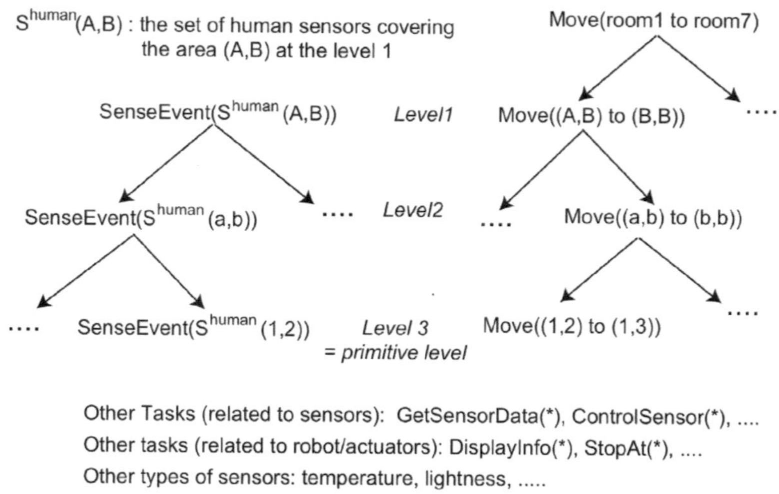

Fig. 2. Hierarchical task structure based on the hierarchical model.

3. Planning at the screening level

3.1 Planning architecture

In our planning architecture, agents first exchange only the presently being generated, scheduled and executed plans described in a certain abstract-level model, called the *screening level* (*SL*). We assume that the plans at this level are simpler than ones at the primitive level but are enough to classify the conflicting situations. The SL plans presently scheduled or being executed are called *SL-valid* plans, and the SL plans that are currently being generated (so are pending) are called *SL-pending* plans.

When agent a_i starts to create its plan for this environment, it first generates a number of SL plans (from the abstract-level plan) and tentatively selects one of them (using conventional utility). It then requests SL-valid and SL-pending plans from other agents to investigate the possible conflicts between a_i's new plan and other plans, by using an estimation based on the utility with the learned conflict discount as described in Section 4. According to this result, a_i selects one of the SL plans to refine further. This plan is marked as `SL-pending'. If $a_i$ is requested to send its plans during this process, it immediately notifies the request for that it is `SL planning' and sends the SL-pending plan right after it is determined. Agent a_i then waits for a short while for other unreceived plans; if it receives no other SL plans that have high conflict discounts, it proceeds to the next stage described below. Otherwise, one of the agents selects another SL plan instead of the current SL-pending plan; this may slow down the system in an extremely busy environment, so a tailored method for this issue will need to be developed in the future.

For further conflicts analysis, agent a_i requests primitive plans only from the agents whose plans are predicted to conflict with a_i 's SL plan. Then a_i modifies the primitive plan to eliminate the detected conflicts. If conflict discount is sufficiently learned, the cost of conflict resolution is relatively low and the resulting plan is acceptable. When a_i completes a primitive plan without conflicts, the plan is scheduled or executed immediately; and its SL-plan is marked `SL-valid'. Section 4 discusses how a_i learns to predict conflicts at the SL and how the utilities with a conflict discount are estimated.

We focus on applications where the same or similar plans are frequently reproduced. Examples of target applications are planning for the intelligent behaviours in sensor-network and ubiquitous-computing systems with many devices, such as sensors, effectors and robots (Figure 1), where agents reside in these devices to control them (Takada et al., 2003). Examples of application scenarios are described in (Kurihara et al., 2005). In this sort of application, e.g., robots moving in a room and assisting in people's daily activities, certain actions are repeated. We assume that other plans that are already scheduled or being executed are not modified (at least, the plans that have already been approved should be preferred) in the current implementation. Often this restricts the quality of the resulting plan. Our aim, however, is to select the most appropriate SL plan in a timely manner. If all of the plans generated at the SL appear to have high-discount conflicts, the agent can backtrack and select another plan at the SL or at a higher level; the agent still creates an abstract plan, which is simpler than creating a useless primitive plan, so we believe that the cost is not so high.

3.2 Conflict detection at screening level

The agent detects possible conflicts, according to resource and task information at the SL, by identifying the possibility of whether multiple plans will use the same resources, such as locations (e.g., squares in Figure 1). An example is illustrated in Figure 3, for which the SL is level 2 in Figure 1; a square at this SL (specified by a pair of lower-case letters) corresponds to 4x4 squares in the primitive model (A square in the primitive level is specified by a pair of positive integers.). In Figure 3, the agent can suggest that task t_l = *move*(**cd** $\rightarrow$ **dd**) in the new plan may conflict with task t'_n = *move*(**cd** $\rightarrow$ **bd**) in the SL-valid plan, where *move*(**cd** $\rightarrow$ **dd**) is the SL plan expressing the agent's movement from somewhere in area ***(c, d)*** to area ***(d, d)***. This conflict can be expected if some squares in area ***(c, d)*** can be simultaneously occupied by two agents during a certain time interval.

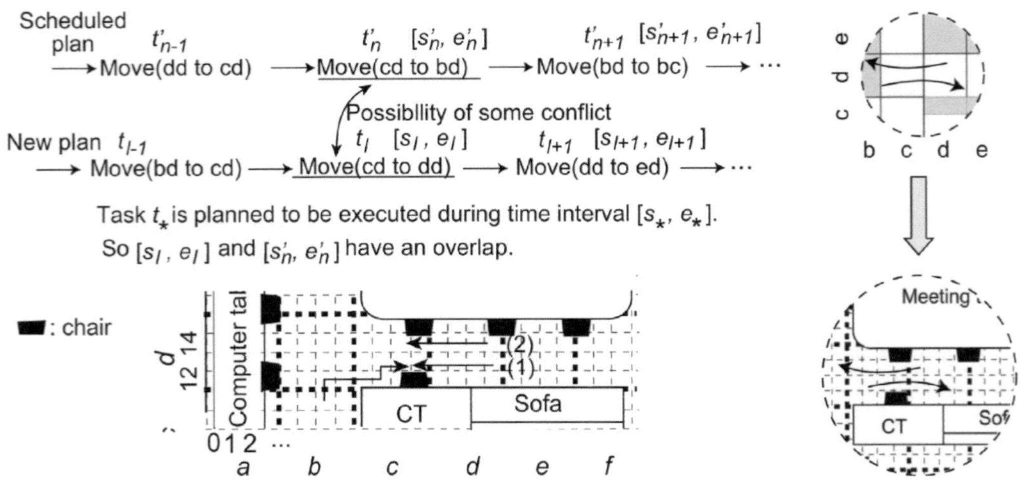

Fig. 3. Example of a detected conflict.

An agent has to take into account time relationships between tasks in the plans. The duration of each task in the SL-valid plans has already been determined, but not that of the new plan. Thus, it uses the expected average duration of each SL task. This value is initially given as part of the SL model; for example, *move*(***cd*** $\rightarrow$ ***bd***) takes four ticks if agents (that is, robots) can move to the next small square in a tick. The expected duration is then statistically adjusted according to the generated primitive plans induced from this SL task. The questions of when and where conflicts likely occur and whether their resolutions are difficult depend upon the system's environment. Suppose that three agents want to pass through area ***(b, d)***. In the SL model, this area (place is a resource) is expressed as a single entity, so conflicts can be expected. However, this area has enough room for three agents if each agent occupies a small square at the primitive level; hence, the conflicts might not actually occur or might be easily resolved. However, in ***(c, d)*** where agents move only left or right, there is not enough room for three agents. Thus, it seems probable that the agents' plans will have conflicts there. Of course, this probability is influenced by the temporal relationships of the agents entering area ***(c, d)***. If a conflict is detected, one of the agents must step out of the other agent's way and wait for it to pass by before resuming its movement.

Method	Description
Synchronization	Stop until another agent performing a task that requires a needed resource finishes the task and releases the resource. Wait for a primitive task or use of some resource by another agent until the task finishes or the agent releases the resource. This method may insert a number for "wait for a tick" for synchronization.
Waiting	Stop until other agents finish tasks that create pre-conditions of the local task. This method may insert a number for "wait for a tick" for synchronization.
Replacement	Replace tasks whose post-conditions do not affect tasks in other agents or whose pre-conditions are not affected by tasks in other agents. This method may replace the conflicting task with others, but these other tasks usually have lower utility (or incur extra cost).
Reordering	Reorder tasks to avoid negative relationships.
Insertion	Insert tasks whose post-conditions recover the pre-conditions of the task. This method adds some tasks, so the utility of the resulting plan decreases.
Commission	Entrust the task to other agents. This form of resolution is preferable when, for example, a conflict can only be resolved by other agents, or if another agent can do the task at lower cost. This method can eliminate some tasks, though some communications, not only for detecting the sharable tasks of the plans but also for committing them to another agent, take place.

Table 1. Examples of methods of resolution.

3.3 Conflict detection and resolution

A number of resolution methods, shown in Table 1, are applied to resolve conflicts. Thus, the agents involved must negotiate which agent (or all agents involved) should commit to modifying their plans and then decide what methods should be applied. These resolution methods are defined as rules and applied under a certain policy. The resulting plans usually have extra cost for the resolutions. In this paper, we do not care what kind of policy is used; our only concern is the cost of resolution and the quality of the resulting plan.

4. Conflict estimation from conflict patterns

4.1 Conflict pattern --- an expression of conflicting situations

A *conflict pattern* (*CP*) expresses a conflict between SL plans. First, we focus on an SL task identified as having a conflict. Let t be an SL task in a new SL plan p, denoted by $t \in p$. Suppose that SL plans $p_1, \ldots, p_k$ of other agents are SL-valid. Then CP, denoted here by $\mathcal{P}(t)$, is expressed as

$$\mathcal{P}(t) = (t, (t'_1, o_1), \ldots, (t'_h, o_h))$$

where $t'_i \in p_j$ $(1 \leq \exists j \leq h)$ and o_i is optional data. CP describes the situation where t is expected to conflict with $t'_1, \ldots, t'_h$ in SL-valid plans.
The optional data o_i can be any information that can be used to distinguish conflicting situations more accurately. For instance, it may be information about (relative) the time of execution and agents' names or types that suggest their ability/performance or physical size (when agents, such as robots and vehicles, have physical bodies). In the example of Figure 3, CP is expressed as

$$\mathcal{P}_1(t_l) = (t_l, (t'_n, \ (\max(s'_n - s_l, 0), \min(e_l - s_l, e'_n - s_l)))),$$

where the optional data is the relative time interval during which the expected conflict may occur. To simplify the expression of this example, we describe the optional data in a more abstract form. For this purpose, we can use the expressions of time relativity; the duration of t'_n overlaps the anterior half (*ah*) or posterior half (*ph*) of the duration of t_l. Other cases of time relativity are expressed as "overlap (*ol*)." Thus, $\mathcal{P}_1(t_l) = (t_l, (t'_n, r'_l))$, where $r'_l = ah, ph$ or ol.
The situation in Figure 4 shows that t_l may conflict with t'_{n+1} and t''_{m-1}. The following CP corresponds to this situation:

$$\mathcal{P}_2(t_l) = (t_l, (t'_{n+1}, r'_l), (t''_{m-1}, r''_l))$$

where $r'_l, r''_l = ah, ph$ or ol.

4.2 Concept of conflict discount

Let $U(p)$ (or $U(t)$) be the initial utility for a primitive plan p (or a primitive task t). $U(p)$ for a non-primitive plan (or task) is the range that cumulatively indicates possible lower-primitive plans/tasks. We introduce the *conflict discount* for a CP, $cd(\mathcal{P})$. The conflict discount is conceptually defined as

$$cd(\mathcal{P}) = U(pp) - U(pp_m) + CCR(\mathcal{P}) \quad (1)$$

where pp is the primitive plan of SL plan p before conflict resolution, and pp_m is the modified primitive plan for resolving conflict $\mathcal{P}$. The term CCR indicates the cost of conflict detection and resolution at the primitive level, which is calculated by combining the costs of requesting, receiving, and analyzing primitive plans from other agents and applying conflict resolution rules to modify the new plan. So even if no conflict actually occurs at the primitive level ($U(pp)=U(pp_m)$), $cd(\mathcal{P}) \neq 0$. This is because, if a conflict is expected at SL, the cost of conflict detection will be incurred. Define $cd'(\mathcal{P}) = U(pp) - U(pp_m)$ as the difference in utilities. The estimation of $cd(\mathcal{P})$ is described in the next section.
When an agent has a new SL plan p that is expected to have CPs, $\mathcal{P}_1, \ldots, \mathcal{P}_N$,

$$cd(p) = \sum_{i=1}^{N} cd(\mathcal{P}_i).$$

The agent uses the modified utility $U(p) - cd(p)$ instead of $U(p)$. When no conflicts are predicted, the agent uses $U(p)$ since $cd(p) = 0$. Our method statistically adjusts the conflict discounts for frequently appearing CPs. Because we focus on the efficiency of plans, we assume that $U(p)$ is the estimated execution time of the primitive plan in the example below.

4.3 Estimation of conflict discount

The conflict discount for a CP, $cd(\mathcal{P})$, is iteratively adjusted by the average or update function as follows when CP is observed s times.

$$cd_s(\mathcal{P}) = \sum_{i=1}^{s} \frac{d_i}{s} \tag{2}$$

$$cd_s(\mathcal{P}) = \lambda * cd_{s-1}(\mathcal{P}) + (1 - \lambda) * d_s \tag{3}$$

where $0< \lambda < 1$ and d_s indicates the s-th CCR_s plus the s-th observed utility difference between the original primitive plan and the plan after the resolution of the conflict corresponding to $\mathcal{P}$. Eq. (3) is more sensitive to environmental changes than Eq. (2). Note that the conflict of $\mathcal{P}$ might not occur at the primitive level after all; if so, $d_s = 0 + CCR_s$. For example, if the partner agent takes route (1) in Figure 3, and this conflict can be resolved by taking a detour or by using "wait for two ticks" to wait until the partner agent passes by. In this case, $d_s = 2 + CCR_s$. However, if the partner agent takes route (2) in Figure 3, no conflict actually occurs and $d_s = 0 + CCR_s$.
To acquire the CCR value for each plan, we assume that agents can monitor their planning activities by themselves. More precisely, CCR consists of the time for (1) requesting and receiving primitive plans from other agents that are suggested to have conflicts, (2) detecting actual conflicts between these plans and the local plan, and (3) modifying the local plan to resolve these conflicts. Agents keep the times for these activities. The conflict discount is re-calculated using the value of CCR plus the differential utility for each CP acquired by each agent from Eq. (2) or (3).

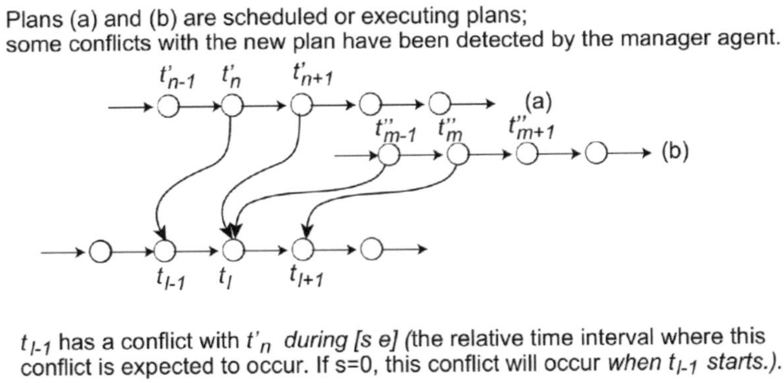

Fig. 4. Example of conflicts between plans.

The calculation of $cd(p)$ of SL plan p, like the conflict resolution process, is an iteration of the procedures for (1) searching for, from the first task, the task t that has a conflict pattern $\mathcal{P}$ with other plans, and (2) predicting the conflict discount $cd(\mathcal{P})$. In procedure (2), the additional cost of avoiding conflicts is predicted, and thus the start times of subsequent tasks may be delayed for this amount of time. Since a number of conflicts may appear and disappear in the remaining part of the plan because of this delay, the agent detects the next conflicting task by using the adjusted duration.

4.4 Sub-conflict patterns

It is probable that many CPs will be created, and storing many CPs in the casebase would require a large amount of memory. This also incurs a large search cost, which degrades scalability. It also lowers the performance of conflict estimations of the CPs. Here, we can try to reduce the memory taken up by the CPs.

Suppose that $\mathcal{P}_1$ and $\mathcal{P}_2$ are CPs:

$$\mathcal{P}_1 = (t, (t_1, r_1), \ldots, (t_n, r_n))$$
$$\mathcal{P}_2 = (t', (t'_1, r'_1), \ldots, (t'_m, r'_m))$$

If $t = t'$ and $\{(t_1, r_1), \ldots, (t_n, r_n)\} \subset \{(t'_1, r'_1), \ldots, (t'_m, r'_m)\}$, then $\mathcal{P}_1$ is the sub-conflict pattern (sub-CP) of $\mathcal{P}_2$, denoted by $\mathcal{P}_1 \subset \mathcal{P}_2$. Now, we assume that $cd(\mathcal{P}_1) \leq cd(\mathcal{P}_2)$ if $\mathcal{P}_1 \subset \mathcal{P}_2$. This is a natural assumption because $\mathcal{P}_1$ is resolved if the conflict with $\mathcal{P}_2$ is resolved.

To save memory, the agent only stores CPs whose conflict discount values are near the turning point of the decision. For example, if $cd(\mathcal{P}_2)$ is sufficiently small, the cd value for $\mathcal{P}_1$ ($\subseteq \mathcal{P}_2$) will not necessarily be stored, so its cd estimation can be eliminated. Similarly, if $cd(\mathcal{P}_1)$ is large, which means that the agent will give up the current SL plan, the cd value for $\mathcal{P}_2$ ($\supseteq \mathcal{P}_1$) does not have to be stored.

5. Experiments

5.1 Conflict discount estimation

We experimentally investigated how cd' (instead of cd) changes depending on the ways that agents interfere in a simulated laboratory room (Figure 1). Agent A randomly selects a starting point in region R_1 and a goal in region R_2 and then tries to generate a new plan for this movement. Another agent, *B*, already has an approved plan whose start and goal are also randomly selected in R_1 and R_2. In this setting, these agents do not cause any conflict when they may take different routes, such as to the north or south of the meeting table. However, they are likely to have conflicts when they both have to pass through area ***(c, d)*** because chairs and computer tables slightly narrow the route through it. Hence, we focused on the cases in which a conflict would be expected there at the SL and iterated the experiment until *A*'s task *move*(***cd*** $\rightarrow$ ***dd***) conflicted with *B*'s task, which were both expressed as *move*(***cd*** $\rightarrow$ ***dd***) (same direction) at the SL. Note that the duration of *A*'s SL plan was an estimated value that may differ from the actual duration of execution. This estimated duration was not used in the experiments in (Sugawara et al., 2005); thus, some of the experimental values shown below are slightly different from the ones reported in that paper. The SL plan was expanded into a primitive plan, and we investigated the conflict discount after conflict resolution. Because *B* requests *A*'s primitive plan, extra costs may be incurred even if no conflicts end up occurring. Therefore, in the following experiments, the number of plans of other agents that were predicted to have conflicts with the new plan was used as the approximate value of *CCR* (hence, a constant for each $\mathcal{P}$) of Eq. (1), because it is proportional to the number of these plans. This assumption means that it takes a tick to request and receive a primitive plan from another agent, check for conflicts between the received and local plans, and resolve these conflicts. We iterated this experiment a few hundred times to calculate *cd'*.

The task *move*(***cd*** $\rightarrow$ ***dd***) usually takes four to six ticks in this environment. Note that we assumed the SL-task *move*(*X,Y*) during interval [*s, e*] occupies resource *X* during *s* to *e* and resource *Y* at *e* and that the primitive-level task *move*(*x, y*) during [*s, s*+1] (a primitive task takes 1 tick) occupies *x* and *y* during *s* to *s*+1. If the agent finds a possible conflict within the first two ticks, the relative time relationship is denoted by *ah*; Additionally note that if it finds such a possibility within the last two ticks, the relative time relationship is denoted by *ph*. Otherwise, the relative time relationship is denoted by *ol*. Hence, we estimated the values of *cd'* for the following conflict patterns:

$$\mathcal{P}_3 = (move(\mathbf{cd} \rightarrow \mathbf{dd}), ((move(\mathbf{cd} \rightarrow \mathbf{dd}), r))),$$

where *r* is *ah*, *ph* or *ol*, meaning that these two agents move in the same direction.

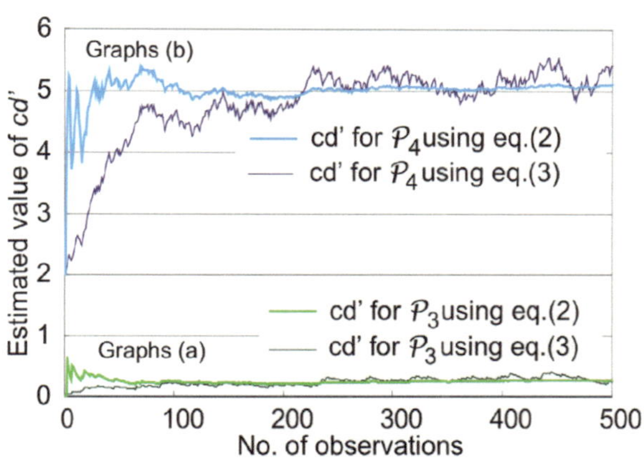

Fig. 5. Estimated *cd'* and average values.

Tables 1 and 2 show the average values from ten experiments based on ten different random seeds, and the graphs in Figure 5 are from one of these experiments.
Graphs (a) in Figure 5 show the estimated values of cd'_m ($\lambda = 0.98$, $1 \leq m \leq 500$) derived from Eqs. (2) and (3) when $r = ol$. In these cases, $cd'(\mathcal{P}_3) = 0.71$ (so $cd(\mathcal{P}_3) = cd'(\mathcal{P}_3) + CCR(\mathcal{P}_3) = 1.71$), which is reasonably small. This is because the two-square-wide path is wide enough for two agents to pass through the area, but agent *A* sometimes has to take a detour to avoid conflicts. Other cases, such as moving in the opposite direction, are shown in (Sugawara et al., 2005).
However, the *cd'* values largely differ when two agents, *B* and *C*, which have approved plans (i.e., plans that do not conflict with each other), move in the same direction *move*(**cd** → **dd**) and agent *A* begins to create a plan to move in the opposite direction though the same area. The conflict pattern of this situation is expressed as

$$\mathcal{P}_4 = (move(\mathbf{cd} \rightarrow \mathbf{bd})), ((move(\mathbf{cd} \rightarrow \mathbf{dd})), ol), (move(\mathbf{cd} \rightarrow \mathbf{dd})), ol))).$$

The estimated $cd'(\mathcal{P}_4) = 5.12$ ($cd(\mathcal{P}_4) = 7.12$) is quite different from the previous cases, as shown by graphs (b) in Figure 5. Because *B* and *C* move almost simultaneously without conflicts, they usually occupy the narrow route in area ***(c, d)*** together. Thus, agent *A* always has to move aside, wait for several ticks until *B* and *C* pass, and then move back to the original route. If the agent's new plan is predicted to have this conflict pattern at the SL, it can select, after learning, another route, such as one taking it north of the meeting table or another taking it south of the sofa in Figure 1, provided the route is shorter than the one in the original plan plus 7.12.
Table 2 shows the estimated *cd'* values in time-relativity cases other than $\mathcal{P}_4$. For example, if one of the relative time relationships in $\mathcal{P}_4$ is *ah* (This CP is denoted by $\mathcal{P}'_4$), the estimated $cd'(\mathcal{P}'_4) = 1.80$. This is small because if *B* and *C* move a slight distance away from each other, *A* can weave its way around them. In the case of *ph-ph*, *A*'s planned task *move*(**cd** → **bd**) may conflict in the latter half of its execution, so the agents will usually not meet in the narrow area (*A* moves right to left). However, because of uncertainty, they infrequently meet at different times in the narrow area. Table 2 suggests that the values of *cd'* depend on the resource structure of the routes, especially area ***(c, d)*** in Figure 1.

	ol-ol ($\mathcal{P}_4$)	*ph-ph*	*ah-ah*	*ah-ol* ($\mathcal{P}'_4$)	*ah-ph*	*ph-ol*
Value of *cd'*	5.12	3.67	3.30	1.80	0.75	1.87

Table 2. Experimentally estimated conflict discount *cd'*.

Suppose that in another situation the agent finds a CP, $\mathcal{P}_5$ such that $\mathcal{P}_4 \subset \mathcal{P}_5$. This CP may appear when conflict among more than four agents at ***(c, d)*** is expected. In this case, $cd'(\mathcal{P}_5)$ must be larger than 5.12. If this value is larger than the predefined threshold, the agent can calculate that $cd(\mathcal{P}_5) \geq 7.12$ (or $cd(\mathcal{P}_5) \geq 8.12$ if this conflict occurs among more than four agents), suggesting that it should try to find another route or shift (delay) its start time to avoid this conflict, even if it has no data about $\mathcal{P}_5$. Conversely, $cd'(\mathcal{P}'_4) = 1.80$ can induce $cd'(\mathcal{P}_3) \leq 1.80$. If this value is small enough, the agent does not need to calculate $cd(\mathcal{P}_3)$. Table 2 also indicates that $cd'(\mathcal{P}_3) \leq 0.70$ if $r = ah$ or ph in $\mathcal{P}_3$.

5.2 Cost (length) of generated plans

We investigated how efficient plans are generated with lower cost after a conflict pattern is found. In our planning strategy, agent A tries to select or generate another SL plan that is expected to have no conflict with other plans and whose estimated utility (in our case, the length of the plan) is less than the estimated utility of the original SL plan plus *cd* (if the CP is $\mathcal{P}_4$, then $cd(\mathcal{P}_4)$ is 7.12). The cost of selecting or generating another SL-plan is relatively low because we can set the upper limit of plan length. If A can find the new SL plan, it is selected and further refined. If A cannot find one, the original plan is selected (so conflict detection and resolution may be required). In the conventional planning strategy, the first SL plan to be generated would always be refined even if some conflicts were expected. (Of course, there might be no conflicts after all).

We examined, in our simulated room, the improvement of our planning strategy that resulted from using the estimated conflict discount value in Table 2. The results of this experiment (Table 3) show that our planning strategy provides an improvement of 2.65 ticks on average when a conflicting situation corresponding $\mathcal{P}_4$ is detected. In other cases, our planning method can generate efficient plans except when the conflict time relativity is *ph-ol*. This improvement is not very large. However, the ability to provide some information for deciding whether the agent should continue to refine the current plan even if the conflict resolution process will very likely be invoked or try to find another plan that does not have conflict with other agents is significant in applications like ours. In the *ph-ol* case, cd' is low so A cannot find any other better route.

CPs	Conventional strategy	Our planning strategy	Improvement
$\mathcal{P}_4$ (*ol-ol*)	33.34	30.69	2.65 %
ah-ah	32.39	30.44	1.95 %
ph-ph	30.93	29.40	1.53 %
ph-ol	23.80	23.80	0 %

Table 3. Cost (length) of resulting primitive plans. Columns 1 and 2 respectively show the average cost of primitive plans derived from the original SL plans and that of primitive plans derived under our planning strategy. In both cases, the cost of conflict detection and resolution is included.

The improvement shown in Table 3 seems fairly small, but our simulated laboratory room is based on an actual room; we believe that our method would be more significant in other situations/environments. For example, (1) if more robots were to move right to left in the narrow area in Figure 3, (2) if the chair there were a bench (a longer chair), or (3) if there were a shorter detour, the improvement would be larger, thus the resulting plans would be of relatively higher quality than the ones obtained by a conventional planning strategy. We finally note that, although the start and goal positions were selected randomly in our experiments, agents (including persons) in actual applications usually have fixed start and goal points. Therefore, we believe that the improvements derived from the experimental results would appear more when this is actually applied to this kind of systems.

6. Discussion and related work

There have been a number of studies on efficient planning in the MAS context. For example, GPGP (Decker & Lesser, 1992) is a general framework for generating effective plans using task and resource relationships among agents. Our method can be used in this framework to identify which abstract plan (task) should be refined first so that the map of the task relationships related to the plan can be created.

Hierarchical planning and coordination issues for improving MAS planning have also been discussed. For example, Ref. (Clement et al., 2001) proposed choosing the most appropriate abstract task/plan on the basis of summary information derived from the primitive tasks and plans in a bottom-up fashion. This method can avoid hopeless planning if some resources are recognized to be insufficient at an abstract level. It also introduced *fewest-threats-first* (FTF) heuristics to choose a lower (deeper) plan. Our approach focuses on the cases where conflicts can be accurately identified at only deeper levels, because the tasks, resources, and their environment in an abstract model are described in an abstract way. Furthermore, a plan with fewer conflicts does not always lead to a better plan; it is possible that only one conflict fails to be resolved but that conflict is nonetheless a critical one. The idea behind our research is that, although conflicts may be invisible at abstract levels (including the SL), there is a tendency that conflicts often occur depending on the environmental factors related to the availability and use of resources, such as the location of agents, the kind of resources, and type of agents, as well as on the kind of task. Hence, we aim at expressing and distinguishing these situations by using CPs in order to enable agents to statistically learn the difficulty of conflict resolution and the quality of a resulting plan.

A number of issues related to MAS planning have been investigated in case-based reasoning (CBR) or its related domains. For example, (Giampapa & Sycara, 2001) proposed a conversational case-based reasoner, called NaCoDAE, which is a type of agent in their MAS applications and helps users decide a course of action by engaging them in a dialogue in which they must describe the problem or situation of assigning missions to platoons. Plan reuse for the same/similar situations in a MAS context has also been proposed for MAS coordination (Sugawara, 1995) and collaboration (Plaza, 2005). A remarkable work similar to our approach is (Macedo & Cardoso, 2004), where a case is used to expand an abstract plan to a less abstract one in HTN, although we focus on avoiding conflicts and/or selecting costless conflicts. In this sense, our motivation is more similar to that in (Aha et al., 2005) which applied CBR to a real-time strategy game.

Our work is also related to hierarchical reinforcement learning, such as (Dietterich, 1998; Kaelbling, 1993; Sutton et al., 1998), because an abstract task is considered to be a subroutine or a subfunction to be learned. For example, in the MAXQ approach (Dietterich, 1998), a task is divided into subroutines that are individually learned by RL methods. Our approach is to select an appropriate subroutine for each situation. In MAXQ, the conflict discount is assumed to have been learned at lower levels. However, in a multi-agent setting, it is naturally difficult to define the task hierarchy for all agents simultaneously.

One clear limitation of our method is that the reliability of *cd* values heavily depends on the accuracy of the SL conflict detection and time-estimation processes. Thus, it is very important to select the appropriate SL and carefully describe the SL model. For example, if level 1 in Figure 1 is the SL, our method does not work well since that level is too abstract. As mentioned above, another issue is that the use of optional data in CPs is important for distinguishing one situation from another. To distinguish situations, our method needs the location of task execution (which may determine available resources), type of agent (which may determine required resources), and (relative) time information. Additionally, if many CPs are expected in a plan, conflict detection at the SL may be ambiguous regarding the scheduled time and resources of the SL tasks, which would affect the quality and cost of the plans. Finally, our method will have to be extended before it can deal with situations where multiple plans are created simultaneously; this extension is important for effective planning, and it will be addressed in a future work.

7. Conclusion

This chapter proposed a method to predict, at an abstract level called the screening level, the cost of possible conflict resolution, and the quality of the resulting plan, to generate better primitive (concrete) plans. In our framework, an agent called the manager agent maintains the plans that are scheduled or being executed at the screening level and predicts possible conflicts between these plans and the newly proposed plan. Then, if necessary, a detailed analysis of primitive plans is performed by individual agents. We conducted experiments to reveal the estimated additional cost (estimated *cd* and *cd′* values) of the plans after conflict resolution and the efficiency of plans derived from our method. Our method enables agents to decide whether the current plan should be refined or another plan should be created at an earlier stage, that is, before an agent creates its primitive plan; this decision makes agents' planning efficient.

Acknowledgement: This research was supported by SCOPE program of the Ministry of Internal Affairs and Communications, Japan, under contract 071607001.

8. References

Aha, D. W.; Molineaux, M. & Ponsen, M. (2005). Learning to win: Case-based plan selection in a real-time strategy game, *Proc. of the Sixth International Conference on Case-Based Reasoning (ICCBR 2005)*, LNAI 3620, pp. 5 - 20.

Clement, B. J.; Barrett, A. C.; Rabideau, G. R. & Durfee. E. H. (2001). Using abstraction in planning and scheduling, *Proc. of 6th European Conference on Planning*.

Decker, K. & Lesser, V. (1992). Generalizing the Partial Global Planning Algorithm, *International Journal on Intelligent Cooperative Information Systems*, Vol. 1, No. 2, pp. 319 - 346.

Dietterich, T. G. (1998). The MAXQ Method for Hierarchical Reinforcement Learning, *Proceedings of the International Conference on Machine Learning (ICML 98)*, pp. 118 - 126.

Giampapa, J. A. & Sycara, K. (2001). Conversational case-based planning for agent team coordination, *Proc. of the Fourth International Conference on Case-Based Reasoning (ICCBR 2001)*, LNAI 2080, pp. 189 - 203.

Goldwin, R. & Simmons, R. (1998). Search Control of Plan Generation in Decision-Theoretic Planners, *Proc. of AIPS 1998*, pp. 94 - 101.

Erol, J. H. K. & Nau, D. S. (1994). HTN planning: Complexity and expressivity, *Proc. of the National Conference on Artificial Intelligence (AAAI 94)*, pp. 1123 - 1128.

Kaelbling, L. P. (1993). Hierarchical Learning in Stochastic Domains: Preliminary Results, *Proceedings of the International Conference on Machine Learning (ICML-93)*, pp. 167 - 173.

Kurihara, S.; Aoyagi, S.; Takada, T.; Hirotsu, T. & Sugawara, T. (2005). Agent-Based Human-Environment Interaction Framework for Ubiquitous Environment, *Proc. of the International Workshop on Networked Sensing Systems*, pp. 103 - 108.

Kurihara, S. (2008). Human Behavior Mining using Sensing Network, *Proceedings of the First International Workshop on Content Creation Activity Support by Networked Sensing (CCASNS08)*.

Macedo, L. & Cardoso, A. (2004). Case-Based, Decision-Theoretic, HTN Planning, *Proc. of ECCBR 2004*, LNAI 3155, pp. 257 - 271. Springer-Verlag.

Plaza, E. (2005). Cooperative reuse for compositional cases in multi-agent systems, *Proc. of the Sixth International Conference on Case-Based Reasoning (ICCBR 2005)*, LNAI 3620, pp. 382 - 396.

Sacerdoti, E. (1974). Planning in a hierarchy of abstraction spaces, *Artificial Intelligence*, Vol. 5, No. 2, pp.115 - 135.

Sugawara, T. (1995). Reusing Past Plans in Distributed Planning, *Proc. of the 1st International Conference on Multi-Agent Systems* (*ICMAS95*), pp. 360 - 367.

Sugawara, T.; Kurihara, S.; Hirotsu, T.; Fukuda, K. & Takada, T. (2005). Predicting Possible Conflicts in Hierarchical planning for Multi-Agent Systems, *Proc. of 4th International Conference on Autonomous Agents and Multi-Agent Systems (AAMAS 2005)*, pp. 813 - 820.

Sutton, R. S.; Precup, D. & Singh. S. (1998). Intra-Option Learning about Temporary Abstract Actions, *Proceedings of the International Conference on Machine Learning* (*ICML98*), pp. 556 - 564.

Takada, T.; Kurihara, S.; Hirotsu, T. & Sugawara, T. (2003). Proximity Mining: Finding Proximity using Sensor Data History, *Proc. of IEEE Workshop on Mobile Computing Systems and Applications*, pp. 129 - 138.

6

Security in Large-Scale Open Distributed Multi-Agent Systems

M.A. Oey, M. Warnier and F.M.T. Brazier
Delft University of Technology
The Netherlands

1. Introduction

Designing large-scale distributed multi-agent systems that operate in open environments, such as the Internet, creates new challenges, especially with respect to security issues. Agents are autonomous, pro-active, communicative, goal-directed, often capable of learning, and sometimes mobile (8). Mobile agents traverse the network to access services and resources they need to achieve the goals they pursue. The potential of mobile agent technology in sectors such as E-Commerce (17; 18), E-Health (29) and E-Governance (10; 52) is well recognized. In these sectors, security issues such as authentication, authorization, privacy, and copyright are of utmost importance. Data access control is mandatory: by moving agents to the location at which data is stored, data access and processing can be done locally and controlled.

Many security requirements need to be addressed for large-scale distributed multi-agent systems in open environments. The focus of this chapter lies on security requirements specific for agent systems rather than security requirements for distributed computer systems in general. Section 2 identifies the most relevant security requirements for agent systems. This set of requirements is a minimum that needs to be fulfilled for secure agent systems in open environments. Sections 3 through 7 discuss the security requirements and possible solutions in detail. The solutions are illustrated within the context of the AgentScape (20) agent platform. This platform has been chosen as it has been specially designed to be used in a large-scale, distributed, open environment. However, similar implementations of these solutions are possible in other agent platforms.

The chapter closes with an overview of a number of well-known agent platforms, such as AgentScape (20), Ajanta (23), SeMoA (41), and JADE (5) with its security extensions JADE-S (34) and S-Agent (16). The discussion focuses on what techniques these agent systems have used to solve some of the discussed security requirements.

2. Security Issues in Agent Systems

An agent system, a specific type of distributed computer system, needs to address not only security requirements related to distributed computer systems, but also multi-agent system specific security requirements. This section identifies a minimum set of security requirements specific to multi-agent systems that needs to be fulfilled for it to operate securely in an open environment.

2.1 Principals in an Agent System

Conceptually, multi-agent systems are distributed, networked, computer systems in which **agent owners** run communicating **agents** that access **resources** on hosts, each of which runs an **agent platform** (i.e., an instance of an agent middleware) that is under the control of a **platform administrator**.[1] The bold terms are the major **principals** in a multi-agent system.
Each of these principals faces security threats. A secure agent system must protect these principals and their communication with other principals against security threats. For example, **secure communication** is needed to protect the communication between two agents, but also between two platforms and between an agent and a platform or the agent's owner. In a large-scale, distributed system, such as the Internet, communication is usually over long distances and can be intercepted or monitored. In a closed environment, all principals in an agent system are known in advance and usually trusted, therefore, security measures are often implicit. However, in a more open environment, more explicit security measures are needed to guard against security threats.
Traditionally, security threats are described using the terms **confidentiality**, **integrity**, and **availability**: the CIA-triad (46). Confidentiality refers to the ability to prevent access by those that are not authorized. Integrity refers to the ability to prevent any unauthorized modification. Availability refers to keeping resources accessible at all times to authorized parties. A prerequisite for guarding confidentiality, integrity, and availability is identity management (9), which encompasses **naming** and **authentication**. Naming is the ability to identify each individual principal in an agent system. Authentication is the ability to verify a principal's identity. For example, reliable authentication is needed as malicious parties may want to impersonate certain principals in order to gain access to that principal's privileges.
The next sections look at security threats in an agent system from the viewpoint of the two most important stakeholders in an agent system: the **agent owner** and the **agent platform's administrator**.

2.2 Security Threats for the Agent's Owner

An agent performs its actions on behalf of its owner, which is usually a legal entity, such as a human or an organization: the **agent owner**. The main security concerns for an agent owner are confidentiality and integrity of his agent, any data it carries, and any communication to and from the agent. Confidentiality is directly related to guarding the privacy of an agent's owner. For example, in an e-health environment, agents acting on behalf of patients carry privacy-sensitive information that should not be revealed to others.
Agent mobility introduces extra security risks, as agents run on hosts that are out of the control of the agent's owner. For example, malicious parties can start agent platforms with the intent to eavesdrop or manipulate agents that they host. This **malicious host** problem is hard to solve, as platforms in general have full control over the agents that run on them. The most effective solutions involve the use of *trusted hardware*. Unfortunately, these solutions are usually also the more costly solutions to implement. Software-only solutions give less protection but are more practical to implement. The malicious host problem exists foremost in open environments. It is reasonable to assume that in closed environments all hosts are trusted to behave well and that adequate **authorization** mechanisms have been installed to prevent unauthorized users of the platform to have access to an agent's private data.

[1] The term *agent platform* or *middleware* refers to software running on hosts to support agents; *agent system* refers to the whole system of agents, agent owners, agent platforms, platform administrators, etc.

Availability of an agent is a requirement for an agent owner that can be implemented by an agent owner himself, possibly supported by a platform. For example, to make an agent more fault tolerant, an agent owner can start two (or more) copies of an agent and send them to different platforms, so that if one agent dies, the other can continue, keeping the agent available to its owner. Alternatively, an agent owner can trust a platform owner to take adequate measures to guarantee the availability of an agent platform.

2.3 Security Threats for the Platform's Administrator

A host's administrator can run an agent platform (i.e., an instance of the agent middleware) on his host. An agent platform enables visiting agents to (paid) access to a host's resources. The main security concerns for an agent platform's administrator (who is not necessarily the same as the host's administrator) are confidentiality, integrity, and availability of the agent platform, its resources, and any communication from and to the agent platform.

In open environments, a platform must prepare for deliberate attacks, from outside, as well as inside. Mobile **malicious agents** can first migrate to a platform and try to attack a platform from the inside. Attacks typically include gaining unauthorized access to a host's resources or accessing the data of other agents running on that host. To protect against the threat of malicious agents a **resource access control** mechanism must be installed that enforces an authorization mechanism that determines who is allowed to access which resource and to what extent.

A typical resource in an agent system that may be the target of availability threats is the **lookup service**. The lookup service is a database that keeps track of the current locations of all agents in an agent system. An agent system needs this information, for example, to deliver messages to agents sent from other agents. In an open environment, an attacker could start an agent platform, join the agent community and subsequently fill the lookup service with false information about locations of agents. This attack renders the information in a lookup service useless and consequently paralyzes an agent system as a whole. This specific attack is a form of a **Denial-of-Service** attack and illustrates the necessity of a **secure lookup service** which guarantees the correctness of its information. Without it, a platform administrator cannot guarantee the availability of the agent platform.

2.4 Summary

The next list summarizes the security requirements discussed in this section. Each requirement is either a prerequisite for security or is associated with a threat to one of the two main principals in an agent system: agent owner or platform administrator.

- *Prerequisite*: **Naming and Authentication** – the ability to verify the identity of principals.
- *Prerequisite*: **Communication Security** – confidentiality and integrity of data sent between agents, services, hosts, etc. must be guaranteed.
- *Agent owner*: **Malicious Host** protecting an agent's confidentiality and integrity even if it runs on a malicious host.
- *Platform administrator*: **Malicious Agent** – protecting a host's confidentiality and integrity from malicious agents.
- *Platform administrator*: **Secure Lookup Service** – guarding the information in the lookup service.

This set of security requirements forms a bare minimum for agent systems in open environments. In addition to these security requirements other requirements common to all distributed computer systems need to be addressed, such as fault tolerance, availability, backups, traceability, etc. For agent systems in specific domains more stricter security requirements may apply as well. For example, in privacy sensitive environments **anonymity** may be an important requirement.
The remainder of this chapter focuses on the specific security requirements in order. Each requirement is discussed in more detail and one or more possible solutions are presented. Sections 3 and 4 discuss the prerequisites naming and authentication, and communication security. Next, Section 5 focuses on the main security threat to an agent owner: the malicious host. Finally, Sections 6 and 7 look at threats to a platform administrator and discuss the malicious agent and a secure lookup service.

3. Naming and Authentication

As mentioned above, identity management is an important security requirement in an open, distributed agent system. The ability to name principals and authenticate them is an important part of identity management.

3.1 Naming

Before authentication can be done, principals in an agent system must first have a (unique) identifier: a name. This name does not have to be human-readable; it can be a meaningless string, as long as it is machine-readable. In principle, names can be static, which means they do not change over the lifetime of a principal, or dynamic. For humans and organizations static names are a more logical choice, however for (mobile) agents in an agent system, dynamic names have their use. For example, agent names could contain a reference to the location where an agent resides (*location-dependent names*, see also Section 7), which makes locating the agent trivial. However, for the remainder of this chapter it is assumed that principals have **globally unique identifiers** (GUIDs), which are static names. The term global does not necessarily have to imply that the identifier is unique in the universe, but it suffices that the identifier is unique within an instance of a running agent system. It can be assumed that in any agent system, something similar to GUIDs is used to name principals.
Another property of naming is whether principals can have more than one name. For example, if an agent has multiple names, it can use these names as *pseudonyms*. Pseudonyms can be used to implement **anonymity** (51): an agent can use a different pseudonym for each interaction with another agent.
To illustrate, AgentScape (20) (see Section 8) actually has two naming schemes. First, agents are identified internally by GUIDs, which are kept private to the middleware. Second, agents are externally visible through their (static) **handles**. Each agent can have more than one handle at a time, which allows them to implement a form of anonymity as each handle is a *pseudonym*. Note that naming is not sufficient for authentication as there is no mechanism to verify that a name corresponds to the correct principal. Authentication is discussed in the next section.

3.2 Authentication: a Public Key Infrastructure

Many ways of authentication are known and used in the world. One well-known method is the use of username and password combinations. Only if the correct password is supplied is the user authenticated. A more elaborate scheme requires a PKI, a **Public Key Infrastructure**, that uses asymmetric key encryption also known as public-key cryptography (27). Every principal (agent, user, host, etc.) that needs to be able to be authenticated creates a key-pair, consisting of a *public* and a *private* key. These keys have the property that data encrypted with one key can be decrypted by the other, and given one key it is computationally infeasible to derive the other key. Every principal publishes its public key to the world, but keeps its own private key private. The identity of a principal can now be verified by checking whether the principal can correctly decrypt a message encrypted with the principal's public key. Only the real owner of that public-private key pair can decrypt the message assuming the private key has been kept private. Whether the public key is indeed the public key of the correct principal and not of an imposter impersonating that principal using its own generated keypair is the task of the PKI.

The public key infrastructure is used to securely publish public keys of principals. A public key is published together with the corresponding principal's personalia. This combination is called a **certificate**. This certificate is also (digitally) signed (25) by a **Certificate Authority** (CA), after it has verified that the public key and principal are indeed legitimate, which, for example, involves showing a passport to an official of the CA. All principals publish their public key in the form of signed certificates. Anyone who trusts the signing CA can use that certificate and be confident that the public key and the principal both stated in the certificate are valid and belong to each other. In short, an agent system is able to solve the authentication problem by using a PKI, where all principals create a public/private keypair and a trusted CA signs all corresponding certificates.

For completeness, signing a certificate is done by adding an encrypted version of the certificate (actually, a hash of it) to the certificate. Encryption is done with the private key of the CA, which means that everyone can verify the signature with the public key of the CA, but nobody can forge the signature. The public key of the CA is assumed to have been distributed securely to all participants. Note that safely distributing the certificates of a handful of CAs is more feasible than distributing the certificates of all participants.

In AgentScape, a public key infrastructure is installed. Agent owners, locations, and hosts have public and private key pairs. This ensures that locations and hosts can mutually authenticate and set up secure communication channels, using SSL (see Section 4).

3.3 Linking an Agent and its Owner

In many situations, an agent must be uniquely and undeniably linked to its owner (e.g., a human or organization). This link is part of authenticating an agent and is necessary, for example, to charge the owner if agents make purchases on the web or to help determine liability whenever agents misbehave. This section discusses, in the context of agent based systems, how agents can be 'bound' to their owner.

As mentioned before, it is assumed that an agent can be identified by a GUID. Conceptually, an agent consists of meta-data, (executable) code, and data that an agent has 'found' on a particular host. The meta-data of an agent contains at least the following: the GUID of this agent, the name of this agent's owner, and a signed (by the owner) hash of this agent's code. The signature ensures that agent and owner are bound to each other. For authentication to succeed, it is important that the public key of an agent owner is stored in a PKI.

For example, in AgentScape, when an agent is injected, the agent platform checks if the agent code is indeed signed. If verification is successful the agent obtains a GUID and a handle is returned to the agent owner. Assuming the owner keeps this handle secret, it can be used to communicate between agent and owner. Next, the injected agent is started by the agent platform. If the agent misbehaves in some way, the owner can be contacted and be held responsible for the agent's actions. The agent injection procedure is similar in other agent systems.

4. Communication Security

In distributed agent systems communication is manifold. The (distributed) components that make up the agent system's middleware need to communicate with each other to maintain a running agent platform, and the agents themselves communicate with each other, with (external) services, and with the platform. Confidentiality of communication between agents, services, hosts, etc. must be guaranteed. Threats can be external or internal. External eavesdroppers may want to listen in on agents to find out privacy-related information, may want to disrupt the agent platform, or may want to impersonate other agents or services, etc.

4.1 Common Security Attacks

Many types of attacks are known that target communication channels. Two very common attacks are man-in-the-middle attacks and replay attacks. This section briefly explains these two attacks to illustrate the kind of attacks possible on communication channels. For clarity, the names Alice, Bob, and Mallory, which are commonly used in cryptography, are used to explain these security attacks.

With a **man-in-the-middle attack**, an attacker (Mallory) tries to put himself in between the communication path of two others (Bob and Alice). When Bob tries to contact Alice, Mallory steps in posing as Alice, and forwards the request to Alice, but now pretending to be Bob. As a result, Bob and Alice both *think* they are talking privately to each other, while in fact Mallory is able to intercept all data that is sent by them. This form of attack succeeds if Mallory is able to impersonate Bob and Alice successfully. A **replay attack** is a threat where an attacker deliberately resends or delays messages that were sent previously. Since the attacker does not alter messages, the receiving party does not have any reason to refuse incoming messages, unless it has the ability to detect that a message is a resent copy or an old delayed message. To see the effect of a replay attack, consider the consequences of a message that contains a money-transfer order for an online bank application.

4.2 Encryption

A common technique to guarantee confidentiality and integrity of communication is encryption. Two well-known techniques are **SSL-based communication** (32) and **IPsec** (26). SSL is widely used to provide secure connections to webservers (e.g., the *https* protocol). All data sent over a connection between two parties is encrypted with a shared-key. The key is exchanged in a hand-shake phase during the setup of the connection. Authentication, that is, the method to ensure that a party actually is who he/she claims to be, usually involves a **certificate** signed by a trusted third party (i.e., a certificate authority) whom both communicating parties trust. After the hand-shake successfully completes, both parties can be assured that their communication remains confidential. In agent systems, the setup of the encrypted SSL-connection is usually done by the agent middleware. As a consequence, the agent middleware's internal communication is also secure. In addition, all agent-to-agent communication is automatically encrypted transparently, under the assumption that communication is supported by the agent middleware, which is almost always the case.

The other technique is IPsec. This protocol uses encryption at a much lower level than SSL does. SSL uses encryption at the application level, which means the encryption is performed

by the application, an agent platform. In contrast, IPsec is performed by the underlying operating system. The advantage of this technique is that both agent application developers and agent system developers have secure communication available to them automatically. However, most agent platforms provide their own secure communication (usually via SSL) as it is relatively simple to implement and they then do not have to rely on the underlying operating system to support IPsec.
For example, AgentScape currently supports SSL-based communication between hosts and locations. This provides the basis for hosts/locations to authenticate each other. Furthermore, all messages transmitted between hosts/locations, including migration of agents, are encrypted to ensure confidentiality. The PKI is used to link host/location identities in a secure manner.

5. Malicious Hosts

To an agent owner, protecting an agent's code and the data it has acquired while traversing a network is his main security concern. Especially, when agents are used in open environments such as the Internet, where agents execute outside the control of the agent's owner. Hosts on which an agent resides may be malicious, yet temporarily have complete control of the agent's runtime environment. It is often infeasible to determine the trustworthiness of hosts in advance in open environments.
Unfortunately, in practice, it is almost impossible to protect a migrating agent if it runs on hosts that are outside the control of an agent's owner. Such a **malicious host** can view and alter an agent's (internal) state, or even delete the agent altogether. However, some hardware and software solutions exist that try to provide security guarantees or at least allow others to detect that an agent has been tampered with by a malicious host. Below some of these solutions are discussed.
In principle, protecting agents from malicious hosts requires (39):

1. Protecting the integrity of the migration path of an agent
2. Protecting the integrity of the agent's data and (binary) code
3. Ensuring confidentiality of the agent's data
4. Ensuring integrity of the agent's control flow

The migration of an agent from one host to another is called a **migration step**. A **migration path** is a sequence of multiple migration steps that identifies all the hosts, in order, an agent has visited. In principle, the integrity of the migration path (item 1, above) forms the basis for detecting malicious hosts and/or preventing them from doing any harm. For example, a number of techniques (6; 22; 39; 43) have integrity of agent migration paths as a premise, and can be used to detect tampering with the agent (items 2 & 4). Solutions to protect an agent's migration paths are discussed in more detail at the end of this section (Section 5.5). Before that, some solutions to protect an agent's integrity, confidentiality, and control flow are briefly presented.

5.1 Trusted Hardware

A technique that in principle can offer the most protection is using trusted hardware (Trusted Computing (49)). Trusted hardware, such as the Trusted Platform Module (TPM), provides guarantees of the hardware's behavior. A TPM is a piece of hardware within a computer that cannot be tampered with. It can perform cryptographic functions and store cryptographic

keys securely. Software manufacturers can use a TPM to guarantee users that their software running on a host has not been tampered with. A TPM can create a hash of the hardware and software of a computer and check whether anything has been modified. Agents can use this information to detect whether to trust a host or not, depending on whether they trust the software manufacturer who created the agent middleware running on the host.
Another use of a TPM is for an agent to let certain critical operations be performed by a TPM. An agent sends any input encrypted to the TPM, the TPM then operates on the data and sends the result back to the agent. The result is encrypted in such a way that only the agent's owner can decrypt it after the agent returns to its owner. Unfortunately, both uses of the TPM require specialized hardware. Requiring all computers to have specialized hardware restricts the use of it for agent systems in an open environment. Therefore, the remainder of this section focuses on software-only techniques.

5.2 Protecting an Agent's Integrity

An agent needs to protect both it's agent code as well as any data it carries. As mentioned before, without trusted hardware, an agent cannot protect this data from being modified by a malicious host. However, it is possible for an agent to detect, after a migration from a potentially malicious host, whether that host has made any unwanted modifications to the agent's code and/or any data that the agent carried. The solution is the use of digital signatures.
To protect an agent's code, the agent carries a signature from the agent owner over a *hash* of the agent's code. After migration, an agent platform checks whether the agent owner is authorized (trusted) to run agents and whether the signed hash in the agent matches the actual hash of the agent's code it received. If not, then the agent has been modified and the agent platform can notify the agent's owner and refuse to start the agent. Since only the agent owner can generate this signature, a malicious host cannot modify the agent's code without being detected.
The data that an agent carries can be protected as follows. A hash is calculated of each piece of data that needs to be protected. Then all these hashes are stored in a table together with some meta-data on each piece of data, such as its location within an agent. This table is then signed and stored within the agent. If a malicious host modifies or removes a part of the protected data or the table, the signature will not match and the modification will be detectable by the agent or the agent owner.
Unfortunately, an agent cannot carry its own private key to sign data, because a malicious host would then also have access to it and be able to fake signatures. Consequently, an agent cannot sign its own data. Instead, an agent owner or a trusted third party should sign the table. The agent has to migrate to the agent owner's host or to the trusted third party's host first to get the signature. Migration to a trusted host makes this scheme a little cumbersome. If, however, the migration path of an agent can be securely tracked (migration path integrity), other solutions become possible (6; 22; 39; 43).

5.3 Protecting an Agent's Confidentiality

To protect a malicious host from reading confidential data that an agent carries, it is sufficient to encrypt that data with the public key of the agent's owner, which ensures that only the agent's owner can read the data after the agent has returned to the owner. Encryption can be done by an agent itself on the (trusted) host where it has acquired the data. Unfortunately, after encryption an agent itself does not have access to the data either. If it needs access to encrypted data and it trusts the host it is on, it can set up a secure connection to the agent's owner and ask it to decrypt the data.

5.4 Protecting an Agent's Control Flow

Unfortunately, protecting an agent's control flow on a malicious host is virtually impossible without dedicated trusted hardware. Basically, an agent would need to control (or at least monitor) the runtime environment of the host on which it runs, which is impossible as the host controls it. For example, a malicious host could deny or limit access to resources that an agent has previously negotiated for. If the agent does not check for this, it would never notice the fraud. Even worse, even if an agent checks for fraud, a really malicious host could change the control-flow of the agent to skip this check.

The best an agent can do is to use the techniques described above to protect the confidentiality and integrity of the data it carries, to at least detect whether the agent has been tampered with. The agent can then can redo its operation again at a more trusted host after migration.

5.5 Protecting an Agent's Migration Path

One fundamental (and unsolvable) problem for agent migration is that a malicious host can always delete an agent in its entirety. This can never be prevented. However, it is possible to detect *which* host deleted an agent. The only thing that is needed for this is the preservation of the integrity of the migration path of an agent. An agent owner can then simply follow the migration path of an agent and conclude which host deleted the agent. Of course for this to work, a malicious host should not be able to forge the migration history of an agent. Once a malicious host is identified as such, the host can be put on a black list, thereby preventing further malicious behavior of the host in question. The main focus of this section is the *detection* of *breaches* of integrity in migration paths of mobile agents.

The host on which an agent is initialized, is assumed to be trusted by the agent's owner. This host can be traced by all other hosts at any arbitrary moment in time. Hosts are assumed to have full control over the agents they run. The consequence of this assumption is that hosts are able to read and alter information stored inside agents. Although agents can decide to only migrate to trusted hosts, that is, hosts that have a valid (signed) certificate, a trust relationship does not give full guarantees with respect to a host's behavior and intentions.

A number of solutions exist to protect the integrity of an agent's migration path. A possible solution uses a centralized **trusted third party** (TTP) (15) to authorize and keep track of migration paths of agents. The trusted third party can be physically located elsewhere and does not have to be part of the agent system itself. However, all users of an agent system must trust that the trusted third party is not malicious and cannot be compromised. Secure communication channels (see Section 4) to the TTP and digital signatures (25) (see also 5.2) are used to secure the migration protocol against fraud. Unfortunately, malicious hosts can simply migrate an agent between them without informing the TTP. Furthermore, a centralized TTP forms a single point of failure and can become a performance bottleneck for large-scale agent systems. Multiple TTPs can be used to improve scalability. For example, in the **home based approach**, each agent uses its own initial (trusted) host as its TTP. Alternatively, Roth (39) uses *co-operating agents* that use each other as TTP.

A decentralized solution to secure the migration path of an agent is **signature chaining** (45), which stores an agent's migration path in an agent itself, together with an agent's code and data. Digital signatures are used to protect the migration path against tampering by a malicious host. In this method, each host adds the next migration step to the migration path that

was already stored in the agent and signs the entire path, including the signatures of previous hosts in the migration paths. By signing the entire migration path the signatures of all participating hosts are chained together. Each new migration step adds another connected link to the signature chain. Unfortunately, verifying long signature chains is computationally intensive, and a malicious host can remove arbitrary cycles from a migration path if an agent (accidentally) visits the same malicious host for a second time (45).
Another scalable solution that uses the notion of distributed trust to secure migration paths is described in (53). In this solution, other hosts in the migration path authorize and check each following migration step. Increasing the number of hosts required to authorize a migration makes the migration protocol more resistant to co-operating malicious hosts. Spreading trust over multiple hosts in an agent system clearly has benefits in terms of scalability and it strengthens the security mechanism, as a 'single point of failure' no longer exists. Orthogonally, a dedicated trust model that can distinguish the –relative– trustworthiness of hosts in multiple agent systems can be of much additional value. Reputation and trust models (1) have been studied in the context of agent systems by, for example, (19; 36).

6. Malicious Agents

The previous section discusses the malicious host problem. This section focuses on the complementary problem: **malicious agents**. Just as agent owners want to protect their agents against potentially malicious hosts, so do platform administrators want to protect their hosts against potentially malicious migrating agents. Malicious agents typically attempt to gain access to resources on a host they are not authorized to use. Such access includes attempts to access private data of the host, private data of other agents, or to use additional computational resources that have not been negotiated. Fortunately, there are a number of techniques that a platform administrator can apply to reduce the threat of malicious agents and control their access to a host's resources. This section discusses a few of these techniques and subsequently focuses on the subject on how to configure and manage access to resources for agents.

6.1 Sandboxing Agents

Most solutions to securing hosts from malicious agents entail monitoring every action that an agent attempts on a host. Whenever an agent makes a call to the middleware API, it is intercepted by a **security manager**. The security manager checks the system policy to determine if an action, such as migration and resource access, should be allowed or denied. For example, a host could decide that it does not allow agents to use remote web-services (i.e., not running on the local host). Every attempt to contact a remote web-service will be blocked by the security manager.
Many agent platforms are Java-based (14), and in Java one of the primary solutions towards securing mobile code is to execute any remote code in a protection domain or **sandbox**. A sandbox limits the set of operations that the remote code may call. For example, sandboxing typically restricts network access as well as access to the local filesystem. Java provides agent system programmers the tools to define sandboxes by using a *security manager* and/or custom *class loaders*. In Java the actual sandbox is enforced and implemented by the underlying JVM, for interpreted scripting languages such as Python and Safe-Tcl the sandbox is implemented by the interpreter. For C or C++ (binary code) agents are 'jailed' (50).
Sandboxing and jailing are examples of solutions with which agents are run in contained environments limiting the amount of damage they can cause to the systems on which they run. An alternative solution is to only run agents of *trusted* owners. Whom to trust is up to

the platform administrator. In this solution, agents are only trusted if they are signed by a reputable software manufacturer, whom the user trusts not to provide malicious agents. The simplicity of this scheme is also its weakness: the security of the system lies in the belief that the signer is trustworthy. The weakness of this system has already been shown as digital signing certificates have been issued to people masquerading as a representative of a well known software maker (12). Furthermore, small and open source software makers may not have the financial capability to purchase such signing certificates. Of course, digital signatures can be combined with sandboxing to create a more robust security solution.

Finally, a more elaborate security approach is the use of proof-carrying code (30) (applied to the mobile agent paradigm described in (31)). Agents carry a *machine-verifiable proof* with them that specifies their expected and acceptable behavior. Each host is equipped with a theorem prover to ensure that an agent's code indeed adheres to its specification. Unfortunately, constructing the proof is very labor intensive (21), which makes this approach less practical.

Sandboxes and security managers restrict an agent's actions. However, a security manager first needs to know when to allow or deny an agent's request to access a resource: **access control**. In a flexible environment, principals may first want to negotiate about which resources they need, to what extent, and at what price. The outcome of this *resource negotiation* is input to the security manager that monitors and authorizes access to resources as negotiated. For example, the WS-Agreement standard (3) which provides a negotiation protocol for the domain of web services can be used. Mobach (28) has applied and extended this standard in the field of distributed agent systems.

Specifying security permissions can be an elaborate job, prone to mistakes. The remainder of this section discusses how the combination of **roles** and sets of predefined **policies** simplify this task. Security policies allow users of agent systems to manage the security features of the multi-agent system of their choice. Developers of agent systems have the opportunity to ship a number of security policies with their software. For example, an effective default policy is one that will not prevent users from performing vital tasks, but will protect the host against some of the most common security issues. In contrast, 'high security' policies should be used in security critical environments. Such policies are very restrictive. Below a security policy framework is discussed and illustrated within AgentScape (20).

6.2 Resource Access Control

Once the basic security features, such as an agent naming scheme and authentication (see Section 3), are in place, the next requirement is an authorization mechanism. Conceptually, an authorization mechanism needs to specify who is allowed to do what and to what extent. There are a number of principals involved in any agent platform. For example, principals in AgentScape are locations, world administrators, resources and their administrators, and agents and their owners. Similar principals can be identified in any other agent platform. In any agent platform agents can perform a number of basic actions to achieve their goals, such as communication, migration, access to resources, etc. Controlling which principal can perform which action is a structure that can be readily managed using a **Role Based Access Control** (RBAC) (44; 54) mechanism.

6.3 Roles, Users, and Permissions

RBAC is an access control architecture that models roles, users and permissions. RBAC is designed to reflect real-world relations between users and permissions. Each role is associated with a set of permissions corresponding to logical tasks that users can perform. Users are

assigned one or more roles. The advantage of this setup is that changing the permissions of a whole group of users with a specific role can be easily done by simply changing the permissions of the corresponding role.
Defining roles, users and permissions can be straightforward. First a number of permissions are defined and assigned to roles. Users are then associated with these roles. Table 1 shows some example (Role, Permission) pairs, denoting the capabilities of each role. Note that each role can have multiple permissions. Table 2 assigns roles to a set of users. These users are shown as textual names, but would in practice be represented by a unique identifier.

Role	**Permission to perform action**
BasicAgent	Migrate, Execute
TrustedAgent	Migrate, Execute, AccessRes
AgentOwner	Inject, GetResult
ResourceAdmin	AccessRes, ChangePerms, GetLogs

Table 1. RBAC Example Role Permission Table

Role	**User**
BasicAgent	SimpleAgent1, SimpleAgent2
TrustedAgent	ClaireTradingAgent, DaveStockAgent
DatabaseAccess	Alice, Claire
ResourceAdmin	Trent, Steve

Table 2. RBAC Example Role User Table

Agent owners form the base of the trust mechanism. They are ultimately responsible for the actions of their agents. Therefore, by default, agents hold the permissions granted to their owners, but these permissions can be further restricted when appropriate. Access to resources is explicitly specified in an RBAC policy.
The RBAC system can be dynamically updated, that is, roles can be changed, users can be added or removed from roles, and permissions can be assigned and removed from roles. Determining, specifying, and managing roles, users, and permissions is the responsibility of an administrator of each host. Part of this management can be delegated to (privileged) users to keep the task manageable. For example, a database administrator can be given the right to manage permissions to databases for which he is responsible. Agent owners can manage the rights of their own agent. Note that an agent owner cannot give its agents more rights than he himself has been given by a platform's administrator.
In an open system, every agent platform is autonomous. Therefore, each host can have its own RBAC policy. In addition, if multiple hosts co-operate in one single administrative domain (called a *location* in AgentScape terminology) each administrator of a host can define different (e.g., stricter) restrictions for its resources than a location administrator and vice versa. Both policies are enforced together; actions are only permitted if both policies agree.

6.4 Security Manager

To enforce resource access control, every action of an agent must first be authorized by an RBAC system before the action can be executed. Whenever an agent attempts to perform a security relevant action, a Security Manager checks whether the agent is authorized to perform this action. This check is a two-step process. First, the Security Manager determines the

GUID of the agent and determines the role, or roles, of which the GUID is a member. Second, the Security Manager determines if one or more of these roles is authorized to perform the requested action.

It is worthwhile to note that not only a platform's administrator, but also an agent owner needs to trust the security manager. After an agent owner has negotiated for resources and possibly paid for access, an agent owner expects the security manager to grant access as negotiated. Similar to monitoring of Service Level Agreements (SLA) a trusted third party module can be used to monitor and log the communication between client (agent) and service provider (host) (37).

6.5 Parameterization of Permissions

A selection of the basic security relevant actions used in AgentScape is shown in Table 3. In most agent systems similar actions can be identified. These actions reflect the basic abilities of agents. The permissions for these actions can be extended with *parameters*. Parameters are used to further refine the granularity of permissions. For example, negotiation can be restricted to specific types of resources. Parameters are defined in parentheses. A special parameter, '*', is supported to allow *all* types of an action to be permitted by a role. This notation is used to avoid having to explicitly specify every type of resource and every location when wishing to grant access to them. Permissions are positive, that is, if access to a resource is not explicitly granted, access is denied.

Action	Principal	Description
Migrate	Agent	Migrate from one Location to another.
Inject	Owner	Launch an Agent in a Location.
AccessRes	Agent	Access a resource provided by a location.
Negotiate	Agent	Negotiate access to a remote location.
Lookup	Agent	Access yellow or white pages lookup service.
SendMsg	Location/Agent	Send a message to a remote location.
RecvMsg	Location/Agent	Receive a message from a remote location.

Table 3. Common Security Relevant Actions

In most cases, locations and hosts typically utilize generic policies for all agents. That is, most locations and hosts are not expected to specifically restrict access to resources, unless these resources are of specific importance. For example, most hosts will allow all agents access to CPU and memory resources, but access to special databases are more carefully controlled.

Parameterization simplifies expressing permissions for roles, and also allows more fine-grained access for system resources to be defined. This can be used, for example, to define policies that limit the locations to which agents may migrate. To illustrate parameterization consider the Role/Permission table shown in Table 4. In this table, normal agents (BasicAgent) are allowed to execute and access CPU and Memory resources. Only trusted agents, that is, agents with the role *TrustedAgent*, are authorized to access the price database.

Role	Permission
BasicAgent	Migrate(*), Execute, AccessRes(CPU,Memory)
TrustedAgent	Migrate(*), Execute, AccessRes(CPU,Memory,PriceDB)

Table 4. Database Resource Role-Permission Table

6.6 Agent Injection

RBAC requires all users (agents, humans, etc.) to be associated with one or more roles. New human users are usually entered into an RBAC system by a location's administrator. However, new agents injected by human users can be automatically added by an agent platform in an RBAC system with the corresponding permissions as described by an agent platform's administrator. The agent injection protocol in AgentScape is as follows. When a principal wishes to inject an agent into an AgentScape location, the principal first contacts the location and they perform a two-way authentication. Once authenticated, a location will accept agents injected into that location by a specific principal if, and only if, the principal is authorized to perform injections.

Once an agent is injected into a location, the location assigns a GUID to the agent instance. This GUID is also automatically entered as a new user into the *Role-User* table of both the location and the host that is going to run the agent, and is assigned to, at most, the same roles as the owner. Owner roles are defined by each location individually. In addition, default roles can be used for unknown agents and owners. To limit the growth of a *Role-User* table, an agent's entry can be removed as soon as the agent finishes or successfully migrates to another location. After successful migration, the GUID of the agent will be entered into the *Role-User* table of the receiving location and host. If owners are removed from a role, any agent belonging to that owner loses that role.

6.7 Security Policies

While security can be a major concern for resource and location administrators, it is not always the case that these principals are either particularly interested, or trained to, define their own security policies. For this reason, it is advisable to have a set of predefined default policies. These predefined policies range from simple, non-restrictive policies, used for agent systems deployed in a well known environment, to stronger, restrictive policies, where agent systems operate in a more hostile environment. These two extremes are described in the context of the following two case studies: a closed world and a hostile world.

In a simple *closed world environment*, locations are controlled by well known entities and are all trusted. Communication between locations is cryptographically secured and each location is known and trusted by every other location. The major threat to the middleware is that of malicious agents. Agent owners must be authenticated. Once authenticated, agents are authorized to perform any and all actions. Therefore, the authorization mechanism is not used for access control, but is instead used for auditing purposes: whenever an agent performs a security relevant action, it is logged for possible later examination by the location administrator. While a simple system is common in small, closed environments, the provision of services on the web, with the associated access of these services by software agents demonstrates that such an environment cannot be assumed.

In a *hostile environment* locations are controlled by entities that are not always known by every principal. Agents are authenticated by their initial location as before, but the authorization mechanism is now used to enforce location-specific restrictions. The security manager monitors usage of specified resources and ensures that all accesses are restricted by the negotiated limits. Any breaches of these limits are logged and execution of the agent responsible is immediately suspended. Migration is only authorized between the original 'home' host–the host where the agent started–and remote hosts. Therefore, migration from one remote host to another forces an agent to first return to the home host. This is enforced to prevent malicious hosts attempting to inject or read data developed from a prior migration. For example, the

result of a price check from a prior website should not be available when performing a price check at a competitor's site.
Within a hostile environment, not only locations and hosts may want to constrain the actions of agents, but also agent owners may want to restrict the actions their agents are allowed to perform on their behalf. These actions include the ability to negotiate, migrate, inject, access resources, purchase items on the web, etc.
In summary, the security architecture outlined in this section and illustrated within the AgentScape agent system provides a flexible means to define and manage agent access to specific functionality. Flexibility is provided in two areas: firstly, hosts and locations have the ability to control access to resources that they control. Secondly, owners can constrain their agents from performing actions that, while they are authorized by the locations and hosts, are not desirable to the owner. For more information see (35).

7. Secure Lookup Service

Every distributed agent system has some way of naming agents, and a way of mapping agent names to their location. Finding the location of an agent is useful, for example, for co-locating agents, that is, migrating agents to run on the same host to improve performance by reducing communication costs. Sometimes the names of agents already contain a reference to their location (*location-dependent names*), in which case, resolving the name to a location becomes trivial. However, with location-dependent names, agents do not have stable names as after a migration their names will have changed. Such agents are more difficult to track for other agents. With *location-independent* names, the names remain stable after migration, but the agent system needs a **lookup service** to map an agent's name to its current location.
A **lookup service** is a generic name for a global service that keeps track of where each agent is located and how to communicate with it. Another name often used is **white pages**. To prevent agents and services from impersonating other agents and services, the information in a lookup service must be trustworthy. However, in an open environment, where anyone can join the agent community, guarding the information in a lookup service is a challenge.
Scalable location services are essential in distributed systems and, in particular, for multi-agent systems. Domain Name System (DNS) is a very successful realization of a location service that resolves symbolic names to contact addresses (IP addresses). DNSSEC (Secure DNS) has been designed to support authentication preventing spoofing and man-in-the-middle attacks (4). Both DNS and DNSSEC, however, are not designed to deal with highly dynamic entities such as mobile agents. The dynamic nature of mobile agents in Internet-scale, open network systems requires a different type of approach for registering, deregistering, and retrieving location information. Scalability and integrity are of utmost importance as (up-to-date) agent location information is a prerequisite of successful agent mobility.
This section presents an approach for a scalable and secure location service.

7.1 Information in the Lookup Service

To make a lookup service secure, the service should store not only agent-ids and their current location, but also provide ways for its users to determine the validity (i.e., trustworthiness) of that information. In an open environment, users of a lookup service know that a lookup service may be compromised and may contain false information. One way to solve this problem is to have information published in the lookup service be signed by its publisher. The validity of the information returned by a lookup server depends on the level of trust placed in the signing publisher. Signing is done with public-key cryptography. This system requires

a public-key infrastructure (PKI). The PKI ensures that public-keys are published in a secure and authenticated manner.
It is possible to integrate (a simple version of) a PKI and the lookup service. In this case, the lookup service holds two types of information: *Agent-Location* information and *Certificates*. The first piece of information is simply an (Agent-id, Location) pair, denoting the current location of a specific agent. This information is signed by the platform that currently holds the agent. Certificates are signed (location, public-key) pairs denoting that the specified public key is the public key of the platform running on that specified location. Note that it is possible for platforms to sign their own certificates: *self-signed* certificates. However, the trustworthiness of self-signed certificates is questionable in an open, hostile environment.
Each certificate is signed by a principal, which is either a root certificate authority or another platform. By allowing platforms to sign certificates containing public keys of other platforms a **web of trust** (13) can be build. Platforms should only sign a certificate for another platform if it trusts that the other platform is not malicious. Users of the lookup service can follow the chain of signatures in the certificates until they find a signature of a platform that they trust. This principle assumes that trust is transitive, that is, you trust everyone that is trusted by someone you trust. This principle may be too naive for some and they can restrict themselves to only trust information that is signed by someone they trust directly.

7.2 Using the Secure Lookup Service

This section describes how a secure lookup service is used in an agent platform, such as AgentScape. Agents are identified by a GUID and locations are identified by their name (locationname). Each location is responsible for publishing the location information for all of the agents it currently hosts. Furthermore, when a location starts, it first publishes its public-key via a certificate so others can verify the signature of all information published by this platform. This certificate is signed by a (root) certificate authority. Note that it is assumed that the public keys of root certificate authorities are well-known and that everyone has obtained a copy of them in a secure manner. For example, platform administrators could exchange certificates in person. In addition, the started platform can sign certificates for other platforms, indicating that it trusts and 'endorses' the information signed by those platforms. Which platforms to trust is usually determined by a platform's administrator and is typically stored in a list by the agent platform.
Below, the main functionality of a location service is briefly discussed.

7.2.1 Registering an Agent.

When an agent is injected into an agent system its location is registered by the lookup service. First, the hosting agent platform creates a (agent GUID, locationname) pair. This information is signed by the hosting platform and published in the lookup service for others to find.

7.2.2 Deregistering an Agent.

Deregistering is done by explicitly publishing that the agent does not have a current location anymore, indicating that the agent no longer exists. To prevent the information in a lookup service from growing too much, information in the lookup service could have an expiration time, that is, a lookup service removes expired information automatically, unless the information is republished periodically. In this case, an alternative solution for deregistering an agent is to simply let an agent's location information expire from the lookup service, that is, to not republish the information for that agent. Note, that until the information expires, the lookup service will errantly report an agent's location, but this is not severe, as any attempt to contact the agent will simply fail with an error that the agent does not exist anymore. Choosing smaller expire times decreases this problem, but requires valid information to be republished more often.

7.2.3 Lookup of an Agent's Location.

Agent lookup is done by searching the lookup service for all information pairs concerning an agent's GUID.

- If no information is found an agent does not exist (anymore).
- If multiple pairs are found, the platform filters the pairs by only looking at information signed by known and trusted platforms. The most recently published information indicates the current location of the agent. The recentness of information can be determined by including version numbers (e.g., timestamps) with each published piece of information.

A less strict trust-model would allow a recursive search for certificates of signing platforms until a certificate is found that is signed by a trusted platform.

7.2.4 Agent Migration.

Agent migration is the most complicated scenario: care must be taken to ensure the agent is not accidentally 'dropped' or duplicated, for example, when one of the locations crashes or network connectivity is lost. Another important issue is to correctly update an agent's location in the lookup service.
The basic agent migration procedure is as follows, given an agent A, and locations X and Y.

- Agent A, running on location X, indicates its wish to migrate to location Y.
- Location X contacts location Y and transfers agent A.
- Location Y acknowledges to location X that agent A has been received.
- Location X stops republishing location information for agent A, but maintains a forwarding pointer for agent A to location Y in case other agents try to contact agent A on the old location.
- Location Y publishes that agent A is now located at location Y. As this piece of information has a higher version number than the previous information published by location X, this marks location Y as the current location of agent A.

7.3 Scalability

The previous section focused on the problem that the information in a lookup service must be authenticated and its integrity guaranteed. Another problem to tackle is scalability. In a distributed environment with potentially many hundreds of thousands of agents (or more) and many migrations, the lookup service can quickly become a performance bottleneck, especially if a centralized lookup service is used. One technique for scalability is Peer-to-Peer technology. For example, a **distributed hash table** (DHT) (38; 42; 47) is a decentralized lookup datastructure that is similar to a hashtable and aimed at performance.
A DHT stores (key, value) pairs and allows quick retrieval of the value associated with a particular key. The data can be spread over the participating nodes, but can also be replicated to increase lookup performance and/or to make the system more fault tolerant. A DHT is a self-managed datastructure. The nodes themselves are responsible for balancing the load and

maintaining the data. Nodes can dynamically join and leave the DHT without disrupting the service. These properties make a DHT very scalable, and therefore, make it a good candidate for implementing a distributed lookup service.

In a lookup service based on a DHT, the (key, value) pairs stored in the DHT are the signed (agent-id, location) information pairs. An agent's location can be quickly retrieved via the DHT. Furthermore, each platform's certificate is stored as a (location, certificate) pair, making verifying signatures straightforward. Note that certificates are relatively static which means that they are easily cached at each host, making lookups in the lookup service necessary only for unknown public-keys, or when the cached copy is too old. Caching increases the performance of the distributed lookup service even further. Experiments in AgentScape with a secure lookup service based on a DHT, as described in this section, have shown promising results with respect to performance (33).

8. Agent Systems Overview

Many dozens of agent systems have been designed and developed over the last ten years or so. Some of them have reached quite a mature state and have an active community supporting and using the agent system. This section briefly introduces and discusses a few representative agent systems: AgentScape (20), Ajanta (23), SeMoA (41), and Jade (5). These agent systems are chosen because they are well-known and/or have a focus on security aspects. Each of these systems provides centralized access control. In contrast, the security solutions presented in the previous sections all emphasize a distributed solution.

The discussion of each agent system focuses on their security architecture and the different approaches taken by these agent systems to deal with individual security requirements. An extensive and detailed discussion of each agent system is out of the scope of this chapter.

8.1 AgentScape

AgentScape (20) is a middleware layer that supports open, distributed, large-scale agent systems. It was designed especially to be used in a large-scale, distributed, heterogeneous, open environment. Its design provides minimal but sufficient support for agent applications within an open environment, and can be extended to incorporate new functionality or adopt (new) standards into the platform. AgentScape is written in Java and therefore runs on multiple operating systems. It also supports agents written in different programming languages, such as Java, Jason (7), and C.

Within AgentScape, *agents* are active entities that reside within *locations*, consisting of multiple *hosts*, and *services* are external software systems accessed by agents. Each host runs an instance of the AgentScape middleware. AgentScape uses a Public Key Infrastructure (PKI). Agent owners, locations and hosts have public key pairs. This ensures that locations and hosts can mutually authenticate and set up secure communication channels, using SSL.

Furthermore, every agent has a GUID that is assigned by the agent platform. This GUID is an identifying reference used by the middleware to address an agent and perform operations, such as deliver messages, stop and/or pause, migrate or even kill and/or remove the agent. A GUID is private to the middleware. Externally, agents use *handles*. An agent can have as many handles as it requires. Handles can be published publicly, making access to the agents for others possible. An agent's handles are uniquely linked to its GUID, but the agent's GUID cannot be deduced from its handles, which makes them suitable as *pseudonyms* (see Section 3.1).

8.2 Ajanta

Ajanta (24) is a mobile-agent system based on the Java programming language. Security and robustness have been primary concerns in Ajanta's development. Ajanta platforms can guard themselves against malicious agents. An Ajanta system consists of several *AgentServers* running on hosts. Each agent server creates a confined execution environment for visiting agents and provides them controlled access to local resources. Agents can migrate to other agent servers, communicate with each other, query their environment, etc. The implementation of Ajanta's security architecture is based on *proxies* and Java's security model to restrict, control, and (remotely) monitor running agents. Agents do not have direct references to a host's resources. Instead they have to go through proxies, which check whether the agent has the authorization to access that resource. Furthermore, agent owners can use encryption to secure parts of the agent's data, thereby guaranteeing the data's confidentiality and integrity.

8.3 SeMoA

Secure Mobile Agents (SeMoA) (40) is an extensible Agent platform, written in Java, designed to counter certain protocol attacks and malicious agents. SeMoA has a RBAC-based access control architecture. SeMoA is also designed to load agents in a secure manner, as each agent is loaded in a separate class loader. This enforces separation between agents, and prevents agents interfering with other code executing within a location. Execution of agents is managed explicitly, with access to features such as threads and resources mediated upon.

8.4 Jade with Jade-S and S-Agent

The Java Agent Development Platform (JADE) (5) is a popular FIPA-compliant agent middleware platform. There are a number of extensions to JADE that provide a security architecture to the system, in particular S-Agent (16) and the JADE-S plugin (34).

S-Agent extends JADE with the intention of providing data confidentiality and addressing the malicious host problem, described in Section 5. S-Agent provides two solutions to the malicious host problem without the need for secure hardware. These solutions are implementations of two different security protocols, the ACCK protocol (2) and the TX protocol (48). ACCK uses a trusted third party to ensure that a host does not act maliciously. The TX protocol uses a threshold scheme, where two or more agents must agree that an action is authorized before that action will be allowed. This eliminates the need for a trusted third party. However, it can require more protocol interactions, depending on the number of parties required for the threshold to be met.

JADE-S is an extension to JADE providing decentralized access control. It uses the SPKI (11) trust management system. Trust management systems have a number of advantages compared to the traditional identity-based systems created using X.509. Policies and certificates are created and maintained separately from the application. The terminology used within the policies and/or credentials is application defined. They are represented in an application specific fashion, allowing the application designer to decide what characteristics are required. Agents are explicitly granted permissions, and only agents trusted by the location are authorized to execute code at that location.

9. Summary

Security in multi-agent systems is a major concern, particularly in multi-agent systems deployed in a large-scale, distributed, and open environment. Finding a balance between re-

stricting access to resources and allowing enough openness to let the whole system function efficiently and effectively is the challenge.
This chapter has identified threats to the two main stakeholders in an agent system: the agent owner and the platform administrator. The security requirements looked at included identity management, secure communication, and maintaining confidentiality, integrity, and availability for the stakeholders. These requirements need to be fulfilled for any secure agent system. Each security requirement has been discussed in detail and solutions have been illustrated in the AgentScape agent platform.

Acknowledgments
This work is a result of support provided by the NLnet Foundation (`http://www.nlnet.nl`). The authors wish to thank Benno Overeinder, David Mobach, Thomas Quillinan, Kassidy Clark, Reinier Timmer, and Reinout van Schouwen for their contributions.

10. References

[1] A. Abdul-Rahman and S. Hailes. A distributed trust model. In *Proceedings of the 1997 workshop on New security paradigms*, pages 48–60. ACM Press, 1998.
[2] J. Algesheimer, C. Cachin, J. Camenisch, and G. Karjoth. Cryptographic security for mobile code. In *IEEE Symposium on Security and Privacy*, pages 2–11, 2001.
[3] A. Andrieux, K. Czajkowski, A. Dan, K. Keahey, H. Ludwig, J. Pruyne, J. Rofrano, S. Tuecke, and M. Xu. Web services agreement negotiation specification (WS-AgreementNegotiation) (draft). https://forge.gridforum.org/projects/graap-wg, 2004.
[4] D. Atkins and R. Austein. Threat analysis of the domain name system. IETF RFC 3833, Aug. 2004.
[5] F. Bellifemine, A. Poggi, and G. Rimassa. JADE–A FIPA-compliant agent framework. *Proceedings of PAAM*, 99:97–108, 1999.
[6] E. Bierman and E. Cloete. Classification of malicious host threats in mobile agent computing. In *Proceedings of the 2002 annual research conference of the South African institute of computer scientists and information technologists on Enablement through technology*, pages 141–148. RSA, 2002.
[7] R. H. Bordini, M. Wooldridge, and J. F. Hübner. *Programming Multi-Agent Systems in AgentSpeak using Jason (Wiley Series in Agent Technology)*. John Wiley & Sons, 2007.
[8] P. Braun and W. Rossak. *Mobile Agents: Basic Concepts, Mobility Models, and the Tracy Toolkit*. Morgan Kaufmann Publishers Inc., San Francisco, CA, USA, 2004.
[9] S. Clauß and M. Köhntopp. Identity management and its support of multilateral security. *Computer Networks*, 37(2):205–219, 2001.
[10] A. Csetenyi. Electronic government: perspectives from e-commerce. In *Proceedings of the 11th International Workshop on Database and Expert Systems Applications*, pages 6–8. IEEE Computer Society Washington, DC, USA, 2000.
[11] C. Ellison, B. Frantz, B. Lampson, R. Rivest, B. Thomas, and T. Ylonen. SPKI certificate theory. Request for Comment (RFC) 2693, Internet Engineering Task Force, September 1999.
[12] B. Fonseca. VeriSign issues false Microsoft digital certificates. `http://www.infoworld.com/articles/hn/xml/01/03/22/010322hnmicroversign.html`, March 2001. Infoworld.
[13] S. Garfinkel. *PGP: Pretty Good Privacy*. O'Reilly & Associates, Inc., Sebastopol, CA, USA, 1996.

[14] L. Gong. *Inside Java™2 Platform Security*. The Java™Series. Addison Wesley, June 1999. ISBN: 0-201-31000-7.
[15] H. Guan, H. Zhang, P. Chen, and Y. Zhou. *Integration and Innovation Orient to E-Society Volume 1*, volume 251 of *IFIP International Federation for Information Processing*, chapter Mobile Agents Integrity Research, pages 194–201. Springer, 2008.
[16] V. Gunupudi and S. R. Tate. SAgent: A Security Framework for JADE. In *Proceedings of the Fifth International Joint Conference on Autonomous Agents and Multiagent Systems (AA-MASâĂŹ06)*, 2006.
[17] R. H. Guttman, A. G. Moukas, and P. Maes. Agent-mediated electronic commerce: a survey. *The Knowledge Engineering Review*, 13(02):147–159, 2001.
[18] M. He, N. R. Jennings, and H. F. Leung. On agent-mediated electronic commerce. *IEEE Transactions on Knowledge and Data Engineering*, 15(4):985–1003, 2003.
[19] T. D. Huynh, N. R. Jennings, and N. R. Shadbolt. Developing an integrated trust and reputation model for open multi-agent systems. In *Proceedings of the 7th International Workshop on Trust in Agent Societies*, pages 65–74, 2004.
[20] IIDS. AgentScape Agent Middleware. `http://www.agentscape.org`.
[21] B. Jacobs, M. Oostdijk, and M. Warnier. Source Code Verification of a Secure Payment Applet. *Journal of Logic and Algebraic Programming*, 58(1-2):107–120, 2004.
[22] G. Karjoth, N. Asokan, and C. Gülcü. Protecting the computation results of free-roaming agents. *Personal Technologies*, 2(2):92–99, 1998.
[23] N. M. Karnik and A. R. Tripathi. Agent Server Architecture for the Ajanta Mobile-Agent System. In *Proceedings of the 1998 International Conference on Parallel and Distributed Processing Techniques and Applications (PDPTA'98)*, pages 66–73, July 1998.
[24] N. M. Karnik and A. R. Tripathi. Design Issues in Mobile Agent Programming Systems. *IEEE Concurrency*, 6(6):52–61, July–September 1998.
[25] C. Kaufman, R. Perlman, and M. Speciner. *Network Security, PRIVATE Communication in a PUBLIC World*. Prentice Hall, 2nd edition, 2002.
[26] S. Kent and R. Atkinson. Security architecture for the internet protocol. IETF RFC 2401, Nov. 1998.
[27] A. Menezes, P. van Oorschot, and S. Vanstone. *Handbook of Applied Cryptography*. CRC Press, Boca Raton, FL, 1997.
[28] D. G. A. Mobach. *Agent-Based Mediated Service Negotiation*. PhD thesis, Computer Science Department, Vrije Universiteit Amsterdam, Amsterdam, The Netherlands, May 2007.
[29] A. Moreno and J. L. Nealon. *Applications of Software Agent Technology in the Health Care Domain*. Birkhauser, 2003.
[30] G. C. Necula and P. Lee. Proof-carrying code. In *Proceedings of the 24th Symposium on Principals of Programming (POPL)*. ACM, 1997.
[31] G. C. Necula and P. Lee. Safe, untrusted agents using proof-carrying code. *Special Issue on Mobile Agent Security*, pages 61–91, 1997.
[32] Netscape Inc. Secure sockets layer website. `http://www.mozilla.org/projects/security/pki/nss/ssl/draft302.txt`.
[33] B. J. Overeinder, M. A. Oey, R. J. Timmer, R. van Schouwen, E. Rozendaal, and F. M. T. Brazier. Design of a secure and decentralized location service for agent platforms. In *Proceedings of the Sixth International Workshop on Agents and Peer-to-Peer Computing (AP2PC 2007)*, May 2007.

[34] A. Poggi, M. Tomaiuolo, and G. Vitaglione. Security and trust in agent-oriented middleware. In R. Meersman and Z. Tari, editors, *OTM Workshops 2003*, number 2889 in LNCS, pages 989–1003. Springer-Verlag, 2003.

[35] T. B. Quillinan, M. Warnier, M. A. Oey, R. J. Timmer, and F. M. T. Brazier. Enforcing security in the agentscape middleware. In *Proceedings of the 1st International Workshop on Middleware Security (MidSec)*. ACM, December 2008.

[36] S. D. Ramchurn, C. Sierra, L. Godo, and N. R. Jennings. A computational trust model for multi-agent interactions based on confidence and reputation. In *Proceedings of the 6th International Workshop of Deception, Fraud and Trust in Agent Societies*, pages 69–75, 2003.

[37] O. Rana, M. Warnier, T. B. Quillinan, and F. M. T. Brazier. Monitoring and reputation mechanisms for service level agreements. In *Proceedings of the 5th International Workshop on Grid Economics and Business Models (GenCon)*, Las Palmas, Gran Canaria, Spain., August 2008. Springer Verlag.

[38] S. Ratnasamy, P. Francis, M. Handley, R. M. Karp, and S. Shenker. A scalable content-addressable network. In *SIGCOMM*, pages 161–172, 2001.

[39] V. Roth. Mutual protection of co-operating agents. In J. Vitek and C. D. Jensen, editors, *Secure Internet programming: security issues for mobile and distributed objects*, volume 1603 of *LNCS*, pages 275–285. Springer-Verlag, 2001.

[40] V. Roth and M. Jalali. Concepts and architecture of a security-centric mobile agent server. In *Proc. Fifth International Symposium on Autonomous Decentralized Systems (ISADS 2001)*, pages 435–442. IEEE Computer Society, 2001.

[41] V. Roth and M. Jalali-Sohi. Concepts and architecture of a security-centric mobile agent server. In *Proceedings of the Fifth International Symposium on Autonomous Decentralized Systems*, pages 435–442, Dallas, Texas, U.S.A., March 2001.

[42] A. Rowstron and P. Druschel. Pastry: Scalable, decentralized object location, and routing for large-scale peer-to-peer systems. In *Middleware 2001*, volume 2218 of *Lecture Notes in Computer Science*, pages 329–350. Springer-Verlag, Berlin, Germany, 2001.

[43] T. Sander and C. F. Tschudin. Protecting Mobile Agents Against Malicious Hosts. *Mobile Agents and Security*, 60, 1998.

[44] R. S. Sandhu, E. J. Coyne, H. L. Feinstein, and C. E. Youman. Role-based access control models. *IEEE Computer*, 29(2):38–47, February 1996.

[45] A. Saxena and B. Soh. Authenticating mobile agent platforms using signature chaining without trusted third parties. In *Proceedings of the 2005 IEEE International Conference on e-Technology, e-Commerce and e-Service, (EEE'05).*, pages 282–285, 2005.

[46] W. Stallings. *Cryptography and network security: principles and practice*. Prentice Hall, 2006.

[47] I. Stoica, R. Morris, D. Liben-Nowell, D. R. Karger, F. Kaashoek, F. Dabek, and H. Balakrishnan. Chord: A scalable peer-to-peer lookup protocol for Internet applications. *IEEE/ACM Transactions on Networking*, 11(1):17–32, Feb. 2003.

[48] S. R. Tate and K. Xu. Mobile agent security through multi-agent cryptographic protocols. In *Proceedings of the 4th International Conference on Internet Computing*, pages 462–468, Las Vegas, NV., 2003.

[49] Trusted Computing Group. TPM main specification. `http://www.trustedcomputinggroup.org/resources/tpm_main_specification`, July 2007.

[50] G. van 't Noordende, A. Balogh, R. F. H. Hofman, F. M. T. Brazier, and A. S. Tanenbaum. A secure jailing system for confining untrusted applications. In *Proc. 2nd International Conference on Security and Cryptography (SECRYPT)*, pages 414–423, July 2007.

[51] M. Warnier and F. M. T. Brazier. Organized anonymous agents. In *Proceedings of The Third International Symposium on Information Assurance and Security (IAS'07)*. IEEE, August 2007.
[52] M. Warnier, F. M. T. Brazier, and A. Oskamp. Security of distributed digital criminal dossiers. *Journal of Software (Academy Publisher)*, 3(3), March 2008.
[53] M. Warnier, M. A. Oey, R. J. Timmer, B. J. Overeinder, and F. M. T. Brazier. Enforcing integrity of agent migration paths by distribution of trust. *Int. J. of Intelligent Information and Database Systems*, 3(4), 2009.
[54] X. Zhang, S. Oh, and R. Sandhu. PDBM: A flexible delegation model in RBAC. In *Proceedings of the 7th ACM Symposium on Access Control Models and Technologies (SACMAT 2003)*, Como, Italy, 2003.